Thinking the Unknowable

Thinking the Unknowable

The Essential Louis Dupré

Louis Dupré

Edited by Peter J. Casarella

University of Notre Dame Press
Notre Dame, Indiana

Copyright © 2024 by the University of Notre Dame

Published by the University of Notre Dame Press
Notre Dame, Indiana 46556
undpress.nd.edu
All Rights Reserved

Published in the United States of America

Library of Congress Control Number: 2024941351

ISBN: 978-0-268-20795-3 (Hardback)
ISBN: 978-0-268-20794-6 (WebPDF)
ISBN: 978-0-268-20797-7 (Epub3)

CONTENTS

Preface by Peter J. Casarella — vii

    Essay 1   Philosophy and Faith — 1

1. Farewell to a Symbolic World — 11

    Essay 2   The Modern Idea of Culture and Its Opposition to Its Classical and Medieval Origins — 13

    Essay 3   The Fragmentation of the Symbolic World — 23

    Essay 4   The Sources of Modern Atheism — 35

II. Philosophical Reinterpretations of Theology — 47

    Essay 5   Hegel's Spirit and the Religious Idea of God as Spirit — 49

    Essay 6   Philosophical Reflections on the Mystery of Creation — 55

    Essay 7   Evil and the Limits of Theodicy — 61

    Essay 8   Intimations of Immortality — 76

III. Phenomenology of Religion — 89

    Essay 9   Phenomenology of Religion: Limits and Possibilities — 91

Essay 10	Phenomenology and Religious Truth	99
Essay 11	The Enigma of Religious Art	113
Essay 12	Ritual: The Sacralization of Time	125

IV. Mysticism: The Silence of Faith 133

Essay 13	Is a Natural Desire of God Possible?	135
Essay 14	Mysticism and Philosophy	142
Essay 15	Justifying the Mystical Experience	151

Notes   161

Index   179

PREFACE

Peter J. Casarella

A few years ago, I visited Louis Dupré and his wife, Edith, in their beautifully modern apartment in the middle of Kortrijk, Belgium.[1] The town is a small one, even by Belgian standards. One can easily view remnants of the ancient walls from the front window of their high-story abode. After lunch, Louis took me across the bridge just in front of the apartment building. On the bridge we passed by the Broel Towers, an important symbol of the city's past. On the other side of the bridge, we encountered medieval Belgium in its full splendor. There Louis proudly showed me his office with the books that had been shipped from Yale and were now housed in a well-kept but obviously historic building. After that, we spent about an hour visiting the cathedral and the Béguinage, the home of lay female mystics that dates from the thirteenth century. Louis came alive in recounting these histories. All of this was within a very short walking distance of his apartment, but still far away from it culturally and spiritually.

When I arrived in New Haven in 1981 as a freshman at Yale, I managed to meet Louis Dupré almost immediately because of a part-time job that I had as a student worker in the Department of Religious Studies. It was a rare stroke of luck. I ended up spending more than a decade as his student and am immensely grateful for his mentorship. At no point in those dozen years, however, did I ever spend time with him in his native Belgium. I knew and heard about his past, but I did not ever fully grasp the immediacy of it in his work or teaching. To be fair, Louis was a U.S. citizen and refers to himself in the essays in this book as a North American. He even wrote as a philosopher of religion operating principally out of a North American context. But the recent visit to his life amidst the ruins of medieval Belgium is now very illuminating. He straddled two worlds his entire life, and so it is no surprise that he spent his last years back in the place that gave him not just his education but a living "symbolic world" that is now fragmented. Our tour was not about nostalgia. It was about roots in faith, in a homeland, and in a place. The entire philosophical journey of this great scholar only makes sense in terms of a life that straddles worlds that have come apart. His fascination with and ultimate rejection of Hegel's philosophy of religion is about that lifelong act of crossing a bridge and knowing that you cannot go back.

Any reader of Dupré today will be viewing his achievement from a different vantage than the one that I had at Yale. The four parts of this book deal with the struggles between philosophy and faith as the separation between them took place in the second half of the twentieth century. Today that severance looks more complicated, whether you invoke terms such as "postsecular" or you attend to the development of a theological phenomenology, especially in France and the United States. At the same time, Dupré's achievement maintains its merit and timeliness. The fragmentation of a symbolic order is now a theopolitical theme. The legacy of the Hegelian *Geist* is still, and probably always will be, a contested terrain. The opening within contemporary philosophy to transcendent mystery and the truth of the work of art is now more viable than it was at the apex of Dupré's time spent teaching at Georgetown and Yale. Finally, the insight of mystics such as Nicholas of Cusa, John of the Cross, Teresa of Avila, and Ignatius of Loyola continues to offer a genuine treasure trove of wisdom for philosophers and theologians.

Essay 1 sets out the task of the book, which is to investigate the relationship of faith and metaphysics. There is a paradox hidden within the thesis of this essay that accompanies the rest of the essays. Metaphysics cannot claim authorship or authority in the realm of the transcendent origin of the belief held by the person of faith. The philosopher, Dupré reminds us, must listen for a voice from beyond. Paradoxically, philosophy of religion discovers its authentic autonomy in precisely this process of remaining open to the mystery. With that opening and with all due caution to modern reason's unlimited "gnostic drive," religion can still be incorporated into metaphysics and provide a critical framework for self-examination and reflection. Faith begins from a higher ground, but ends up on the same level as reason. Dupré's synthesis is not a philosophy of religion tailored to the hegemonic temptations of the theologians of the revealed word, but neither is it a rationalist submergence of belief to critical reason. The God of the philosophers is still, in the memorable words of Henry Duméry, "a theft and a blunder" (essay 1), but the analysis of the experience of the transcendent (especially in its symbolic self-disclosure) can proceed in a rational manner.

Part I (essays 2, 3, and 4) deals with what Paul Levesque calls "the modern predicament" in Dupré's theory of the symbol.[2] The modern mind must traverse interiorly the passing of the Broel Towers in Kortrijk or the trip uptown to view the stunning medieval tapestries in New York City's Cloisters Museum. In other words, the material representation of belief is drawn from the symbolic world of the past, but the knower of these symbols is still a subjective self who cannot but dissect the beauty of the living form. Between the frontiers of the Thomistic *analogia entis* and the Kantian Copernican revolution, Dupré reluctantly occupies a desert that was in the second half of the twentieth century the proud home of transcendental Thomism. He calls it "a defensive strategy" in part II (essay 6) but offers a modified defense of its return in part IV. In part I, his concern is different, for he wishes to show how the philosophical account of the real and the account of the mind's power to know the real became separated from one another.

Language as a cipher for human existence connects the three essays in part I. Essay 2 establishes that the subjectification of reality was catalyzed by the Nominalist separation of words from things. Each of the following two essays offers an alternative: the poetic word of early humanism and the religious deism of Spinoza and Locke. Dante, Coluccio Salutati, Cristoforo Landino, Leon Battista Alberti, and Nicholas of Cusa each makes a unique contribution to a new theology of language, including the language of painting.[3] Ernesto Grassi once noted that these authors had primitive insights into Heidegger's thesis that language is a house of Being.[4] But Dupré does not turn this poetic theology into a Heideggerian hall of mirrors. Dupré wrote in *Metaphysics and Culture*: "Kantians fail to account for the expressiveness itself of symbolic expression."[5] These early theorists of a modern theory of cultural expressivity were trying to re-establish the freedom of individuals and communities to assert themselves in a spiritual manner. Later neo-Kantians such as Paul Natorp would concede that a transcendent source of unity was needed to keep together the cultural expression in the *symballesthai* (the "gathering together" at the root of the English word "symbol").[6] Dupré too wants to make such an affirmation about the religious symbol's place in the modern and contemporary consciousness.

For example, Locke in Dupré's narrative is a *religious* Deist; he is neither the Socianian rationalist that his admirers claimed him to be nor an inevitable precursor of the currents of atheism that took root in his wake. What is the difference between these nuanced parsings of eighteenth-century British and French Christianity and what difference does this make? Dupré, first of all, takes Locke to be sincere and earnest in his self-defense in *A Second Vindication of the Reasonableness of Christianity*. He simply did *not* believe that autonomous reason stood on a higher ground than biblical revelation. Locke argued for their compatibility, and his interpreters (rationalist and antirationalist) transformed his insights into a foundationalism (essay 4). This is the decisive difference. The reasonable complement to a biblical faith became its unconditioned mode of justification.

Humanist theological hermeneutics and deist biblical spirituality are not permanent solutions to the subjectivist ills of modernity. They are forgotten flashes of religious wisdom that have been lost in the rush to a secular modernity. So when Dupré writes of "wobbling beacons" in the desert of modern atheism (essay 3), he is not speaking about the challenge of evangelization, at least not in a narrow sense of that term. Atheism is *not* in the first instance a denial of the existence of God. Like Michael Buckley, Dupré maintains that the philosophical presuppositions of Denis Diderot or Paul d'Holbach are related to traditional theism by means of a strict dialectic.[7] A common set of philosophical presuppositions regarding nature and culture informs both sides of this divide. The rejection of the theist postulate first required the mounting of a defense of the newly minted idea of God as a principle that stood over and against human subjectivity, a thesis that, rightly or wrongly, became associated with Descartes. The wobbling beacons are illuminations of human freedom and creativity that reaffirm the nondiabolical nature of humanity and recast the relationship between the divinity and humanity in meaningful new ways.

Part II (essays 5, 6, 7, and 8) treats the idea of God in modern philosophy. The first two essays deal with what Hegel said about God as the Absolute. The second two try to pick up the pieces that remain of the idea of God in the wake of Hegel, first looking at the problem of the suffering of the innocent and then at the meaning of immortal life. Even though Dupré served as president of the Hegel Society of America, he did not worship at the altar of Hegelianism. His relationship to Hegel on the

Absolute is just as vexed as his relationship to modernity itself. He acknowledges, with a clear nod to Cyril O'Regan, that Hegel deliberately reframed the Christian narrative in a gnostic fashion. But he nonetheless seeks to draw out the lasting truth of Hegel's bold reformulation of philosophy's surpassing of religious representation through a dialectical mode of reflection. Dupré readily acknowledges the paradoxical position of *The Phenomenology of Spirit* whereby the drama of unhappy consciousness is suddenly taken as the narrative of God's unfolding in history. He turns to the complex forest of the *Lectures on the Philosophy of Religion* to shed light on the unresolved puzzles. There Hegel identifies Spirit's self-realization as Spirit with its presence in the community that recognizes the Spirit of God. Dupré is troubled by the conscious limits put on a God who cannot exist without believers to support the claim for God's existence. But Dupré still pushes forward to advance the claim "that Hegel wanted to preserve the Christian idea of God" (essay 5). Hegel was a failure in offering the definitive word on how to interpret Christian doctrine philosophically. But Hegel's *felix culpa* was not without its progeny. Dupré's own philosophical philosophy of religion is not without its Hegelian roots and branches. In Dupré's account, Hegel liberated the modern idea of God from religious representation as such but paradoxically maintained the necessity of a revealed Word. Dupré leaves behind Hegel's philosophy of the Absolute, but his philosophical account of how to interpret Christian revelation and the idea of God found within it has a Hegelian residue.[8]

Nowhere is that more evident than in the treatment of the idea of a passive God in essays 6 and 7. Once again we face a negative dialectic and a positive hypothesis. Negatively, modern thought found itself incapable of incorporating the richness of the fourfold sense of divine causality that Plato and Aristotle bequeathed to Latin Christian thought (essay 6). As a consequence, modern European thinkers first equated a narrowed version of efficient causality with the ministrations of a mechanistic universe, only to later reject it. Hence, the need for a whole new proposal (essay 7). Dupré is adamant that the Aristotelian-Thomistic response whereby there is no real relation between God and the world is thoroughly inadequate. He is even less sanguine about fideist accounts of divine redemption that de facto ignore the real suffering of innocents by elevating the resolution of the philosophical problem to an unthinking spiritual plane. He is much more tentative in suggesting that Christian thinkers revisit the theosophical principle whereby the creation of the world as good and the creation of the possibility of evil being inflicted upon innocents is coterminous. When he states that faithful Christians ought to concede that in his redemptive action God reacts to real suffering and real evil, he is aware of the danger of anthropomorphism and the more serious charge of modern Gnosticism (essay 7). Dupré's positive solution is that in God's "pure actuality" God also has "the potential to 're-act' to events and circumstances in a manner that requires the acting subject to move out toward the other in order to return to itself in a new manner" (essay 6).[9] This form of divine agency does not apply to God in God's very own being but to the simultaneous emergence in the act of creation of an active and a passive God. Whitehead's dipolar deity is a much more formalistic expression of this same idea.[10] Regardless of the philosophical problems, the religious value of this hypothesis is quite clear. God is not an intermittent participant in human affairs. Whitehead's words are far less tentative than Dupré's, but they speak to a common vision of the place of God's co-creative lure in the world: God "does not create the world, he saves it: or, more accurately, he is the poet of the world, with tender patience leading it by his vision of truth, beauty, and goodness."[11]

In the wake of the failure of Hegel's Absolute Spirit to offer a compelling idea of the Triune God's self-realization in history, Dupré considers two offshoots: North American radical empiricism and European phenomenology. The former is treated in the last essay of part II, essay 8, "Intimations of Immortality," and the latter serves as the basis for part III. The essay on immortality is a dialogue with Spinoza and William E. Hocking, Harvard professor and successor to Josiah Royce. Hocking occupies a middle ground between Aquinas's defense of the immortality of the soul as the form of the body and the idea of Spinoza's that the soul is the idea of the body. Basically, Hocking maintains that the mind is a relating entity, "a field of fields," that connects the empirically verifiable world this side of death with an independent space of possible existence after death.[12] The excursive self stands firmly on one side, and the reflective self seeks to transcend the flow of conscious events in order to bridge worlds. The empiricist, by radicalizing the method and leaving behind all a priori assumptions, forces the philosopher to do the same. But Dupré is still drawn to Spinoza's idealism, for it dispenses with the double self in Hocking's empiricism. The ideal embodiment of Spinoza is probably not enough to account for individual identity, even after death. The *relative* independence of the mind from the body in our conscious and subconscious states may be the best proof we are going to find of eternal life. In the end, Dupré leaves the most important questions open and is satisfied to allow Christian believers to rely on the testimony of the apostolic witnesses for their justifications of immortal life. But the purpose of this exercise was finally to put to rest the blindness of a blind faith and not the dynamic mystery of what awaits us on the other side of death.

Part III deals with the phenomenological method and is dedicated in the first place to Husserl and Heidegger. Dupré reports that he first published an article on Husserl's thoughts on the idea of God in 1969, which means that essay 9 looks back in a critical way at his own research by almost half a century. He also speaks of the defense of Scheler's phenomenology in an article published in 1977.[13] Much has changed, but certain challenges seem to still be with us. Husserl's method of reduction provokes religious thinkers and Christian theologians alike. Moreover, the principle that Dupré elucidates regarding the fundamental givenness that adheres to the object of the religious act now applies more generally to the work of Jean-Luc Marion and those who have taken the new path to phenomenology that he opened.[14] But he eludes to an early tension between Henry Duméry, who insisted on the philosophical justification of the new method, and Gerardus van der Leeuw (who later set Eliade on his course). The latter insisted that the new method concentrate on "religion-as-experience" and leave "religion-as-transcendent" to theologians and others who wanted to explore divine revelation. Dupré once advocated for Duméry's position, but became more tempered. He does, however, take issue with the switch to scientific observation: "Living religion centers on a nucleus, which believers consider to be *given*" (essay 9). By shifting the emphasis from the given to what appears in experience, an enormous set of problems emerges regarding both the content of belief and the means of investigating it. Today we have this problem in what Robert Orsi calls "lived religion" and Thomas A. Tweed calls a "locative" theory of religion.[15] The phenomenology of religion has in a certain sense been a victim of its own success. These two scholars stand at the forefront of a "new ethnography" that drives a much sharper (and far less tenable) distinction between transcendent essence and phenomenal manifestation than did the founders of their own craft. In the first wave of reception of the work of Husserl and Heidegger in Europe, a dialogue between theology and phenomenology appeared to have been opened. Today, if the foregoing analysis is even partly on track, one must choose between a scientific understanding of the phenomenal or abandon what Dupré considers the nucleus of belief itself even while struggling to find one's way in the expanding world of discordant case studies. In a sense, the Parmidean bias of Duméry's henological solution has now given way to a Heraclitean dogma that prevents a unified theory from ever again being sought. It is not clear whether Dupré's survey of the options available to scholars of religion today is overly naïve or just prescient. Perhaps a little bit of both.

In essays 10, 11, and 12, we see Dupré returning to very familiar themes: the nature of truth, the relationship between aesthetic and religious experience, and the ritualization of time. All three topics follow from the tentative but still decisive opening to a new method for the study of religion I just elaborated. The truth of disclosure is superior to a theory of correspondence and a theory of coherence because it maintains the closest link to the ancient notion of being in the truth. Dupré depends explicitly upon Heidegger in defining what he means by disclosure as an unconcealment of the truth, but he also departs from it, noting the more ancient roots of Heidegger's postmetaphysical account in the Christian metaphysics of light. But Dupré is actually unconvinced by both Heidegger's denial of transcendence through the finitization of reality and neo-Augustinian hailings to a light from above. The post-Hegelian appropriation of the faith of the mystics commended by Dupré reveals a religious disclosure of truth that has a symbolic valency and a transcendent ultimacy.

The treatment of transitoriness in essay 12 actually points to a set of questions that permeates the whole book. Moreover, the event whereby truth discloses itself illuminates the work of art and the ritualization of time. Both phenomena speak to the temporal meaning of selfhood.[16] Modern art, Dupré says, cannot rely on any intrinsic link between the sacred and aesthetic modes of disclosure. Seeing the pure form of the ancients is a Romantic quest that has to be pursued with a great deal of circumspection, in spite of its valorization by Hegel and others.[17] To bring together a new religious ontology with the self-disclosure of a work of art, Dupré reverts to the following highly original notion of the symbol proposed by Gadamer (essay 10):

The work of art is conceived as an ontological event and the abstraction to which aesthetic differentiation commits it is dissolved. A picture [*ein Bild*] is an event of presentation [*ein Vorgang der Darstellung*]. Its relation to the original is so far from being a reduction of the autonomy of its being that, on that contrary, I had to speak in regard to the picture, of an "increase of being" [*Zuwachs an Sein*].[18]

The process of depicting a new reality in a work of art is thereby taken out of the realm of a purely subjective imagination and into the still interiorizable realm of symbolic manifestation and thereby an experience of truth.

With respect to both contemporary religious art and the experience of ritual, Dupré's shift in reading of the event of symbolic disclosure from an epistemological focus back to an ontological one is presented with characteristic skepticism. A painting by Barnett Newman or by Mark Rothko might capture a sense of transcendence in painting, but these experiences are fleeting and ambiguous. Once again, we encounter fragments of truth in a shimmering process of unveiling, rather than the blinding illumination of the Truth. The Gadamerian *Zuwachs an Sein* is not an ontological "increase" in any measurable sense of the term. It is, rather, an emergent maturation of our understanding of reality that brings itself into our field of experience often without warning or clear signs of development. The Judeo-Christian memorial of God's past redemptive activity on behalf of God's people is a telling example of the hermeneutics of the *Seinszuwachs*. The re-presentation in the present cannot be a mere reminder of the past. What is past becomes contemporaneous by virtue of the intentionality of a transcendent origin in the life of faith of the believer. Even the hardened atheist who is approaching this reality with an animus against the truth of the faith needs to have some sympathy with the religious parameters of the incorporation of the original narrative into the believer's form of life in order to achieve a genuine understanding.

Ritual, like art, points to the future but still cannot delay the arrival of the truth wholly to what lies beyond the present moment. The ritualization of time is not an escape into a private inner sanctum where one is alone with one's Savior. Rituals allow us to reenter the ordinariness of time with a new awareness of one's own time and of time itself. The fruit of the *Zuchwachs* is not just moral. The discovery is not focused on the values that can be applied to discrete moments. Dupré is also skeptical about linking the hermeneutics of time too closely to the cycle of seasons, but he may lose sight of important commitments to ecological stewardship in this uncharacteristic a-cosmism. Regarding the North American spirit of the frontier that is constantly advancing against the incursions of violent memories from the past, Dupré is neither despairing nor an Americanist frontiersman. Like Balthasar, he finds solace in the quiet musings about time and eternity in Thornton Wilder's *Our Town*.[19] North American cultural amnesia and saturation with television need not prevent a North American religious poetics or a North American liturgical rhythm that is more than just faddish. But the Yankee challenge to resurrect meaningful temporality with existential authenticity and sufficient attention to cultural pluralism is great.

Part IV (essays 13, 14, and 15) deals with the mystical contribution to a new philosophy of religion. The mystics and mystical topoi covered in these essays confirm the title of the volume: *Thinking the Unknowable*. What does Dupré actually mean by "mysticism?" It is not unique to monotheism or to the revealed religions. Basically, it is an experience of union with God that can and should be examined through the natural inclinations of human cognition, but it ultimately is not a construct of the human power to seek the origin of transcendent knowing, being, and loving. The methodological lessons from the phenomenology of religion from part III are applied with great rigor, but Dupré also moves freely between the history of mystical theology in the Christian tradition and the philosophical interrogation of the same extending from the late nineteenth century (von Hügel, James, Blondel) to the present (Maréchal, Heidegger, Rahner, and Milbank). What he offers is not simply an endorsement of either the phenomenology of the mystical experience or the intellectualist strand within Christian mysticism. In fact, he explores the limits of both and is most intrigued by the cognitive interstices *and* experiential bonds that distinguish and unite the philosophical elaboration of transcendence and the mystic's genuine openness to the gift of grace.

The question about the natural desire to see God according to God's essence arises out of the Scholasticism of the thirteenth century, but Dupré transforms this problematic into an investigation of the possibility in a secular age of acknowledging a transcendent horizon to all finite knowing and loving. Aquinas inherited from Aristotle the idea that the mind must desire the cause of its being by virtue of some connaturality that joins the seeking intellect to its origin. For Dupré, the condemnation of 1270 marks the turning point at which the resolution of the philosophical problem is relegated to faith and the dynamics of the seeking intellect become supplanted by the vicissitudes of a nominalist God. Even the contested reconstruction of Aquinas's original view by Henri de Lubac, with minimal recourse to the thesis of a historical pure nature, still is unable to respond adequately to the view of radical empiricists and phenomenologists that questions the supposition of knowledge presupposed in the intellect apart from the givens of actual experience.[20] This critique leaves open a path to transcendental Thomism, one that Dupré here traces through Blondel, Jaspers, Heidegger, Scheler, and Rahner. Rahner, Dupré argues, in *Hearer of the Word*, is the most consistent. He skirts the problem of apriorism by claiming that the preapprehension of being that leads us to God is not a priori knowledge but the actual existing horizon against which judgments are made. Dupré notes the reprise of Descartes's proof for God's existence on the basis of divine infinity in the Jesuit-trained Frenchman's *Third Meditation*. Dupré nonetheless concludes that Rahner has proved only the possibility, not the actuality, of God as the end of all desire (essay 13). Dupré once told me that he would run into Joseph Maréchal in the library when he was a young student of philosophy in Louvain, but he never took a course with him. Dupré was nursed by this Catholic school of thought and therefore never dismisses out of hand its central premises. His critique is far more mild than that of the so-called Yale School of Theology, which reacts negatively to the existential undergirding of biblical ways of knowing God. In some ways, it is more devastating than that of his dear colleagues Hans Frei and George Lindbeck.

Essay 14 ponders a contemporary approach to the "soul" of the mystic. This question arises at the intersection of two noble but failed quests. The first is the attempt by modern philosophers to rehabilitate mysticism as the limit concept that borders the emergent rationalism. Dupré surveys how Fénelon in the eighteenth century and Bertrand Russell and Ludwig Wittgenstein in the twentieth explored this terrain. One cannot help notice the straitjacket that the modern philosophers put on mystical experience in order to accommodate it. A second strand emerges with the Spanish mystics Teresa of Avila and John of the Cross and then is turned into a universal principle of faith by Jacques Maritain. In this view, mystical visions contribute "intuitions of an immediate consciousness." By linking this to the doctrine of participation through the receptivity to God's sanctifying grace, Maritain makes most religious believers into potential mystics, Dupré states. The latter argument is philosophically unobjectionable to Dupré but still too dependent upon theological premises to constitute a proof of any transcendent origins of the soul.

Ultimately, the mystic discovers a self beyond its states of subjective consciousness. This discovery may also require a twofold definition of the self, one that is filled with images that approximate what it, through their symbolic representations, means to be alone with God and one that is imageless and revelatory of a "divine resplendence" known only through negativity. In sum, Dupré has invested himself in an interreligious spiritual psychology. Contemporary psychology allows religion to enter only through an empirical door and then with a great deal of hesitation. Dupré offers through his study of the mystics a new path to explore the "psyche" of psychology. He is never dismissive of the post-Freudian discourse of the unconscious, and he himself endorses radical empiricism. His main contribution, I think, would be to open up an investigation of the religious experience of the self-denying self whereby denial is understood ontologically and teleologically, not in terms of a Cartesian epistemology or merely in terms of a suppressed emotional state.

At the heart of essay 15 is a reexamination of the inverted analogy of Cusanus's *De visione Dei*. Cusanus sets the stage for thinking the unknowable, according to Dupré, even though Jan van Ruusbroec remains his preferred guide in linking mystical union to a common life in the world. The attraction of Cusanus's meditative treatise of 1453 is that it brings together Neoplatonic ideas of the intellectual unity of the soul with God with fervent faith in a Christ who mediates between divine and human nature in the expression of infinite love. By now it is clear that an either/or to the question of philosophical yearning and its opposition to a passive participation through grace has been ruled out. But Dupré goes further in maintaining that Cusanus already suggested an original solution to the problem of the justification of mysticism as a cognitive path. The Austrian monks who commissioned *De visione Dei* were fully unaware of a secular problematic. To them, William James's *Varieties of Religious Experience* would have appeared sacrilegious in its frank empiricism.

The monks wanted Cusanus to resolve a heated dispute between their abbot and Vincent of Aggsbach on whether mystical theology was primarily intellectual or voluntarist. Herein lies the genius of Dupré's interpretation of Cusanus. He explores the metaphor of God's seeing as creating and finds it multivalent, for it speaks both to the unified being of the Creator and the multiplicity of creation. The soul finds its rest in being seen by God because of the attractiveness of an invisible beauty. But the divine *eros* in its incarnate form is infinitely more powerful and unifying than the intellect's striving. Ultimately, the two trajectories are joined in the God-man, Jesus Christ, who is not a construct of the human power to envision God. Dupré writes: "By its very nature the intellect is called to this 'supernatural destiny,' yet only by subjecting itself in faith to the Word of God will it realize its natural perfection (essay 15)." Analogy signified an ascent from likenesses in the world to an original archetype. Dialectic denies that movement and posits the opposition of the finite to the infinite. Both of these positions find support in the works of Nicholas of Cusa, but Dupré's hypothesis of "an inverted analogy" brings us closer to a truly Cusan synthesis. The natural desire for God in the human intellect is called to realize its full perfection both on philosophical and religious grounds. But "the summit of contemplation" is not reached by the dynamics of ascent.[21] God's love permeates and unifies intellect and affect. In faith, knowledge is granted that is possible only by inverting analogical yearnings but without embracing the implicit iconoclasm of a nude and lifeless dialectic. Dupré's justification of a cognitive phenomenon ends with an invocation of the Cusan spirit of inquiry that is wholly unlike the rationalist spirit of modern philosophy. Dupré considers this synthesis very fragile, but it is, in his view, the most compelling synthesis of reason's freedom to explore and faith's concrete commitments that Christianity has ever devised.

To conclude, I would recall that Dupré, the Flemish Catholic phenomenologist who ended his illustrious career teaching the philosophy of religion in New Haven, Connecticut, is drawn to Robert Frost's Yankee evocation of "the road not taken." His desire to forge a new discourse that countered the excesses of modernity while culling its most important fruits was passionate while echoing the poetic measure of Anglo-American restraint. In fact, he concludes *Passage to Modernity* with these words of Ralph Waldo Emerson: "We must hold to this poverty, however scandalous, and by more vigorous self-recoveries, after the sallies of action, possess our axis more fully."[22] In fact, sometimes it seemed as if he fastened his entire theory of modernity on this staid but paradoxical gesture.[23] Secular modernity went down one path with rise of a new subjectivity and a new atheism, and we can never easily retrace our steps to the past that was consequently left behind. The principal difference between Dupré and traditionalism lies in this principled refusal of a nostalgic return. The metaphysician, for that matter, can still profess allegiance to, for example, Gilsonian Christian philosophy, but only after directly confronting the critiques of Kant, Hegel, and Heidegger. Dupré's range and depth as a scholar of Kant, Hegel, Husserl, and Heidegger on the trodden path has few rivals. His view of the spiritual gains made by modern progress was always a tempered one. On the untrodden path, for example, we find Cusanus's mystical synthesis of divine grace and human creativity as well as modern (but still pessimistic) readings of Augustinian selfhood and Ignatian humanism.

A pattern emerges in the midst of this paradoxical discourse. Louis Dupré *always* took the road not taken. He crossed the bridge to the past in order to retrieve insights for the present. The journeys I have made with Dupré on the path not taken have been some of the most important ones of my entire life. They never get old, and I am eager to revisit them because I know they will inspire new reflections each time. I encourage the readers of this book to join Dupré in crossing the bridge from philosophy to faith (and back again) and thereby discover new worlds of meaning and new expressions of truth.

ESSAY 1

Philosophy and Faith

For many years, metaphysicians have dealt with the object of the religious act as if they had invented it. Natural theology and theodicy were considered to be branches of philosophy independent of religious experience. This view may have appeared first in Aristotle (depending on the interpretation); it survived in the Stoa, and disappeared in early Christian thought. It reemerged in late Scholasticism and reached new heights in various systems loosely combined under the vague name *rationalism*. Kant, originally one of its chief proponents, became the main cause of its decline in philosophy.

In *Science and the Modern World*, Whitehead wrote:

> Aristotle found it necessary to complete his metaphysics by the introduction of a Prime Mover—God.[1] This, for two reasons, is an important fact in the history of metaphysics. In the first place, if we are to accord to anyone the position of the greatest metaphysician, having regard to genius of insight, to general equipment in knowledge, and to the stimulus of his metaphysical ancestry, we must choose Aristotle. Secondly, in his consideration of this metaphysical question, he was entirely dispassionate; and he is the last European metaphysician of first-rate importance for whom this claim can be made.[2]

Contrary to this thesis, I posit that philosophy by itself never reaches the idea of God, that it has received this idea from actual religious experience, and that philosophy ought to acknowledge this debt. In the words of the French philosopher Henri Duméry, "The philosopher *encounters* this idea; he is not the author of it. He must therefore seek to know what it signifies and which function may be assigned to it. But the philosopher is not to mould it as he pleases nor turn it to uses which do not correspond to the fundamental aspiration of the religious mind. In these conditions, the so-called God of philosophy is from the start a theft and a blunder. One pretends to believe that the idea of God is the property of philosophy, whereas it is borrowed from religious life."[3]

Even though philosophy may conclude to an ultimate, absolute principle of truth and of value, it thereby has not yet attained the idea of the *sacred* with its unique connotations of religious worthiness and its equally unique combination of fear and attractiveness that commonly accompany the religious idea of God. A similar argument applies to the metaphysical principle of ultimate value. Does it coincide with the religious idea of absolute Being? A partial identity is evident; a total one is not. Even if we were to assume a total identity, the way in which the principle of value appears still differs from the religious idea of God. The German philosopher Johannes Hessen justifies this negative conclusion: "That the principle of value just as the principle of meaning stands close to the religious idea of God is undeniable. Nevertheless, we must beware of identifying them. 'Principle of value' is a metaphysical concept, 'reality of value' a religious one. The former lacks the specifically religious quality, the quality of the sacred."[4]

Not even the philosophical attribute of all-surpassingness coincides with the sacred. Although what philosophy calls *transcendent* (i.e., all-surpassing) may in some respects be named *sacred*, yet this predicate should never appear alone: God is no more transcendent (i.e., beyond all things) than he is immanent (i.e., within all things). The term *transcendent* is by no means the determining characteristic of the sacred. It is a neutral, relational term. Thus, in epistemology the object known is said to *transcend* the knowing subject, insofar as it surpasses mere self-awareness. Analogously with this, philosophers call God absolutely *transcendent* insofar as they conceive God as surpassing any possible other reality. But for describing the sacred, the term *transcendent* is inappropriate. For that reason *rational arguments* alone are inadequate for proving God's existence, as medieval theologians appear to have done in presenting the *viae* (ways) that lead the pious mind to God. Still Aquinas, in his five ways, seems to have had an additional purpose in mind, namely, to show that the existence of the finite and the contingent *requires* the existence of God.

Nevertheless, philosophy may compare the ascending trajectory, which includes the so-called rational proofs of the existence of God of an infinite, necessary Being. Indeed, before John Duns Scotus, no Scholastics claimed to have produced a philosophical, fully equipped proof of God's existence. Their procedure essentially differed from that of the so-called philosophical arguments, which by a process of sheer reasoning expected to reach a full-fledged religious conclusion, as if the phenomenal world could provide adequate information about what surpasses it.

The very assumption of such a possibility was denounced by Kant. A second error, criticized by Hegel, consists in the fact that all attempts to "prove" God reduce God to an object. To "prove" is to posit an ideal content as objective reality independently of the positing subject. But the idea of God can never be an *object* of thought, for the nature of the *religious absolute* is such that it cannot be separated from the asserting subject.[5] All arguments misrepresent the relation between the finite and the infinite. The proof posits the finite first, as if it were the condition for the infinite's existence. Hegel therefore concludes: "The metaphysical proofs of the existence of God are defective interpretations and descriptions of the mind's elevation from the world to God, because they fail to draw attention to the moment of negation which is implied in this elevation."[6] Not because the finite *is*, the infinite is, but because the finite cannot be without the infinite, therefore the infinite must be. This is the way the religious mind envisions the relation between the infinite God and the finite. True infinity preserves the finite within itself.

Even if "purely rational" arguments for the existence of God could be made more successful than they are and actually *proved* the existence of an infinite being, they still would not reach what the *religious act* aims at. Unless philosophy first finds God *within* the religious experience, where his name originated, it will fall into the error denounced by Max Scheler: to identify two differently *intended* objects without proving that they are identical. The absolute of philosophy attempts to solve an intellectual problem; the God of religion is the one humans adore.[7]

Another metaphysical approach to the problem of God appears more promising. Recently philosophers have pointed out that a perception of finitude is possible only against a background of infinity. The light in which we see the finite is projected by an absolute intelligibility, which religious believers identify with the Supreme Being intended by the religious act. For that reason the limits established by Kant are also the limits of the metaphysical knowledge of God. A Scholastic school of philosophy, influenced by Maurice Blondel and Joseph Maréchal, started exploring the dynamics of the intellectual act, not in the hope of finding a new argument for the existence of God. Yet both they and their recent follower, Karl Rahner, have, on the ground of these early investigations, laid the groundwork for further philosophical inquiry.[8] In *Hörer des Wortes*, Rahner mentions the presence of an infinite dimension in the *pre-apprehension* (*Vorgriff*) of Being that accompanies each assertion of a finite reality: "The pre-apprehension of Being is not an *a priori* knowledge of an object, but the *a priori horizon of perception* of an object presented *a posteriori*. It is the *a priori* condition of the knowledge of an *a posteriori* appearance."[9]

Being-as-such is implicitly coasserted in any assertion of a *finite* reality. In his other philosophical work, *Geist in Welt* (*Spirit in the World*), Rahner explicates the principle on which his argument rests. In every judgment, knowledge of the infinite *esse* is pre-apprehended (177). If we grant the truth of a pre-apprehension, the assumption that the infinite that thereby appears is more than a merely formal concept (what medieval Scholastics called an *esse commune*), which includes all possible modes of Being but leaves their actual existence unproven. Rahner attempted to refute a reductionist interpretation of his thesis by arguing that his thesis applies only for the affirmation of actual beings, not possible ones, "since possibility is known from actuality, and not vice versa."

Still, might one not oppose to Rahner's argument Heidegger's thesis that any affirmation of being is surrounded by *nothingness*, as he claims in *Was Ist Metaphysik?* Still, in asserting the presence of a metaphysical horizon, whatever its nature, Rahner undoubtedly raises a metaphysical problem: What lies beyond the finite horizon? This question, far from being meaningless, as positivists claim, is metaphysically inevitable. While focusing on the horizon of Being, one naturally raises the *question* of transcendence. This, as I understand, is as far as philosophy may go in its metaphysical grounding of the essence of God. It is sufficient to make religious concerns *meaningful* to the metaphysician, but not to justify any positive religious assertion.

Turning now to the position of those who do not pretend to prove the existence of God, but nevertheless remain "open" to the religious idea of an infinitely transcendent and immanent reality, which the believer claims to encounter in the experience of the *sacred*, we face a variety of positions concerning the ultimate ground of the mind and the universe.

Which one shall we take? One philosopher here deserves particular attention because he has established a principle of choice among the infinite variety of religious experiences. Maurice Blondel refers to Christianity as a "necessary hypothesis" for any educated Western person. His selection was made at the time when most educated Europeans were at least marginally acquainted with the Christian faith. This hypothesis therefore deserved to be explored prior to a number of other hypotheses, which the philosopher may not consider, even though he does not consider them logically flawed.[10] Concretely, philosophy's task, then, consists in analyzing the internal coherence of the God-hypothesis, as the religious mind actually encounters it. For Muslims, that would probably be the Koran and the actual religious presence of God in his believers; for Jews, it would be the Bible and the living practice of Judaism; for Christians, it would include the Gospels and the tradition, both theoretical and practical, as realized in the life of the Church. For performing this reflection the mind turns to philosophy of religion. The transition seems smooth enough, but there is always waiting the temptation of not keeping the argument within well-defined limits. Otherwise, the philosopher may conclude, as he had done so often in the past, to some abstract concept of God, which faith or theology merely "fills out more fully." Whoever searches for the meaning of religion must be acquainted with *the full impact* of a religion, not with an outline or a mere abstract theory of it.

The main objective of philosophy of religion hereby consists in determining the specific nature of the religious act in and through its expressions. To achieve this purpose the philosopher must above all study the nature of the symbolic activity on which the religious consciousness relies. This is what Schelling in his *Philosophy of Myth* and in his *Philosophy of Revelation* attempted to accomplish. In so doing, philosophy responds to faith's own need of reflection: the drive toward *gnosis* belongs to the essence of the religious act. Faith seeks ever-greater clarification. The expression *fides quaerens intellectum* ("faith seeking understanding") is not an invention of philosophers but of theologians, and one that theistic traditions have practiced since their beginning. The educated believer naturally wants to explore what such concepts as "divine Creator," "immortal soul," and other tenets in the faith of his or her tradition might possibly mean. He or she must do so with constant reference to that fundamental interpretation of reality in its entirety, which we name *metaphysics*. The neo-Kantian philosopher Windelband therefore called religion "an intercourse with the inmost nature and foundation of all reality, a life in and with God, *a metaphysical life*."[11]

This questioning does not undermine religious faith; indeed, it follows the self-transcending movement of faith in its restless desire to move beyond its present state and seek to attain the clarity of vision. Nevertheless, such a reflection is fraught with danger to faith. The believing metaphysician may be tempted to take his religious interpretations for metaphysical answers. As Heidegger reminded us, God is not the final answer to the question, Why is there something rather than nothing?[12] If anything, God is part of the problem, for metaphysics must question infinite Being and also finite beings. Too eager a desire for philosophical confirmation may lead the religious person to substitute independent speculation to living experience. The believer may pretend to understand what in another respect he or she declares to be beyond understanding.

These dangers must be braved since the believer has no choice but to take the risk inherent in a critical reflection on his faith. Whitehead forcefully insisted on the need of reflection when he declared that faith, to maintain its religious identity, must remain aware of its metaphysical implications. In this respect faith differs from science: "Science can leave its metaphysics implicit and retire behind our belief in the pragmatic value of its general description. In doing so religion would admit that its dogmas are merely pleasing (i.e., adequate) ideas for the purpose of stimulating its emotions. Science (at least as a temporary methodological device) can rest upon a naïve faith; religion never stops longing for justification. When religion ceases to seek for increased clarity of expression it is sinking back into its lower forms."[13]

The degeneration to which Whitehead refers consists in a flight into the purely emotional and the wildly fantastic, typical of all primitive and uncritical religion. What Otto Karrer calls the *Verwilderung* (feralization) of the imaginary elements stands in the way of a mature development of religion. Edward B. Tylor was not entirely wrong in describing the development of religion as a *rationalization* process, which gradually subdues the unruly forces of religious inspiration. Otto Karrer considers the interpenetration of the rational elements with the nonrational ones inevitable at the initial stage of the religious consciousness, but it must be eliminated as religion grows to maturity.[14]

The category of the sacred is not fully realized until the nonrational, numinous events become *schematized* by rational elements. For Hegel this meant that faith has to develop into metaphysics. He claims that his "system" of philosophy, which begins with the *Logic* and ends with the *Philosophy of Spirit*, has the same content as religion. Philosophy has its own content, its need and interest common with religion; its object is the eternal truth, that is, nothing but God and his explication. Philosophy explicates itself only when it explicates religion, and while it explicates itself, it explicates religion.[15]

Still, the philosophical reflection upon the religious act remains distinct from general metaphysics. Whereas metaphysics ought to abstain from God-talk in religious language, philosophy of religion is explicitly invited to do so and thereby account for the full content (rational and suprarational) of religious activity. Although its general object coincides with that of philosophy, philosophy of religion does not stay with pure thought. It enters into the religious representation in order to penetrate to the fullness of religious expression.

Related to this incorporation of religion into metaphysics is the position held by theologians who subordinate philosophy to theological reflection. Thus the autonomy of philosophical thought becomes jeopardized altogether. The nonbeliever is declared to be subject to an illegitimate intrusion of religion into the domain of metaphysics. To one so widely extending the boundaries of theology, there is no proper domain for philosophy left. A somewhat similar view, albeit more restrained, was defended by Etienne Gilson, who, on the basis of Aquinas's *Summa Theologiae*, considered all true philosophy an integral part of Christian theology. This position obviously precludes an autonomous philosophy of religion. If this is assumed to be Christian philosophy, there is no Christian *philosophy*.

It is not always clear which one of the two positions an author adopts. In the case of Hegel, this has remained a matter of dispute to the present day. Hegel claims to accept the authority of Christian revelation. Yet he also argues that faith does not fully come into its own until it has philosophically *rethought* the representational content of revelation. Philosophy then is not merely a reflection upon faith; it is *faith itself* reaching its truth in philosophy. This does not mean that philosophy is a substitute for religion. (How could it be a substitute for what it presupposes?) But it nevertheless asserts that religion has not reached its own truth until it has philosophically justified each theological thesis by a philosophical insight. This rule places an undue emphasis upon the cognitive, gnostic element of the religious act. Religious faith spontaneously tends toward philosophical reflection, but its identity does not depend on reaching philosophical insight. To remain religious, the gnostic drive of faith must be kept within the boundaries of faith. A religious act can never be transformed into one of philosophical reflection while still preserving its original identity. Hegel appears to set no limits to the gnostic drive.

The God of faith still remains *hidden*, at the end of the philosophical clarification process as much as at the beginning. Hegel's philosophical religion admits no such restrictions. The cognitive dynamism of the religious act will continue to drive the mind until the original darkness of faith has completely evaporated. Hegel's position has given pause even to his most faithful commentators, as it does in the case of Albert Chapelle: "Does speculative thought grasp the mystery as well as it claims to do? Does the perfect knowledge, the spiritual gnosis, of the Trinitarian mystery not impose another negation, an abnegation, of which the patient Idea does not seem to be aware? Perhaps it is not a mere figure of speech that a surplus of knowledge remains promised from the Spirit to the Spirit. But does the relentless idealist thought ever know a surplus?"

Hegel's case shows how difficult it is to keep the relations between metaphysics and religion in perfect harmony. I think that the effect of religion upon general metaphysics, via the philosophy of religion, is more modest than he describes. It consists mainly in the awareness of another dimension in the [sic] Being, to which philosophy provides no direct access.

Philosophy must keep a precarious balance between admitting the experience of religious transcendence and abstaining from a full exploration of it. To adopt this attitude the philosopher must be willing to listen while retaining his full critical jurisdiction. In the past, philosophy of religion has often failed by an unwillingness to admit a transcendent origin of theological sources. By taking credit for doing independently what in fact it borrowed from religious sources, it betrayed philosophy's real autonomy and misinterpreted the nature of the religious experience.

PART I

Farewell to a Symbolic World

ESSAY 2

The Modern Idea of Culture and Its Opposition to Its Classical and Medieval Origins

Several writings in early Greek philosophy bear the title *Peri fuseos* ("About Nature"). *Physis* was, indeed, one of the oldest and most comprehensive concepts of Greek thought. It included nature, gods, and humans, subjects later divided over cosmology, theology, and anthropology. Another foundational concept was that of *form* (presented as *eidos* or as *morphē*). In contrast to the more fluctuating term *physis*, barely detached from the verb *fuein* (to grow), *form* referred to the permanent essence of a thing. Nothing is fully real until it appears in a well-defined, stable form. This principle of reality also functions as the basis of aesthetics, because only what has reached *formal* perfection may be considered beautiful. In Plato's philosophy, the forms alone are fully real and objects of knowledge. Their being carries an inner necessity: depending on their own intrinsic power, they are not subject to change or destruction. Aristotle also took *form* to be the defining notion of reality. In his interpretation, however, forms, in contrast to Plato's, are not separate from the world of appearances, but constitute its very essence.

The Hebrew view of reality substantially differed from the Greek one. The world was intrinsically dependent on a single divine Creator. Its forms had no inner necessity. The Greek conception of an uncreated cosmos contrasted with the Jewish-Christian one of a *created* world. As late as the sixth century, the philosopher Simplicius accused a Christian thinker of blasphemy for having compared the light of the sky to ordinary light. In spite of this opposition between Greek and Christian concepts of the cosmos, Christians found much to agree with, especially the idea of nature as established by measure and number, and ruled by divine Wisdom. Its hierarchical order reflected the light of that Wisdom. For Christians also, the cosmos played a significant theological role. Cosmological speculation abounds among the Church Fathers. The Hexaemeron commentaries on the six days of creation as described in Genesis provided ever-new opportunities for speculation about nature—some of it in the tradition of Plato's *Timaeus* and Aristotle's *Peri Philosophias*.[1] The planets, for good or for ill, still influenced terrestrial events of birth and death, of character, success and failure. Even medieval philosophers continued accepting the causal influence of the stars upon sublunar events.

One reason why Greek culture had been able to maintain itself to such an amazing degree was its overruling rationality. The term *logos* refers to *word* or *speech*, and beyond individual speech, to the fundamental reason inherent in all aspects of the cosmos and, especially, in the human mind. Stoic philosophy was to place so much stress on this inherent reason that it became the basis of law in ethics and politics. The Stoic idea of natural law preserved much of its authority in Christian times. Even Paul referred to it in his Letter to the Romans. Some theologians identified the angels with the pre-Christian movers of the planets, and attributed to them the characteristic qualities of astral bodies—*claritas, subtilitas, agilitas, impassibilitas*.

According to Boethius, the Christian Roman philosopher, a divinely established cosmic order determined man's place and prescribed his norms of conduct. Political structures had to conform to the cosmic hierarchy, according to Dante's *De monarchia* and to Thomas Aquinas's *De regimine principum*. Even Plato's idea of an *anima mundi* (world soul) was not discarded: several medieval theologians felt that the Holy Spirit easily fulfilled this function.[2] There was, to be sure, also a pessimistic streak in the Christian worldview. But even this may have been inspired as much by Greek (possibly Gnostic) sources as by the biblical story of the Fall and by Paul's theology of original sin. In any event, the Christian worldview became solidly incorporated within an originally Greek cosmology. In Whitehead's judgment, a fundamental rationality dominated medieval culture, more so than the age that was to give birth to modern science. To the Greek rationality, faithfully preserved by medieval Christians,

Arabs, and Jews, we owe the unique quality of objectivity that links early with modern thought.

Eventually the Christian idea of a rational universe ran into problems with some principles of late medieval theology. Was the person of Jesus, who had been raised unto membership of the divine Trinity and identified with the divine Logos, still compatible with that of a poor inhabitant of an occupied country and sentenced to death on a cross? Where was reason in all this? As the notions of sin and condemnation started to occupy an ever-increasing place in the religion of grace and redemption, a dark cloud of pessimism descended upon a culture that had begun with such high expectations. Nature ceased to play the role of the safe rational counselor it had been for centuries. In fact, it became the prime suspect in leading people astray on the way of salvation. Augustine, the main Western theologian of the early Middle Ages spent years fighting Pelagians and semi-Pelagians for believing that nature provided sufficient assistance for leading a virtuous life and thereby reaching salvation. The slow death of the once so glorious Roman Empire, the ruin of the cities, the collapse of the economy, and the spread of contagious diseases nourished this rampant religious pessimism. Augustine himself felt urged to protest in his voluminous *City of God* that this was not yet the end of the world.

Then, around the year 1200, after centuries of darkness, a new era of optimistic naturalism dawned. People regained interest in the secrets of nature, enjoyed her beauty, and started trusting her benevolence. With the new life came a fresh sensitivity for natural feelings. Religion woke to a new hope and an unprecedented humanism. Bernard of Clairvaux, the herald of the Christian renewal, expressed his love for the divine Word in terms of courteous love. Yet the real revolution began with Francis of Assisi (1182–1226), who, in lieu of Bernard's still abstractly universal Neoplatonic language, addressed his divine lover as an individual, human person. The universal notion of form made place for the singular individual. The humanism of Dante and Petrarch announced the advent of the modern age.

Still one more crisis separated modern speculation from this modern humanism: the theology of Nominalism. Medieval piety had nurtured a profound trust in the theological doctrine that the cosmos reflected the perfection of its Creator. Without needing to observe nature in detail, humans had a priori known that its laws and proportions had to be perfect. Late medieval theology, by one-sidedly stressing God's transcendence, came to conclude that divine omnipotence was above all human standards of wisdom and perfection. Hence, humans felt no longer confident in predicting on the ground of God's perfect nature how creation had to be. Henceforth scientists had to rely on their own observations and calculations. Only one science still provided absolute certainty, after all others had become shaky, namely, mathematics. If scientists succeeded in reducing all surfaces to measurable dimensions, physical knowledge would expand indefinitely.

Yet mathematical structures remained hidden behind the so-called secondary qualities of the physical world, such as color, taste, and sound. The observation of nature, therefore, had to undergo a scientific *reduction* before its quantitative nature was to appear. To obtain this result, Galileo devised an analytic method (*metodo resolutivo*) to break physical reality down into purely quantitative elements. The synthesis, however, that followed this analysis by no means reconstituted the early reality; it construed a new, *reduced* reality: the mechanical world of physics. Nature thereby became truncated, consisting of what the mind entraps and controls as calculable, predictable forces. Nature also lost its self-evident clarity. It became mute, while its inner teleology migrated to another segment of the real, namely, the mental one. The mechanically reduced physical world remained the exclusive subject of *science*.

There remained, of course, that other segment of reality, as certain as mathematics, of which it was the foundation, the entire area of mind. Yet of that *res cogitans*, as Descartes was to call it, there existed no *science* as yet. Unsurprisingly, the science of physical nature, the *res extensa* (Descartes) with its clearly established principles, eventually was to encroach upon the terrain of the *res cogitans* and, according to some scientists, eventually absorbed it. To them, life, including thinking life, had gradually become part of one all-comprehensive nature.

At the early stage of modern consciousness, all motion in Descartes's universe was still assumed to derive from a divine Creator. Yet if physical nature was to be truly unified, the mechanical model of nature was to be complemented by a more inclusive organic one. A crucial condition of this change was that motion hitherto conceived as *externally imposed or given* by divine causality be replaced by *self-motion*. Giordano Bruno made this possible by adopting a different view of creation. Whereas in the traditional view creation had depended on a primary motion given by a divine Creator to the cosmos at its beginning, Bruno proposed that motion had always been present in a *self-moving* cosmos. This, of course was still a hypothesis waiting for proof. But later materialists thought it sufficient to dispense with any *supernatural* cause of the cosmos and to assume, on the basis of Newton's principle of inertia, that if the world had been moving at the start, it would continue to do so forever. Thus, what Bruno had guessed, Diderot proved a century later, namely, that no external agent was needed to introduce motion into the world.

Other changes were equally fundamental. Inspired by the same resistance to a transcendent causality, some began to question the notion of an infused rationality in the concept of a world order. Why should all rationality not be due to the only being we know to be rational, namely, the human mind? Yet when the human subject became the sole source of rationality, reason turned into a method of categorical structuring and lost its contemplative quality. It is hard to imagine Greeks or medieval Scholastics describing the process of cognition as "a judge compelling a witness to answer," as Kant had formulated it. More and more, then, an imperious human mind appeared to bestow its own rationality upon an amorphous world. Whereas the Greek *theoria* had required the soul to be purified before being allowed to the divine act of contemplation, the subject now adopted a dominant attitude that culminated in the conception that *real* is only what had been constituted as such by an autonomous human reason.

Overall, reason acquired a practical orientation, even in its theoretical activity. Practical control ended the supremacy of contemplation and introduced a period of fabrication. This, as Hannah Arendt argued, resulted in an unlimited instrumentalization of the cosmos: a confidence in tools, a dominion of the principle of utility, a reduction of nature to a workshop for human tinkering.[3] Hans Jonas illustrates the transition in the cognitive attitude, from purely theoretical to practical, by contrasting Francis Bacon's attitude with that of Thomas Aquinas. The British scientist writes: "I would address one general admonition to all: that they consider what are the true ends of knowledge, and that they seek it not either for pleasure of the mind, or for contention, or for superiority to others . . . but for the benefit and use of life. For the matter in hand is no mere felicity of speculation, but the business and fortunes of the human race, and all power of operation."[4] For Bacon, the end of knowledge is its practical use—to overcome the physical miseries of life. For Plato, Aristotle, and Aquinas, knowledge had been an end in itself, essential to the good life. The good life may require the satisfaction of basic physical needs, but it culminates in contemplation. Nor is the modern goal one in which we simply *apply* the conclusions of science. Theory itself has become a practical, problem-solving concern that forces nature to respond to the "vexation of art."

For two centuries, modern science had created almost no technology. Nevertheless, it prepared both the methods and the attitudes needed for technological development once other, primarily economic and social, factors had made it possible. It initiated that ordering of nature, which in the nineteenth century would explode into a technical revolution that has now come to dominate our entire lives. We deceive ourselves in continuing to view technique as an instrument to self-directed goals—not essentially different from the ancient and medieval crafts in which the term *technē* had its origin. Modern technology, instead of participating in the work of nature as it did in ancient and medieval theories, aims at full control over nature, even if that implies an outright confrontation with nature. The Greeks did not aim at controlling nature or its processes, but rather at keeping all instrumental activity within boundaries set by nature. Undoubtedly, the products of *technē* and *poiēsis* are original creations of man. But the traditional craftsman did not intend to change or even to humanize nature. To create, then, was primarily to adjust oneself to nature.

Modern technology, on the contrary, is a conquest of nature on man's own terms without regard for nature's immanent processes, except for the purpose of exploiting them. Above all, it has ceased to be a means. The world we inhabit has been built *by* technique and *for* technique. Unquestionably, technology has rendered us unprecedented services. Yet it is anything but man's handmaid. For the services, in a classical reversal of the master-and-servant role, have made its dominion irreversible. The benefits acquired by modern science and technology are not of the kind one can choose to use or not to use. Refusing to use them would set civilization back at a primitive state, when we started using them out of sheer necessity.[5] Once we have passed that stage, technology offers us so many advantages of increased speed or utility, which it becomes almost impossible to resist. At that moment, the purpose of new inventions becomes reversed. Instead of improving life by offering greater comforts, they complicate it to a point where disadvantages outweigh advantages.

Yet there is no escape. Take the case of the computer. What has caused greater changes in all aspects of modern life than cybernetics, the greatest revolution of the twentieth century? Yet controlled by modern goals of production, aiming at increasing profits rather than increasing use value, in quick succession it offers new models that make the older ones obsolete, forcing its users to study new techniques and removing former models from sale, thereby making their inventions inaccessible to older, less educated, or poorer persons. Thus, the most advanced theory of the modern age has to an undue extent become a function of practice. In the instrumentalist universe of modern science, all becomes *function*; nothing refers *beyond* the closed circuit of technical connections. Technical improvement contributes to the smooth functioning of a circular *system*, of which the person himself forms an essential part. The user has neither the desire nor the power to escape from what he or she knows to have become indispensable to human well-being. The technical imperative summons him or her as much as it summons all of nature and demands its full attention. Technology has become the very face of reality.

Indeed, to speak of the "ends" of technology makes little sense. Whatever surplus of leisure and theoretical insight it has produced is fed back into the self-perpetuating system. It is unrealistic to hope that the leisure created by the freedom from menial tasks will eventually result in a higher amount of time available for devoting to theoretical or contemplative knowledge. Hans Jonas wisely states: "If we equate the realm of necessity with Plato's 'cave,' then scientific theory leads not out of the cave; nor is its practical application a return to the cave: it never left the cave in the first place. It is entirely of the cave and therefore not 'theory' at all in the Platonic sense."[6] Hence the paradox noted by Hannah Arendt that in the age when man became most worldly (that is, most able to humanize the world), the world itself has lost all intrinsic meaning. It has become reduced to a mental abstraction. What started by being a thing in its own right ends up being devoid of any substance, a mere projection on the technological circuit. Everywhere man encounters only himself and his own fabrications in this closed, autistic universe. Yet, Heidegger adds, nowhere does he encounter himself in truth, that is, in his essence.

This leads us to a second transformation of modern culture: that of the meaning and role of the self. In Plato's *Timaeus* and the many writings it influenced, the human person is a microcosm of the entire world order: "The world is like, above all things, to that living creature of which all other living creatures, severally and in their families, are parts. For that embraces and contains within itself all the intelligible living creatures, just as this world contains ourselves and all other creatures that have been formed as things visible."[7]

Christians had enthusiastically adopted the microcosmic view of man. We find it in a number of Greek Christians, such as Gregory Nazianzen, Basil, and Gregory of Nyssa. Maximus the Confessor structured his entire anthropology of mediation between the material and the spiritual world around it.[8] The macrocosm/microcosm parallelism pervades the entire Scholastic cosmology.[9] Man, in whom creation culminates, had in this medieval system the task to return it to its Creator in a contemplative and oblative attitude. The entire universe was conceived as a gift endowed with a meaning that it is man's task to discover and express. In fulfilling this task, man finds at the same time his own meaning, as described in the two books of nature and revelation.

This beautiful parallelism disintegrated in the Nominalist theology of the late Middle Ages, when the world became a blind product of an omnipotent and inscrutable God. Bacon explicitly rejects both the world's being an image of God and man's being an image of the world: "The works of God show the omnipotence and wisdom of the maker but not his image: and therefore therein the heathen opinion differs from the sacred truth; for they supposed the world to be the image of God and man to be an extract or compendious image of the world."[10] Henceforth the human subject alone bestows meaning upon a reality drained of any immanent meaning.

What began as a radical *subjectification* of the real, ended up reducing the subject itself to the mere function of *constituting objectivity* in the theoretical and the practical order. The instrumentalization of reason is depriving it of all content of its own. In Max Horkheimer's caustic phrase, "The more all nature is looked upon as mere objects in relation to human subjects, the more is the once supposedly autonomous subject emptied of any content, until it finally becomes a mere name with nothing to denominate. The total transformation of each and every realm of being into a field of means leads to the liquidation of the subject who is supposed to use them. This gives modern industrialist society its nihilistic aspect."[11]

The problem became even more acute by the awareness that a dependence upon an external cause is hard to reconcile with genuine human freedom. Kant, in the antinomies of pure reason in the *Critique of Pure Reason*, opposed freedom to causality, but then resolved the conflict by assigning to each a separate realm. Even if this solution had sufficed to justify the presence of free will and causal necessity in the same universe, it failed to show how a causal dependence could be at the origin of this freedom. The theory of autonomy in the *Critique of Practical Reason* made an open conflict between freedom and causal dependence inevitable. If any heteronomous interference with self-determination would be fatal to freedom, it logically follows that freedom could not have its origin in a process of efficient causality. Yet Kant never drew that conclusion. Later he even claimed that it was possible to regard all moral duties as divine commands and that this was, in fact, the very essence of religion.[12]

Later philosophers of freedom were more consistent: since most of them continued to accept the causal model of creation as the only possible one, they became almost without exception atheists. Freedom can tolerate contingency and limitation, but not a causal determination, not even a preestablished givenness of ideals and values. If they were imposed upon a free agent, his or her only choice would consist in *either* ratifying or realizing them *or* in refusing to do so. Sartre added that in such a choice only a refusal to ratify them would be a genuinely free choice. Nothing can be *given* in freedom except freedom itself, and that, by its very nature, cannot be given causally. That this problem did not emerge earlier in Western thought may be due to the small amount of control that man actually exercised over a world that dominated him more than he dominated it.

In the eighteenth century, the idea of God ceased to be a dominant factor in Western culture. Yet not until the nineteenth century did the absence of a meaningful idea of God become a scientific a priori. At that time originated scientific positivism, social determinism, and axiological humanism. These antitheist trends have survived until our own day, yet they no longer dominate the present religious condition. Today's secularist philosophers consider their position sufficiently established in Western culture to stop defining themselves by a negation of religious faith. Many have abandoned their antireligious stand for an attitude of all-comprehensive openness that, rather than fighting values traditionally represented by religion, has incorporated them into a more accommodating synthesis. For many, religion has become reduced to an experience, indispensable in the past and even today enlightening to some, but not sufficiently powerful to draw their entire existence into its orbit. Having not found a substitute for the earlier integration, they have resigned themselves to a fragmented worldview.

ESSAY 3

The Fragmentation of the Symbolic World

A Symbolic World

In New York, at the northern end of the city, on a plateau overlooking the Hudson valley, stands my favorite museum, The Cloisters. In the heart of it, a mysterious room contains the famous Unicorn Tapestries of the late Middle Ages. To visit that room is at once an enriching and a disconcerting experience. As in a dense literary text, literal meanings are indissolubly mingled with symbolic ones. Reality itself here appears as a scripture, inviting a never-concluding commentary that constantly shifts from one meaning to another. All things refer to one another in a play of continuously transformed analogies and affinities. Nature itself here appears symbolic in its very essence, rather than *rendered* symbolic by the mind. Meanings are *given*, not invented, but none are given simply. Hence, unlike what happens in a symbolization made by the mind, we are unable to predict the strange ways in which reality may symbolize.

Today we tend to ascribe the origin of meaning exclusively to the human mind. Rarely do we question this assumption, least of all when we confront "symbolic" meaning.[1] The symbolic nature of medieval reality did not exclude literalness, however. Long ago, the eminent French art historian Émile Mâle cautioned against a symbolic interpretation of all features of the Gothic cathedral. Medieval sculptors delighted in poking fun at the serious visitor: at any opportunity they attempted to write their whimsical signatures in half-hidden but easily discoverable places. Medieval symbolism was so tightly intertwined with reality that the very term *symbolic*, as we use it, hardly applies to a world that in its entirety was perceived as *mirroring* God's complex reality. Alain de Lille's playful verses express this fundamental principle of medieval art:

Omnis mundi creatura	Each creature of the world
Quasi liber et pictura	Is to us a book and image
Nobis est et speculum.	As well as a reflecting glass.

Nature functioned *as a book* that even the illiterate were able to read. Medieval learning depended heavily on exegesis: knowledge consisted mainly in a commentary on the relation between the two books of nature and scripture. In an inexhaustible number of words and things, each possessing multiple meanings, they endlessly referred to one another by means of analogy and affinity. This complexity invited scholars to a never-ending *commentary* and charged them with the double task of decoding a twice-revealed text. Like the book of scripture, which conceals as much as it reveals, nature challenged scholars with the task of interpreting "the book [of nature] in which the creative Trinity shines."[2] Without language (biblical or other), nature would have remained symbolically silent. Still, language itself appeared as an integral part of God's creation, not as a separate, humanly invented ability to shape and reshape the meaning of nature at random. Language and nature together were the two complementary parts of one divine creation; one articulates the meanings that the other inspires.

This intrinsic link between nature and language dissolved at the end of the Middle Ages. We usually hold Nominalist theology responsible for this dissolution. Once nature was reduced to the blind effect of an inscrutable divine decision, it lost the internal richness of symbolic meanings it had possessed at an earlier age. The proportions among things, which previously had given nature its metaphorical character, were attributed to thought, that is, to human interpretation. Language's primary function came to consist in supporting man's practical activity. For that purpose, words had to be stripped of all metaphoric ambiguities and words frozen into atoms of potential meanings. Eventually people developed parts of them into abstract sets of signs remote from any direct contact with reality, yet indispensable for finding their way to nature. The more limited the task they served, the more language could be reduced to an international shorthand, hardly different from one culture to another. This multinational speech requires little learning, consisting as it does mainly of acronyms, abbreviations, and equation-like formulas.

Yet the relative independence of language with respect to *reality* opened new possibilities for its autonomous development. By separating speech from nature, Nominalism rendered possible what, at first blush, it might have seemed to exclude, namely, a cult of language for its own sake, independent of its relation to nature. Nevertheless, such a cult stands at the origin of late medieval humanism. Rather than honoring the coarse language of everyday use, humanists turned to the new aesthetic possibilities, which the formal perfection of the classical writers of Greece and Rome had given to speech. In contrast to the naturally symbolic language of the Middle Ages (in which nature and language had complemented each other), the artificial language of the Renaissance humanists appears as a separate, ennobled, and exclusively *human creation*. Some attributed the rise of this independent cult of language to Dante. In fact, Dante's thought, however original, had remained solidly rooted in the medieval assumption that language was intrinsically linked to nature in a single divine act of creation. Nevertheless, the fact that the language of his poetry *surpassed* nature induced Dante's followers Petrarch and Boccaccio to interpret their master's art as a language that had become *separate* from nature.

This language, once it developed into an autonomous entity, became the foundation of a new *culture*. The separation between language and nature became definitive when the early humanists started following the models of those who had given speech its greatest formal perfection, namely, the classics of Athens and Rome: "The rhetorical revolution of the fourteenth century reflects what Mario Praz was to call *a revolution in sensibility*. Men of the Renaissance turned to the pagan feelings because they discovered types in their literature and art, which expressed feelings similar to the ones they wished to express."[3] This is the point where the Renaissance began to split from early humanism. Later humanists returned to what Dante had really written about the cult of language. During his journey through hell, he sadly encountered his beloved master Brunetto Latini, who had defended the *dulce stil nuovo*, the poetic use of the vernacular, which he considered the ancient, most authentic form of Latin speech. The native tongue of the people had preserved the full creative power of words. It alone was capable of a poetic symbolization of the poet's inner life. In his Latin treatise *De vulgari eloquentia* ("On the Vernacular Language"), Dante argued that language is man's creative response to his physical and his spiritual needs. Yet only in the metaphorical, that is, the poetic use of language, do humans display what Dante calls their divine powers. Through the power of metaphor, man builds a separate spiritual universe.

A hundred years after Dante, another Italian humanist, Coluccio Salutati, in his *De laboribus Herculis* ("On the Works of Hercules"), reaffirmed even more strongly the primary role of the creative word in the development of culture. Hercules, alleged to have been the protagonist of poetry, replaced Prometheus as the mythical founder of culture. Only through poetic metaphors does man succeed in raising a particular experience to a universal level, as culture requires. In the fifteenth century, Christoforo Landino added that poetry, the synthesis of the liberal arts, contains the quintessence of all human creativity. Increasingly, rhetoric came to be viewed as the basis of thinking. Only *words* give men access to spiritual *reality*; in many instances by *constituting* it.[4]

Before him, Cardinal Nicholas of Cusa, a man of uncommon genius, philosophically restored the foundation of language that had been lost in the Nominalist derogation of it. According to him, the symbolic power of language enables the mind to compare "ideas" and thereby becomes the "measure" of all things: *Mens mensurat etiam symbolice, comparationis modo* ("The mind also symbolically measures by way of comparing").[5] Cusa's knowledge-by-comparison stands closer to the new rhetoric of the humanists than to traditional metaphysics. Being the living image of the Creator, the human person *creates* his own symbolic world: "For as God is the creator of real entities and natural forms, so is man the creator of rational entities and artificial forms, which are but similitudes of his intellect, even as creatures are similitudes of the divine intellect."[6] Images and symbols are products of the *mind*'s creative power.

Mind: The Mirror of Unlimited Reality

Surprisingly, yet not coincidentally, Cusanus and fifteenth-century humanists placed the human person at the center of the spiritual universe, just at the time when Copernicus's theory was to dislodge the Earth from the physical center it had occupied in the medieval universe. The emphasis on the *spiritual* rather than the *physical* position was to render the new heliocentric theory acceptable.[7] Man is great, Pico della Mirandola had declared, not because of his physical position, but because of his power to define his role and function in the world. In the same spirit, Copernicus, in the dedication of his *Revolutiones* (1543) to Pope Paul III, claims that the world was made for man, not so much to sustain him physically as to allow him to comprehend it intellectually. Had Plato, the pope's favorite philosopher, not compared the mind to the sun of the universe? Likewise, the sun of the mind was now declared to be the center of that new, spiritual universe. Even after the heliocentric theory had come under a cloud, its spiritual significance remained. Thus, Cardinal de Bérulle wrote: "This new idea, hardly popular for the knowledge of the stars, should be so for the knowledge of salvation."[8] Obviously Bérulle considered a universe with the source of light at the center of the planetary system more suitable to symbolize God's relation to the world than man's marginal place in the physical universe.

The cosmological revolution continued to enjoy the full approval of the spiritual authorities until Giordano Bruno's theories lowered the celestial realm of the fixed stars to the lower level of the moving planets. The apparent immobility of the "fixed" stars was to be explained by the immensity of a universe, in which cosmic motions were not perceivable to the naked eye. From the immeasurability of its distance, Giordano Bruno concluded to the existence of an infinite, moving universe that consisted of uncountable systems of which our solar system occupied only an infinitesimally small part.[9] To Bruno, this spectacle of an infinite universe, ever in motion, provided limitless human possibilities. Where nothing is fixed, man, the spiritual center, may adopt any perspective he chooses. In one of his mythical dialogues, Bruno describes how the gods have given man hands and an intellect in order to allow him to create himself a second nature similar to that of the gods:[10] "Going beyond nature, as what already exists, becomes the existential sense provided for man by nature."[11] The infinite universe, then, no longer held the horror of the indefinite, which the *apeiron* (meaning "infinite" as well as "indefinite") had for the Greeks. For Bruno, infinity no longer means mere negation of limits, but unrestricted space for human creativity. In an infinite universe, the human intellect becomes aware of its own infinity. Once the finite world order had ceased to contain man, human intelligence stood ready to inform the empty space with its mental infinity. The primacy of the human subject in the constitution of meaning had already become acceptable. The new cosmology provided the conditions for realizing the modern idea of absolute freedom.

Thus far we have directed our attention mainly to language. Yet architects, sculptors, and painters also expressed their symbolic creativity in an unlimited variety of works of art. In the Italian Renaissance, the idea that the artist is able to give form and shape to any human projection infinitely expanded the world's aesthetic potential. Henceforth the human subject alone imposes a self-given form upon the universe. Perspective was freely chosen in an infinite universe. If the human subject occupies the center of an infinite symbolic world, modern perspective might start from the eye of the beholder. Man would remain the spiritual center of the universe from any place. Artists had started using the one-point perspective before scientists had established the immensity of the universe. The central perspective was, to my knowledge, first consistently applied by the fourteenth-century Sienese painter Ambrogio Lorenzetti. Yet the beginnings of it appear in the miniatures for the *Heures* (Breviary) of the Duc de Berry, painted by the Brothers van Limburch.

The question of what things are *in themselves* had guided the development of Eastern and early Western iconography. In Byzantine and primitive Italian painting, all details of human observation, such as the shape and color of clothes and physical environment, the particular expression and posture of the represented individuals, even their pictorial resemblance, were deliberately omitted. They confront us as impersonal figures, presented in a hieratic view against a background of gold—the color that most purely reflects light, the very refraction of spirit in matter. Renaissance art instead aims only at creating *representations*, that is, images and perceptions arranged within the perspective of the human eye. To *know* no longer consists in a spiritual presence, but in a reflection on the reality of human observation. Henceforth the criterion of art lies in the truth of this observation, not in the nature of things themselves. Thinking itself became a mirror—Shakespeare's "glassy essence"—wherein man refashions reality according to his own capacity.

To what extent does this mirror image reflect the primary, given reality of things? This question introduces the critical investigation required by the modern attitude toward the world. Galileo distinguished *secondary* qualities dependent on the structure of the observer from *primary* ones, which remain after the critical investigation and therefore may be considered to belong to the nature of reality itself. Galileo and Descartes identified the latter with the geometrical, measurable qualities. Yet clearly, that distinction failed to solve the problem. Who would be willing to reduce the real to mathematical abstractions? Even the physical sciences, for whose benefit the mathematical simplification had been conceived, made little progress until Newton had shown the imperfection of a conception of the real on the sole basis of mathematical principles.

Despite their heavy schematizations, scientists and even artists continued to speak of *nature* as their ultimate model and criterion. Renaissance painters and sculptors all claim to "imitate" nature. The Italian architect Leon Battista Alberti (1404–72) justifies this ancient saying by describing painting as an activity that imitates the *creative process* operative in nature. Nature invites the artist to do what she herself does, namely, to *create*. Only when we surpass and improve nature do we truly imitate her. For that reason the artist's most important task consists in the composition, the arrangement of the various objects into an orderly totality. To ensure grace and beauty, the artist must imitate how nature composes the parts of beautiful bodies, namely, by leaving out everything but what appears significant to the artist. In his form-giving activity, the artist re-creates nature. When the painter treats a two-dimensional picture as if it were a window, through which a three-dimensional scene appears, as Alberti invites him to do, then, in fact, the painter reshapes reality and defines it in terms of his own visual representation.

The idea that art consisted in a self-conscious process of shaping and defining reality continues after the Renaissance. It culminates in Romantic art. In the influential preface to his play *Cromwell*, Victor Hugo argues again that we should imitate nature, but precisely thereby surpass naturalism altogether: "La vérité de l'art ne saurait être, ainsi que l'ont dit plusieurs, la réalité absolue. L'art ne peut donner la chose même" (The truth of art could not be, as some have claimed, the absolute reality. Art can never give us the thing itself). But the modesty of this statement only prepares the ambitious claim that at least dramatic art is "un miroir de concentration qui, loin de les affaiblir, ramasse et condense les rayons colorants, qui fasse d'une lueur une lumière, d'une lumière une flamme" (a mirror of concentration, which far from weakening them, picks up the colored rays and condenses them; converting a shimmer into a light, and a light into a flame). In this respect, literary art, Hugo concludes, is almost divine: it resurrects through history, it creates through poetry. Balzac agrees with Hugo. The mission of art is not to copy nature, but to express it and thereby to force it to reveal its mysteries. The artist wants "to steal the secret of God."

The *imitatio naturae*, understood in the sense of penetrating to the core of the natural processes, would, after considerable historical detours, lead to a view of art as a projection of life. Renaissance poets, artists, and thinkers had been impressed by the mathematical proportions of the cosmos. This insight links Descartes's method with the mathematical perspective of the Florentine painters. Yet in the end, a merely mathematical conception of nature proved to be inadequate for science and even more for art.

The Fragmentation of Symbolic Structures

Of all literary genres, the novel most closely followed the movements of the modern mind. György Lukács, the Hungarian philosopher, showed how the crisis of meaning in late modern culture promoted the success of literature. In fiction, we attempt to recover a meaning that is no longer available in life. The very coherence of its structure—the move from a beginning to an end, via a number of complications—renders the novel into an island of sense within an ocean of meaninglessness. According to Michel Foucault, "*Don Quixote* is the first modern work of literature . . . because in it language breaks off its old kinship with things and enters into that lonely sovereignty from which it will reappear, in its separated state, as only literature."[12] Yet before we agree to recognize the novel as "only literature," an escape from boredom and disorder, the novel had a short but promising career as a new source of meaning.

Its very structure guaranteed some measure of protection against the unlimited liberty the person had come to claim for him- or herself. The form of the novel requires coherence of plot and character. In its early days, the *Bildungsroman*, the report of the hero's educational journey through life, assumed an unprecedented importance. Goethe's *Wilhelm*

Meister, the prototype, was soon followed by Novalis's *Heinrich van Oefterdingen* and Jean-Paul's *Titan*. Even Romantic poets such as Wordsworth in *Prelude* and Byron in *Don Juan* turn the journey into a symbol of life's spiritual development. The historical novel raises the development of the individual onto the grand scale of a nation, tribe, or city. Of course, the novel cannot do full justice to this inner development through freedom, "for if the man were entirely free he might simply walk out of the story."[13]

Indeed, rather than moving toward an ever-greater freedom of the imagination in an "open-ended universe" as the novel had promised at its birth—a promise that throughout the eighteenth century it had more or less faithfully fulfilled—the great nineteenth-century novelists, rather than continuing this trend, began to aim at the far more ambitious goal of providing new meaning to human existence as it was. No longer satisfied with the escapist flights of the epic imagination, post-Romantic novelists shifted the weight of meaning entirely to the side of language. On the wings of this ambition, the novel soared to its greatest height with the realistic novels of Balzac, Flaubert, and Zola in France, Dickens, Thackeray, and Hardy in England, and Manzoni in Italy.

Yet the final goal proved to be elusive. Once writers fully realized that even realistic narratives did not fulfill their philosophical aspirations, the genre rapidly went into decline. The most ambitious among those who succeeded the nineteenth-century realists, particularly the German giants of language, Kafka, Musil, Broch, and Mann, attempted to regain existential significance by sacrificing the straight objective narrative, which for centuries had established an ideal level of *imagined* meaning. Once the novelist knows that the patterns of meaning of any fiction remain at variance with reality and realizes that his reader knows it, he turns the narrative into a personal quest, which, by its intrinsic interest, allures the reader to follow him on his road to insight. He has ceased to count on the solutions that ancient drama and modern epic had promised. The writer, not the hero, features as main figure in this essentially fragmentary enterprise: "In telling the story of his successes and failures the novelist succeeds—as a momentary reconciliation of matter and spirit toward which the hero strives in vain."[14]

When the writer and the reader so self-consciously take their distance from the mythical hero, skepticism quickly turns into irony. Irony, to be sure, bridges the gap between conflicting positions but, once it becomes self-conscious, it also widens the distance. Eventually, it turns against the writer and his literary enterprise. This inversion has given birth to complex works that barely deserve the name of fiction: their subject consists mainly in writing about writing, literary criticism presented as fiction, antinovels posturing as novels. Literary criticism and even philosophy seem to have converged in the contemporary novel, much to the detriment of the narrative.[15]

Some contemporary writers have drawn the conclusion that, after all, the novel consists of words about words, neither about life nor about the world. As literary language detaches itself not only from any given order, but even from a *representational* narrative, its word-structures become self-referential. Its word-structures become self-referential. Symbols merely refer to other symbols, while dispensing almost entirely with the course of the world outside.[16] This final, radical assertion of the supremacy of language over nature had been anticipated by the nineteenth-century poet Baudelaire. Not only does the poet refuse to "follow" or "imitate" nature; his intention is to erect a veritable antinature. For him the poem, and the work of art in general, must be a pure creation, unattached to anything outside itself. The artificial thereby becomes the natural home of poetry. Nature, wherever it enters artistic creation, must be transformed until its *reality* status vanishes. In that direction, Henri Lefebvre observed, poets went further than novelists would ever go: "The narrative of the novel accepts everyday life: it describes it. It takes it as object, at least as an object. Poetic language pursues the metamorphosis of the ordinary. Its operation has a dual character. The ordinary, having been refused, is by that refusal lifted up to language and language itself elevated to the absolute. But this soon evokes doubt and insecurity with respect to a language that is fetishized. The eternal silence hovers over the word, surrounds it, threatens it."[17] Language thus alienated from nature sets its verbal structure up as an independent universe, at war with the established reality constructions of men. The poet turns into an outcast of society, a *bohémien*, even a demoniacal *poète maudit* (such as Rimbaud or Lautreamont). His existence and that of his fellow artists moves around night cafes, music halls, boulevards, and salons. It is the world of Degas's *danseuses*, Toulouse-Lautrec's floozies.

Still, language has rarely accepted a complete isolation from the *givenness* of nature or culture. Being by nature object-oriented, it intends and *names* reality. It inevitably makes statements about the world, even when it attempts to speak only about itself. Nevertheless, as the literary work becomes more enclosed within itself, its meaning grows esoteric and more and more requires interpretation. Thus, in our age, criticism has come to occupy a dominant place in literature, as if it were destined to become the literary genre of the present. What Renan predicted has now become a reality: "In a sense criticism is superior to composition. Till now criticism has adopted a humble role as a servant and *pedis sequa* of literature. Perhaps the time has come for criticism to take stock of itself and to raise itself above those whom it judges."[18] Literary interpretation today no longer needs "literary" works to write about: it has become able to be its own subject. A newspaper article may serve as well as a poem. For criticism also has taken the inward road: it appears to have become its own subject conclusion from a purely subjective source.

In many respects, even the infatuation of the subject with its own projections appears to have come to an end. More and more a feeling emerges that man does not measure up to the role of the "transcendent" subject into which he has cast himself. A projected symbolic structure in the end appears to be no more than the contingent utterance of a contingent subject. What was more logical, then, than the attempt to exorcize that subject from its own work after it had proven inadequate to provide its content? Thus began the paradoxical search for a symbolic world that would at once be wholly man-made and wholly untainted by subjectivity. It inaugurated the quest for a new immediacy, for a *reality-in-itself,* undisturbed by human emotions, yet nonetheless man-made. For this purpose artists attempted to convey the impact of the real *before* consciousness transforms it by reflective clarity. Even such highly self-conscious movements as surrealism and abstract expressionism manifest a desire to retrieve the immediacy of reality's first contact with the still unconscious self, before it becomes decanted by reflection. Of course, the unconscious has always been a hidden source of artistic creativity. Yet to use it as the leading principle of the creative process will not result in bypassing the conscious subject at all, but only in rendering its creations ever more private.

Late modern culture certainly presents an exciting spectacle. Yet its unrestricted creativity exacts a high price. Symbols and symbolic structures that have traditionally functioned as beacons of meaning on our journey through time are no longer able to do so. Once we take upon ourselves the task of creating such structures at random, they cease to provide guidance. They turn into games—with words or forms that have all the glitter of glass beads but fail to leave any impact beyond the moment of their appearance. We are left with Eliot's "heap of broken images." Still, the desert of meaning that has produced this glitter cannot afford to dispense with these wobbling beacons. For even these aesthetic symbols with the forever-shifting perspectives in an unstable universe yield at least a momentary glimmer of eternity. They are still to be treasured as "fragments against ruins."[19]

ESSAY 4

The Sources of Modern Atheism

Religious Deism

The principles that since the eighteenth century have determined modern culture obviously conflict with those that gave form to traditional theism. Some have described the modern ones as implicitly *atheistic*. The term *atheism* is not new. Socrates was branded with it for undermining the polytheist religion of his time, and so, in a different way, had Epicurus undermined it. Yet both believed in gods. Closer to our own time, the pious Spinoza was charged with atheism for having articulated the relation between God's transcendence and immanence in terms that varied from the traditional understanding. The stigma adhered to his name all through the eighteenth century. Lessing's reputation as a religious thinker changed overnight when Jacobi discovered some Spinozistic leanings in his work. As late as the nineteenth century, Fichte lost his chair at the University of Jena in the *Atheismusstreit*. Those who attempted to rethink the nature of religion have always been suspected of being atheists.

The "atheism" described in this essay was both more radical and less pious. It was mainly due to an incompatibility of the foundational principles of modern thought with the idea of God as the ultimate cause of reality. Unlike earlier forms of "atheism," the modern one failed to replace what it abolished. It was in fact the final stage of an intellectual movement derived from theological assumptions. Nominalist theology had, in a one-sided emphasis on divine omnipotence, ruptured the bond of analogy that formerly had linked Creator and creature. It caused endless controversies and, if it had been victorious, it would have broken up the complex synthesis of early modern culture. When the protracted religious wars of the sixteenth century finally forced Europeans to search for a new spiritual unity, the compromise that emerged still bore the marks of the theological battles. The original attempts to restore religious peace continued to turn around the theological categories of nature and grace, reason and revelation. As reason became dominant, a different version of the old theological language emerged. It was called *deism*.

A religious "deism" had existed for a long time, even longer in Islam than in Christianity. The ninth-century Baghdad theologian al-Kindi had shown the rational and hence universal nature of prophetic revelation. Al-Farabi and Ibn-Sina (Avicenna) later professed similar beliefs. Both had been faithful Muslims. Even Thomas Aquinas, probably influenced by those Arabic scholars who had preserved and theologically justified Aristotle's manuscripts, incorporated a substantial part of Aristotelian philosophy within his Christian synthesis, thereby opening the way to a religious universalism based on reason. A number of early Renaissance thinkers, such as Marsilio Ficino and Nicholas of Cusa, accepted the Neoplatonic theory that the human mind *naturally* longed for its divine source. This early deism, far from excluding revelation, had in fact justified its theory by assuming an aboriginal revelation to the entire human race. Vestiges of that primitive monotheism had left traces in all existing religions and even survived in Egyptian and Greek polytheism. As late as the eighteenth century, the devout Cambridge Platonists still assumed that such a universal deism lay at the ground of all religions.

In fact, the earliest forms of this religious deism admitted revelation as *practically* necessary because of the weakness of human reason. Fausto Sozzini, to whom friends and enemies traced a deist line within modern Christianity, and Matthew Tindal, author of *Christianity as Old as Creation* (1730), the "bible of the deists," still accepted a primeval revelation, the core of which Christians shared with other religions. Indeed, the text that may have been most responsible for the spreading of a rationalist deism in Britain and France, John Locke's *On the Reasonableness of Christianity* (1695), had been intended to serve as a work of apologetics written by an orthodox believer. What earned it a place in deist literature was Locke's thesis that the content of revealed religion is always *compatible* with reason and the *credibility* of its revealed authority could be rationally justified. The deist appropriation was unjustified, Locke argued. His *Essay on Human Understanding* and his *Letter on Toleration* undeniably influenced later deist theories. But Locke's work is neither deist nor rationalist in the sense his adversaries understood those terms.

Later deists dropped the idea of a primitive revelation and justified the universal presence of religion on the ground that morality required the support of religion. They had been inspired by Roman sources, in which Christians, ever since Augustine, had found an arsenal of weapons against polytheism and atheism. Modern deists used them for a different purpose, namely, to establish a natural theology that dispensed with revelation altogether. This deism became a rival religion. Its principles included the existence of a Creator, who rewards good and punishes evil, and whose providence guides history toward progress of morals and culture. It claimed to rest on a rational foundation. In fact, however, it was the outcome of a filtering process that had strained off all theological remnants from religious faith and retained only that minimum which, by eighteenth-century standards, reason demanded. It appeared to be more an attenuated version of Christianity than a religion of reason. Its idea of God displayed sufficient remnants of its origin to be recognizable as the ghost of the Christian God. It was a rationalist abstraction of a specifically religious idea. "I know of no greater tribute ever paid to the God of Christianity," Etienne Gilson quipped, "than his survival in this idea, maintained against Christianity itself and on the strength of pure natural reason."[1]

For Locke, revelation is an indispensable complement to reason, not only for those who lack the leisure or the mental aptitude to follow a complex philosophical argument. It is needed for enriching the thin religious content of philosophical theology and for teaching essential points of Christian doctrine (such as the teachings concerning resurrection and the afterlife). To be sure, reason prepares the mind for accepting revelation and always remains the critical norm of what truly belongs to revelation. No position contrary to reason could have been divinely revealed. Locke considered scripture essential and infallible, but the Church's interpretations of it remained subject to the critique of reason. While preparing *The Reasonableness of Christianity as Delivered in the Scriptures* (1695), he wrote to an acquaintance: "This winter I have been carefully considering in what the Christian faith consists. I have drunk for myself from the Holy Scriptures, but I have held aloof from the opinions of sects and systems."[2] The outcome was, for its time, a remarkable exegesis of the four Gospels intended to prove that Jesus was indeed the Messiah announced by the Hebrew prophets.

At the very beginning of his work, Locke rejected the thesis that Christianity is no more than "a natural religion" that contains nothing *above* reason. That theory had been emerging at the time, as appears from the title of John Toland's *Christianity Not Mysterious, Or a Treatise Shewing, that there Is Nothing in the Gospel Contrary to Reason, nor Above It* (1596). For Locke, faith, being an assent *"not thus made out by the deductions of reason but upon the credit of the proposer, as coming from God,"* goes by its very nature beyond reason.[3] Nonetheless *The Reasonableness of Christianity* was immediately accused of atheism and Socinianism by John Edwards, a Calvinist divine.[4] Locke answered that his position, contrary to Socinius's, was entirely based on scripture and not on independent reason.

Further controversy followed, and Locke in *A Second Vindication of the Reasonableness of Christianity* explicitly and, I think, sincerely declared that he wrote this treatise for the benefit of "those who thought that there was no need of revelation at all."[5] In a reply to Thomas Woolston, bishop of Worcester, he had written: *"the reason of believing any article of the Christian faith . . . to me and upon my grounds is its being a part of divine revelation"*[6] (Locke, *Works*, 4:303). In light of those declarations, it appears astonishing that Locke was considered to be the father of rationalist deism.

Rationalist Deism

The slide to a rationalist deism occurred almost imperceptibly. According to Herbert of Cherbury, a seventeenth-century English philosopher, the idea of one Supreme Being, avenger of good and evil, to be worshiped by a moral life, had been implanted into the human mind, independently of any revelation. The theory that no revelation stood at the basis of religious belief was frequently accompanied by a reduction of religion to the domain of morals. With characteristic assurance, Voltaire defined natural religion as "the principles of morals common to the human race."[7] Whereas religious believers claimed that the initiative in religious belief came from divine grace, for rationalist deists, a human *"ethos superseded the religious pathos."*[8] Religion had scarcely any function left but that of sanctioning morality. D'Alembert declared in his *Discours préliminaire de l'Encyclopédie,* "One would do a great service to mankind if one could make men forget the dogmas; if one would simply preach them a God who rewards and punishes, who frowns on superstition, detests intolerance, and expects no other cult of man than mutual love and support."[9] Moreover, Voltaire added, moral virtue is defined entirely by its use to society.[10] For deists, religion was the conclusion of an argument, not of an original revelation.

For traditional Christian, Jewish, and Muslim thinkers, however, reason *encounters* the idea of God; it has not deduced it. To be sure, philosophy may conclude to the existence of an ultimate, unifying principle. But the specification that this principle coincides with God does not follow. Deists, however, claimed to deduce God's existence and God's attributes from rational premises. The first part of Aquinas's *Summa Theologiae*, on God, thereby gained an unprecedented support among deists. In fact, the *Summa Theologiae* is a *theological* text written with the support of philosophical concepts. God need not even be mentioned in an exclusively metaphysical text. Modern readers rightly consider Thomas's "five ways" inadequate or incomplete if used as arguments for the existence of God. Aquinas concludes each of them with the words *Et hoc est quod omnes vocant Deum* ("And this is what all call God") well before all the elements required by a formal argument are in place. They are not arguments, but, as Thomas calls them, *ways* in which the believer may test his belief in the light of reason. Deists, however, interpreted them as attempts of reason to establish the *foundations* of faith.

Deists, for all their hostility to scriptural authority, continued to rely heavily on the theological legacy of the gospel. Their "rational" monotheism remains in essence biblical, endowing God with the traditional attributes of justice, goodness, omnipotence. Their moral code continued to borrow from the gospel. Indeed, they displayed an amazing loyalty to their rationalist idea of God. Voltaire, who had assaulted the Christian and biblical faith with unprecedented vehemence, wrote equally scathing attacks on atheists in his *Questions on the Encyclopédie*, in the dialogue *The Sage and the Atheist*, and in his *Philosophical Dictionary*. Deists felt as passionately concerned about the survival of their religious rationalism as hostile to the errors of "superstition." Their position, however antagonistic to Christian theology, maintained an ambivalent relation with it.

Atheism

What, then, was the decisive factor in the genesis of modern atheism? The decisive break with theism was, in my opinion, a direct result of a philosophical change. Modern philosophy with few exceptions (Leibniz was one of them) had reduced all forms of causality to the efficient one conceived on the model of a mechanist theory of motion. It had thereby also restricted God's creative impact to a one-time communication of divine power.

Descartes had shared this view of causality, except that for him creation is a never-ending process. If God interrupted his creative activity for one moment, the cosmos would immediately return to nothingness. In the third *Meditation*, he writes: "The same powers and action are needed to preserve anything at each moment of its duration as would be required to create that thing anew if it were not yet in existence. Hence the distinction between preservation and creation is only a conceptual one."[11] Descartes's notion of causality, then, does not link him to eighteenth-century deism, much less to atheism. Nevertheless, in a mechanist system, motion once instilled moves by its own power: no divine intervention was ever required.

The *start* of motion ceased to be the crucial problem it once had been after Newton proved that a state of rest was not more "natural" than one of motion. Newton's principle of inertia had invalidated the traditional assumption that rest had a natural priority over motion. If we also abandon, then, the unproven principle that the cosmos must have a beginning, the need for an efficient cause of motion beyond the universe ceases to be valid. Such was the conclusion of Diderot, which was accepted by later French materialists.

Diderot also attempted to solve the remaining problem, namely, how life could emerge from inorganic matter, by attributing dynamic qualities to what once had been assumed to be a static mechanism. Matter possessed creative powers that far exceeded the ones needed to maintain motion. Diderot believed them at work in each generative process. If life originates from the union of sperm and ovum, neither one of which, he thought, was truly a living being, why should life not result from a development of matter's autonomous evolution? Do even the highest forms of mental life become more intelligible when we ascribe their origin to an unknown cause outside nature rather than to nature's own development?[12] Is this scenario not more probable than the one whereby God first creates a chaos from which a universe, worthy of God's wisdom and power, was never to emerge? The presence of some order in this universe, though not enough to show it to be the work of a perfect Creator, finds some negative explanation in the fact that total disorder destroys itself. Such were Diderot's conclusions.

The transition to atheism became inevitable once deists became aware of the inconsistency of a position that asserted an exclusively human source of meaning and value, yet at the same time proclaimed that this source was dependent on a transcendent principle. As La Mettrie observed, the deist concern was not with the existence of God as such, but with the alleged need for a transcendent support of an autonomously human activity. Such a support, he argued, was no longer needed in a consistently mechanist worldview:

> I do not mean to call in question the existence of a Supreme Being. On the contrary it seems to me that the greatest degree of probability is in favor of this belief. But since the existence of this being goes no further than that of any other toward proving the need of worship, it is a theoretic truth with very little practical value. . . . Let us not lose ourselves in the infinite, for we are not made to have the least idea thereof, and are absolutely unable to get back to the origin of things. Besides, it does not matter for our peace of mind, whether matter be eternal or have been created, whether there be or be not a God.[13]

La Mettrie's agnosticism with regard to the need of God in mechanist philosophy holds also for the deist claim that a belief in God is needed as a support of morality. How could moral norms be preserved, especially among the uneducated, without some divine sanction? As the answer to this question became ever-more uncertain under the attacks of agnostics and atheists, deism lost its *raison d'être* and developed into atheism. The atheist conclusion implicit in the deist premises appears evident in Hume's

Natural History of Religion (1757). The very title indicates how far modern thought had moved away from asserting the need of a supernatural principle of meaning. That principle has been replaced by one that has a *natural* (i.e., purely immanent) origin in the human mind. Early deists had sidestepped the question of the historical origin of religion. They had repudiated the Renaissance notion of an archaic revelation, yet had provided nothing to replace it. Later, many had assumed the existence of some universal religious instinct, but had failed to prove its existence.

To Hume, the assumption of a religious instinct appeared useless. In his opinion, historical evidence suggested that religion was derived from natural emotions, which were neither inspired nor transformed by religion: "Some nations have been discovered, who entertained no sentiments of religion, if travelers and historians may be credited; and no two nations, and scarce any two men, have ever agreed precisely in the same sentiments. It would appear, therefore, that this preconception springs not from an original instinct or primary impression of nature, such as gives rise to self-love, affection between the sexes, love of progeny, gratitude, resentment; since every instinct of this kind has been found absolutely universal in all nations and ages and has always a precise determinate object, which it inflexibly pursues."[14]

Shortly afterwards, Baron d'Holbach completed Hume's theory: "The first theology of man was grounded on fear modeled by ignorance."[15] For d'Holbach, however, fear or ignorance alone failed to explain what inspired people to join a religion. Hume had left a door open to a rational justification of religion: some philosophical arguments might prove the existence of God independently of human emotions. Hume himself had conceded (though with dubious sincerity) that this was indeed the case: "The whole frame of Nature bespeaks an intelligent author; and no rational inquirer can, after serious reflection, suspend his belief a moment with regard to the primary principles of genuine Theism and Religion."

Skeptical readers doubted that after the exhaustive, "natural" interpretation of Hume's *Natural History of Religion*, such an argument was likely to be forthcoming. They were right. In his posthumously published *Dialogues concerning Natural Religion*, Hume not only closed that door, he made sure to plug all loopholes through which a deist argument might slip in. His assertion that a genetic interpretation left the logical validity of the idea of God intact must have seemed to himself "a lame excuse, if there ever was one," as Freud called such a possibility after having completed his own genetic explanation of religion.[16]

Even the assumption of an original monotheism (in contrast to the idea of a primitive revelation, which some early deists had held) proved untenable. [Hume says,] "It is a matter of fact incontestable, that about 1700 years ago all mankind were polytheists"—with the exception of a few philosophers and one or two nations, "and that not entirely pure" (section 1).[17] Primitives do not raise such abstruse theoretical questions as whether there might be one or many causes behind the multiple phenomena visible in this world. Nor had monotheism emerged as a conclusion of reason, but rather as a natural development of polytheist religion. Gradually religious worshippers had attributed more and more powers to one god. Originally that one god had been no more than the top of the polytheist hierarchy. That this concentrated product of fear and superstition "coincided with the principles of reason and true philosophy" (section 6), Hume ascribed to chance.

To the pragmatic argument that once had supported some deist position, namely, that only religion provides an adequate basis for morality, Hume dealt a final blow. No link joins virtuous conduct to religious belief. How could superstition ever induce moral behavior? Has religious fanaticism not been responsible for the most heinous crimes? "Hence," Hume concludes, "it is justly regarded as unsafe to draw any inference in favor of man's morals from the fervor or strictness of his religious exercises" (section 10). For Hume, religion is not a neutral, but a negative, moral power.

Does atheism still preserve a dialectical relation to faith? This is the question Michael Buckley raises in the final chapter of his study *To the Origins of Modern Atheism*.[18] Modern atheism differs from the earlier versions by its absolute character. Eighteenth-century unbelief rules out *any* kind of religious interpretation of reality. This absolute character of modern atheism seems to exclude all dialogue with its opposite. Yet experience tends to confirm the legitimacy of Buckley's question. Was atheism's development out of deism more than a straightforward movement toward an unqualifiedly secularist position? In the modern epoch at least, the slide toward atheism was slow and gradual, accomplished with many hesitations and, until the age of deism, rarely followed through to the end. Even some of the deist *philosophes* of the eighteenth century still hesitated to walk this slippery slope to nowhere, and no one more so than Denis Diderot. His spiritual development had brought him from theism to deism, to pantheism, and finally to atheism. Do his many hesitations and constant changes indicate the inevitability of an atheist conclusion to the premises from which he started?

Even though his believing contemporaries considered the outcome plain atheism, it preserved a dialectical relation with theist creationism. Diderot's contemporaries were not wrong, however, in suspecting a direct link between his early skepticism and his later atheism. Once a slide to unlimited immanence is set in motion, it will inevitably render any further talk of transcendence meaningless. In following this line of reasoning to the very end, Diderot was more consistent than others before and after him.

The question, then, inevitably occurs: Was there no alternative? And further: Is theism still compatible with the scientific outlook of the present time? If it is true, as I have assumed, that one of the main principles of the modern age consists in holding humans responsible for their own future, then the Enlightenment's position on this issue was a radicalization of a distinctive trait of early modern culture. An early manifestation of it appears in Nicolas of Cusa's comparison between the poet's creativity and God's creation. (I remember having read a similar analogy made by Dante but was unable to relocate it.) Early humanism was still devout. Soon it would be followed by the creative outburst of Renaissance artists and of great scientists, Copernicus, Galileo, and Kepler, all the way up to Newton. All remained religious believers. Why?

They considered their own scientific and religious *creativity* dependent on a divine creation. Most of the early scientific discoveries were made during the late Middle Ages, often as part of a theological program. Yet the early concept of dependence on divine creation implied that humans and nature in *all* respects of their being and activity remained dependent on a superior creative act. This awareness, however, did not prevent them from being free in the choice of their activity, even in resisting a dependence that restricted their relative independence as free agents. The modern concept of *causal* dependence, however, was conceived according to a concept of efficient causality, such as scientists used in their study of the physical world. Such a reduction of human dependence to an effect of efficient causality would inevitably come into conflict with the modern principle of human freedom and full responsibility.

Perhaps the most surprising phenomenon of this conflict was that it lasted so long before exploding. The reason, in my opinion, was that few thinkers followed the premises of modern thought to their radical conclusion. Eighteenth-century rationalism was more consistent. It hardened what had remained flexible and canonized what had remained open possibilities in the early modern period. The dialogue between atheists and believers is still possible. Yet the subject will no longer be about scientific evidence, I believe—both believers and atheists agree about scientific conclusions, but not about the nature and extent of human freedom.

PART II

Philosophical Reinterpretations of Theology

In part I, we have seen how in modern thought the discussions concerning the relation between the infinite and the finite detached philosophy from theology. In this second part, I shall consider how modern philosophers converted religious ideas into philosophical concepts. From the fact that contemporary philosophy had partly been inspired by Christian theology, Hegel had concluded that in periods of religious crisis (such as Hegel considered the present to be), theology ought to take refuge in philosophy. Philosophy starts with the central theological thesis that God is spirit. Yet fundamental questions remain about the philosophical idea of spirit. Does it only refer to God? (essay 5). If it does, what does Hegel mean by the theological notion of the Holy Spirit? (essay 6).

ESSAY 5

Hegel's Spirit and the Religious Idea of God as Spirit

In his triple Critique, Kant concluded that an area inaccessible to the categories of human knowledge had no place in philosophy. Theologians of the nineteenth century (among them Friedrich Schleiermacher and Ferdinand Christian Baur) protested against this rationalist verdict and strengthened philosophy's dependence on theology. They did so primarily by extending the concept of truth beyond Kant's narrow restrictions. In Hegel's view, religious doctrine, far from being excluded from philosophy, had, in fact, been the very source from which philosophy had received its most significant ideas. In representations, religion expressed what philosophy was to formulate in ideas. An unfortunate side effect of Hegel's interpretation was that it seemed to soften the distinction between ideas and representations, as if religion consisted only of representations. This is particularly noticeable at the highest level. In his theory of spirit, Hegel appears to identify the Holy Spirit of Christian faith with a representation of the Absolute Spirit of his philosophical system.

There can be no doubt that Hegel sincerely considered his philosophy to be inspired by the Christian religion—witness the fact that his early writings had focused on theological problems and that during the almost forty years of his active life he lectured again and again on religion as providing the content of philosophy. What to him had seemed so obvious, namely, the ideal quality of religion, appears to have lost its compelling evidence after his death. Better than either his left- or his right-wing disciples, Hegel understood the central role of religion in the development of all aspects of culture. His early studies of classical Greek thought had convinced him that the driving power of Hellenic culture at its most creative periods had been religion. Later he generalized that insight and asserted the primary influence of religion on the entire life of the mind.

His former disciples on the left perceived in Hegel's idea of spirit no more than an inflated human subject, while the critiques on the right accused him of falling far short in his representation of the Christian God, as if He were no more than a revival of the unholy alliance between faith and metaphysics, which had given rise to Enlightenment deism and eventually to pantheism. Hegel started working on his *Phenomenology of Spirit*, especially on sections VI (Spirit) and VII (Religion). He treated the question of spirit as culminating in religion. Thereby religious life came to occupy the center of Hegel's theory of consciousness. This is not obvious because the specific subject of the *Phenomenology* was an epistemological problem: how the mind progresses from sensation to consciousness and self-consciousness, concluding with reason and spirit. This ascent from consciousness to spirit *resembles* a religious process, where after periods of hardship and failure, the mind reaches the full clarity of spirit. The passage in the preface to the *Phenomenology* is well known: "*The idea which represents the Absolute Spirit—the grandest conception of all and one which is due to modern times and its religion [Protestant Christianity (L.D.)] . . .*"[1]

The impulse to progress in the dialectic of consciousness derives entirely from a *negative religious moment*: the mind's "despair" about its actual achievement. The section on the *unhappy consciousness*, which moves the mind from consciousness to self-consciousness, appears as a premature longing of the finite mind for an infinite fulfillment, an implicitly religious aspiration. In Hegel's representation, medieval Christians naïvely expected to find this fulfillment by meeting Christ in Jerusalem, after they had freed the city from the occupying infidels. Hegel poignantly describes the disappointment of the Crusaders, who, after years of hardship and combat, found nothing in Jerusalem but Jesus's empty tomb. The unsuccessful quest of the earthly Jesus led them to the painful conclusion that God himself had died and that Christ's body was no longer to be found.

Beyond the "longing" of the Crusaders, Hegel aims at the immediate quest of the infinite, common to his Romantic contemporaries, who continued to expect a direct encounter with the sacred. Disappointment soon developed into actual despair. Yet in mourning the death of God, the soul realizes the significance of its own inwardness and forces the mind to overcome its "natural" state, which lacked subjective depth. The sense of loss thereby caused a sacred sadness that had been unknown in the ancient world. Most readers of the *Phenomenology* considered it an imaginary description of a philosophical ascent to religion as well as a logical process to mental integrity.

Undisturbed, Hegel continues. In the section on the alienated mind (*Phenomenology* VI B), the unhappy consciousness urges the soul to withdraw from the finite world, where the infinite had been pursued yet never found. Only by following the example of hermits, nuns, and monks, who dismiss the worldly realm as detrimental to spiritual progress, could humans hope to attain the kingdom of Spirit. Yet, Hegel immediately corrects this interpretation. Such a radical alienation from the world would merely accelerate an ever-increasing desacralization.

After the soul has refound a modicum of spiritual harmony, it still has to overcome a final obstacle before reaching the liberation of spirit. It was anticipated in ancient Greek religion when comedy had been an essential part of the tragic Dionysian cult. There, in sacrilegious words and obscene gestures, the comedians ridiculed what their cult had adored. The comedy presents an arrested state of self-consciousness, incapable of ascending to the level of spirit. Its significance lies not in the decline and death of a particular religion (religions have died before and after), but in the collapse of the entire Greek mythology. With the Greek gods died the most articulate forms of the sacred. Yet worse was to come. Hegel regarded the ancient comedy as a mere foreplay to the Enlightenment. During that period, the sarcasm of Voltaire and Diderot brought the spiritual progress of the modern epoch to a premature end. If this had been the real end of the soul's progress, religion would continue to exist only as an insignificant *part* of modern culture, still accepted by some, yet rejected by the enlightened.

The reader may wonder what entitled Hegel to equate the development of consciousness with the Spirit of religion. Was *Phenomenology* more than a process of the human mind stalemated by the cynicism of the modern age? To equate this interrupted ascent to spirit with an ascent to God as Spirit seems unjustified. Has the dialectician changed his position without informing us, or is the idea of God flexible enough to undergo the strange process described in the *Phenomenology*, while still remaining recognizable to the religious believer? In the *Lectures on the Philosophy of Religion*, to which we now turn, Hegel attempted to clarify some of the paradoxes of the *Phenomenology*.

Hegel delivered those *Lectures* four times during his tenure at the University of Berlin. He never edited them into a continuous text. In his own handwriting we possess only a short set of notes prepared for the first delivery in 1821 and since then used again at each later occasion. He never published these preparatory notes, or the final versions of the actual *Lectures*. Yet the German custom of organized note-taking by a small group of students provided later editors of the *Lectures* with a number of relatively reliable transcripts. One year after Hegel's death, the theologian Philip Marheineke, rector of the University of Berlin, published an edition that combined the four series into one coherent text. Controversies about the interpretation of Hegel's thought in this unified text led to a new edition. A year later, the *Lectures* again appeared under the editorship of Marheineke, though most of the actual work was done by the theologian Bruno Bauer, Karl Marx's atheist mentor.[2] As for the relation between the philosophical spirit and the religious idea of God as Spirit, mentioned at the beginning of Hegel's manuscript of the *Lectures*, he defines his position in a dogmatically religious manner: "God is Spirit in the element of thought— that which rightly is called the eternal God. . . . God is Spirit—that which we call the *triune* God, a purely *speculative* content, i.e., the *mystery* of God—God is Spirit, absolute activity, *actus purus*, i.e. subjectivity."[3] How is this dense theological language to be translated into a theology of the Trinity, with its distinctions between Father, Son, and Holy Spirit? Hegel's distinctions may have some significance for the philosophical idea of the spirit, but not enough to call one a philosophical version of the other.

What then justifies the philosopher to identify the two notions of *spirit*, the theological and the philosophical? In his manuscript, Hegel claims what he intends to be an answer: "The Christian religion is the religion of *revelation*. What God is and the fact that he is known *as* He, not merely in historical or some similar fashion as in other religions, is made manifest [*offenbar*] in the revelation [*Offenbarung*]; *manifestation* is its character and content. Revelation, then, is the very being of God for consciousness . . . The nature of Spirit is to manifest itself, to make itself objective; this is its activity and vitality, its sole action, and its action is all that spirit is."[4] Again, this response does little to justify Hegel's claim that religion represents what philosophy thinks. Its inadequacy appears in Hegel's treatment of the Holy Spirit.

Hegel speaks of the Spirit as God. Yet Christian doctrine distinguishes the Holy Spirit from the other two divine persons (*hypostases*)—Father and Son (or Word)—between whom the Spirit mediates. This distinction appears to restrict the Holy Spirit to one moment of the Trinity rather than exhaustively defining God entirely as Hegel's philosophical Absolute Spirit does. In Hegel's words, the Father is the universal, that is, the all-encompassing; the other, the Son, is infinite particularity, the realm of appearance; the third, the Spirit, is singularity as such: "But all three are spirit. In the third, we say, God is Spirit; but the Spirit is also 'presupposing,' the third is also the first."[5]

Cyril O'Regan, in his penetrating commentary on Hegel's concept of the Trinity, claims, "It is precisely with respect to the Trinity that all Hegel's problems come home to roost. Precisely Hegel's trinitarian articulation justifies the charge of gnosis (and) the accusation of monism."[6] God now comes to reside entirely within the limits of knowable reality. The distinction between God's inaccessible inner Being and his relation to all finite reality, including creation—what theologians call the immanent Trinity beyond the economic one—ceases to exist. To be sure, the ultimate validity of that and similar theological distinctions may itself be questioned. All too often they were hardly more than the outcome of a never fully concluded dispute between one theological party and its opposite, in this case, between Sabellius, who, stressing the absolute unity of God, reduced the distinctions between the divine Persons to mere modalities, and on the opposite side those theologians who stressed the distinctions to the point when they barely differ from an assertion of three gods. The compromise between these two overstated cases has often ended up being the content of a theological definition. The philosopher should not simply adopt such ecclesiastical definitions. Nevertheless, Hegel's claim that philosophy formulates the essence of the Christian tradition requires that philosophy should clearly establish the limited authority of such theological exercises. This Hegel never did, yet from his explanation it appears that he observed no restrictions.

Elsewhere he asserts even more explicitly the identity between the mind's spiritual consciousness and God's self-consciousness. Following

Eckhart, he writes, "That man knows God implies, in accordance with the essential communion, a communal knowledge; that is to say, man knows God only insofar as God knows himself in man."[7] It is not immediately evident how a consciousness of the Absolute must itself be absolute, that is, without any otherness with respect to the human mind. Nor do I understand how Hegel could write, *Gott ist Geist nur insofern er in seiner Gemeinde ist* ("God is Spirit only insofar as God is in his community") (*Lectures* 1, 164). I suppose what Hegel means is that God can fully be Spirit only if God meets conscious beings through whom he is able to reveal himself. Orthodox believers thereby wonder whether God could have existed before there were conscious beings to recognize God. I have similar questions about the text in which Hegel describes the emanation of the divine Spirit, and even that God could not be God if this emanation ever ceased (*Lectures* 3, 231).

Elsewhere Hegel decisively refuses to equate Spirit with the self-consciousness of an age. We may recall the pessimistic conclusion of the *Lectures* of 1821 in which Hegel assigns to philosophy the task of preserving the Christian message through the dark age of modern secularism. This passage conflicts with his optimistic philosophy of the Holy Spirit. Hegel has been sliding from the religious representation of the Trinitarian God into a *gnostic philosophy*. That some sense of subjectivity may be needed for the mind in order to receive the effusion of God's Spirit, and to acquire a proper idea of Spirit, may be true. But I wonder whether there is still place for the religious idea of God in a philosophy that has replaced all religious "representations" of dependence by a philosophy of spontaneous self-birth.

There is no doubt, however, that Hegel wanted to preserve the Christian idea of God. Yet when he equated this idea with the spirit as it appears in his own philosophy, it ceased to correspond to the God of the "consummate religion" in that all aspects of God's nature must be intrinsically intelligible to the human mind—a gnostic assumption. Christianity had confronted it since its beginning and steadfastly rejected it for being incompatible with its own doctrine. In all these respects, Hegel's philosophy failed being a philosophical interpretation of Christian doctrine. The following two essays show different, more successful attempts.

ESSAY 6

Philosophical Reflections on the Mystery of Creation

When Kant's philosophy closed the entrance to metaphysics, he also closed the doors to theology, which had traditionally provided philosophy's fundamental concepts. In the modern age, philosophy was to derive many of its concepts from positive sciences, thereby weakening the traditional function of metaphysics: to reflect on human existence and its place in the totality of being. In the early twentieth century, two theories called philosophy back to its primary purpose—radical empiricism in North America and phenomenological theory in Europe reopened philosophy to metaphysics. To the religious believer, the content of faith constitutes a most significant source of meaning. Why, then, should it not deserve to be investigated? To be sure, not every object of religious belief is worth studying. Left to its uncritical development, religion produces a considerable amount of wild growth. The unwarranted claims of religious devotion or the wholly unsupported "events" reported in its legends need not be taken any more seriously in the area of religion than they are in the sciences. For religious philosophers, such as Jaspers, Blondel, and Ricoeur, yet also for such phenomenological critics as Sartre and Merleau-Ponty, religion became again a central object of philosophical speculation. They drew new philosophical attention to the primary experience of religion.

    A basic question that had always occupied the human mind concerns the beginning of things. Without answering the scientific questions of origin, which fall entirely beyond its competence, religion reformulated the fundamental issue to be whether all finite reality is ultimately *dependent* on the infinite or not. On this issue the earliest Greek philosophy appeared to agree with the earliest revelation. Parmenides declared Being to be one, because both a mysterious goddess revealed it and philosophy confirmed it. Israel also had heard the mysterious message from beyond. The voice in the burning bush had spoken to Moses, "I am the one who is." Mystics—Jewish, Christian, and Muslim—interpreted this to mean that God's presence in creation essentially coincides with his presence to Himself. Plato had supported this insight when teaching that the One is present on all levels of Being. His thesis, as transmitted by the Arabic commentator Avicenna, is ambiguous and could be interpreted in a pantheistic sense, meaning that the Creator *coincides* with the Being of all that exists: *Ipse Deus est esse existentibus*. Yet even mystics such as Pseudo-Dionysius, the father of Christian mysticism, and Eckhart adopted the traditional meaning that God is the Being of all things, and yet He fundamentally differs from them. Two of Eckhart's Latin works begin with the words *Esse est Deus*. The mystic here followed an earlier, Plotinian understanding of Being that sharply distinguishes the Creator's Being from created beings. It excludes even an ordinary analogy between the two: "If God is Being, the creature *is* not; if the creature *is*, God is not." For Eckhart, God's goodness, the source of beings, even as the Good in Plato's *Republic*, is declared to be "beyond being" (*heneka tēs ousias*). Yet God, stated to be the source of all being, is present to each being. Eckhart's theory of participation differs from the Thomist one, but it is not pantheist.

Yet another historical figure occupies a central place in the religious metaphysics of Being: Nicholas of Cusa, the spiritual giant of the fifteenth century. This distant follower of Eckhart most daringly formulated the mystical implications of the philosophy of Being. He interprets creation as an unfolding (*explicatio*) of the very Being that in an enfolded mode (*complicatio*) is God as God is in himself. The totality of all that exists or even could exist is God's Being unfolding itself. Finite beings are distinct from God's Being only through their finitude. They are *other* with respect to each other. But God cannot be *other* than anything he has created. Cusanus therefore prefers to name God by the predicate *not-other* (*non aliud*). The Absolute defines both itself and all relative beings. Yet God grants creatures their own identity. God is not only the cause of all things, but also the ground of each self-awareness. The self-identity of a finite being for Cusanus (as for Eckhart) consists neither in those determinations that distinguish them from each other nor in the contingencies of their existence, but their innermost being coincides with God's Being. Despite this coincidence, creatures are not similar to God, as the fact of their being images of God might lead one to believe. As in Eckhart's theology, creatures, because of their determinateness, are totally unlike God. To call the creature an image of God refers to God's immanence in its being.

In Cusanus's theology of creation, Being is absolute, act without potency. Whatever exists "besides" that Absolute can only be an overflowing of the one, divine Being. Thus, as Cusanus argues in *De possest* (the title combines *posse* and *esse*), God is the ground of possibility and of actuality. Nor does possibility precede actuality as a vacuum within which God creates, as Leibniz assumed. Neither is there a need for a divine *sensorium* of absolute time and space, within which the physical world originates, as in Newton's *Principia*. In God, the possible coincides with the real.

The intimate union of God and his creatures vanished when modern philosophy ceased to recognize causality in any other than an efficient way. For Plato, Aristotle, and the Neoplatonists, efficient causality was by no means the only form of causality: to them the primary meanings of the concept of causality were *formal* and *final*. Yet since a mechanistic theory of the universe required no other causality for referring to the communication of power than a purely externally efficient cause, all other forms vanished from common discourse. Theists had always interpreted God's creative act as a causal one, yet never exclusively as an *efficient* one, in which the cause remains external to the effect.

As a result, creation had come to be understood as "making" and "moving" of the cosmos—both purely external activities—whereby the weight of meaning fell entirely on the *beginning* of divine activity. The role of the Creator appears to be reduced to a one-time initial act. This is how most theist believers still represent the act of creation. But does the universe have a beginning? Thomas Aquinas for theological reasons affirmatively answered that question, but he nevertheless conceded that reason alone was unable to prove it. Is an external force needed to justify motion, the presumed source of the cosmos's existence and functioning? Had Newton's principle of inertia not abrogated the assumed temporal priority of rest over motion? We have elsewhere argued that none of these questions required a theological (that is, revealed) answer. If the universe had always existed as a body in motion, no transcendent cause was needed to bring it into being or to set it in motion. Of course, that still left the existence of order and coherence unexplained. But why should matter not have possessed the power to move *itself* from chaos to order, especially over an infinite stretch of time? Biology and zoology had sufficiently shown that nature was endowed with more than the static powers of mechanistic physics. Of course, we do not know the answer to these questions. But what do we gain, Diderot had wondered, by ascribing natural events to a force outside the world, of which we know nothing, rather than by assuming it to reside within the world?

When Kant in the *Critique of Pure Reason* refuted the argument for the existence of God based on causality and showed, in "The Antinomies of Reason," that it was impossible to prove or disprove the beginning of the world, the idea of creation appeared to have become a dead problem for philosophy. Believers might continue to accept the religious interpretation. But they ought not to count any more on the unqualified support of reason. Thus matters stood at the end of the eighteenth century when Kant's two most intelligent followers, Fichte and Schelling, directly attacked the notion of a cosmology conceived without absolute foundation.

Post-Kantian metaphysics possesses none of the ontological richness characteristic of Aquinas's idea of *Being*. Even so, it spelled the revival of a genuine metaphysics. As Cornelio Fabro noted, Hegel describes the Absolute as *esse ipsum*.[1] Yet in his dialectical philosophy, an idea attains its truth only after it has gone through the full circularity of thinking. Thus the all-comprehensive idea of Being attains its completion only in the final syllogism of absolute identity-in-difference. The same sources of Aquinas's theory of Being are also at the foundation of Hegel's, namely, Parmenides and the Bible.

At the end of the *Logic*, then, Being discloses the qualities of unity and truth, which the indeterminate concept of the beginning had intimated. Hegel now clarifies that the abstract concept of the beginning had been no more than the immediate presence of Being. Nevertheless, even that early concept had not been immediate, as sense intuitions or representations are. It had the immediacy of *thought*, as its universality indicated. Nor was it static or lifeless: its very nature implied development both in thought and in being. Hence its truth lies in the concrete totality at the end. Indeed, Hegel's thesis is that Being may be called absolute only when it comes to be conceived as in-itself and for-itself. Only at that point may we call it inspired by the religious idea that Being attains its full significance only in the theology of the sacred Trinity.[2]

The revival of the religious metaphysics of Being would not have been possible if the twentieth-century culture had not undergone a metaphysical reawakening. I believe that the new need for metaphysics was, at least in part, a response to a vacuum of meaning left by the senseless First World War and the horrors preceding and accompanying the Second World War. New concepts of philosophy had also made a deeper probing of existential meaning possible. I have mentioned the phenomenological movement and the theory of radical empiricism. Yet in the meantime, the "bracketing of existence" characteristic of phenomenology's early method came to be seen as obstructing a full exploration of the attack on meaning that a new generation of philosophers had witnessed.

Sartre rightly pointed out that there was also a *phenomenon of existence*, which philosophy's exclusive concentration on the essence of things had neglected.[3] Whereas for Edmund Husserl, the father of the phenomenological method, the phenomenon of *Being* had, during the early period, been thought to coincide with the being of the phenomenon, for Sartre, the fact of existence differs from the appearing essence of *Being*, in the sense that an existence cannot be reduced to its being known, its *percipi*: *L'être n'est pas un apparaître* ("being is not an appearance").

At the same time, Heidegger, influenced by his early studies of Scholastic philosophy, initiated a more thorough exploration of the idea of Being. In *Being and Time*, he did so by a searching reflection on the human condition. Rightly, because the human person is the one being to whom existence has become a question (*Dasein*). Later Heidegger turned to an analysis of Being (*Sein*) that surpassed the still subjective study of human existence. Yet both his later and his earlier work forced him to pay attention to emerging questions of transcendence, which previously had been left to theology. More than any other recent thinker, Heidegger was responsible for having removed the Kantian barriers obstructing the way to Being. Maurice Blondel, in his doctoral dissertation, *L'action* (1893), argued that all human activity receives its impulse from a desire that surpasses any specific object of choice. This transcending aspiration of the will opened philosophy to theological insights, albeit under severe methodical limitations. Moving in the same direction, Joseph Maréchal, in *Le point de départ de la métaphysique* (particularly in the final volume VI), showed that a similar aspiration motivates all human knowledge.[4]

Thomists considered this epistemological reinterpretation incompatible with an essentially realist philosophy. Yet in meeting the challenge of the Kantian critique, Thomist philosophy showed that it was not defenseless against the antimetaphysical, antitheological position of modern thought. Metaphysics again came to occupy a place in philosophy. After the defensive strategy of transcendental Thomism (i.e., Thomist philosophy performed within Kant's restrictions), it was no longer necessary to squeeze Aquinas's realism within the conceptual restraints of the Kantian critique. Nor did it force believing philosophers to maintain a total separation between their philosophy and their faith, as had been necessary a century earlier. Metaphysics had come to recognize the profound existential meaning of religious ideas and the etiological origin of some of its fundamental concepts.

ESSAY 7

Evil and the Limits of Theodicy

Theodicy is the part of philosophy that intends to answer the question whether the Creator is responsible for evil and the suffering of humans and other sensitive creatures. The fact that believers and nonbelievers almost unanimously declare that philosophy suffers shipwreck on the problem of evil does not dispense the philosopher from the task of investigating whether, within a different, *theological* context, belief in God is *compatible* with a full awareness of the presence of evil. In addition, the philosopher must critically examine whether the theological presuppositions that lie at the ground of his valuation of what counts as good or as evil are universally valid. As Hegel once remarked, only in actual worship are believers capable of overcoming evil. In the third section below, I shall present an alternative theological hypothesis wherein the Creator, far from being responsible for the suffering of his creatures, shares in their sufferings.

Concrete-Religious versus Rationalist-Abstract

Theodicy today labors under the poor reputation of an experiment that failed. Few outside the small circle of persistent believers in it would grant that it has succeeded in accomplishing what it set out to prove. That failure has become more painfully apparent as our sensitivity to evil, both moral and physical, has increased and made our questioning more urgent. The sheer magnitude of evil, which our age has witnessed in death camps, nuclear warfare, internecine tribal, or racial conflicts, has lowered our tolerance level for what once was accepted as a necessary part of human life. Indeed, I believe that the presence of evil has impressed itself more powerfully upon the minds of our contemporaries than the presence of God. The primary question is no longer how God can tolerate so much evil, but rather how the reality of so much evil is still compatible with the existence of God.

Beyond religious and ideological differences, our contemporaries remarkably agree that evil "was not meant to be," that it represents a hostile invasion of injustice. To an unprecedented degree we feel the need to *justify* the presence of evil in the world. Yet we have lowered or abandoned our expectation to receive an adequate answer from philosophy to the ancient question, *Unde malum?* (Whence evil?). Indeed, most attempts to answer that question tend to render the reality of evil less, rather than more, acceptable. Evil invites philosophical speculation, yet it is the cliff on which philosophy founders. By a paradox unique to our time, we remain simultaneously aware of both terms of the opposition.

Schopenhauer anticipated the paradox when he wrote, "Without doubt it is the knowledge of death and, along with it, the consideration of the suffering and misery of life, which gives the strongest impulse to philosophical reflection and metaphysical explanation of the world. If our life were endless and painless, it would perhaps occur to no one to ask why the world exists, and is just this kind of world it is."[1] Two distinct philosophical responses have emerged. Some contemporary thinkers attempt to repair by one philosophy the damage wrought by another, believing that what has been philosophically misstated can be philosophically corrected. Logicians have endeavored to point out the many *non sequiturs* that lead to the conclusion, "Hence an omnipotent, omniscient, good God cannot exist." Yet no remedial strategy will suffice, as long as we fail to question the anthropomorphic assumptions that inspired the objections. Even those who succeed in replacing a simplistic conception of God by a philosophically more mature one fail to dispel our basic doubt whether *any* philosophical speculation would be capable of challenging a difficulty born from metaphysical despair. An even more fundamental problem remains: theodicy is based upon a concept of religion in which the believer will hardly recognize as his or her own.

As Kant defined it, theodicy consists in "the defense of the supreme wisdom of the Creator [*Urheber*] of the world against the charges raised by reason on the basis of what conflicts with a meaningful order [*Zweckwidrig*] in the world."[2] The God hereby presented is not merely "less" than the "Father" whom Jesus revealed or than the Lord of Israel: He essentially differs from both. To be sure, there is nothing wrong with a philosophical attempt to articulate the dependence of creation on God, while leaving all other aspects out of consideration. Problems begin when that dependence is conceived *exclusively* in terms of *efficient* causality. The link between God and his creatures is obviously more intimate than that between a merely efficient cause and its effect.[3] To conceive creation *exclusively* in terms of efficient causality makes it impossible to justify evil and all suffering present in the creation of an all-wise, omnipotent God. The so-called physico-theological argument intended to prove the existence of God on the basis of the existence and nature of the cosmos becomes thereby inverted into a normative rule that determines the limits of divine action in the world.

A second problem consists in the different assumptions various religions have made about the origin and significance of evil. They exclude a single "religious answer" to the question of evil. Positions vary from a strong assertion of evil as a principle coequal with that of good in Manichaeism, to a denial of evil as an illusion in the more radical Buddhist and Vedantic monist schools. Between these two extremes, theist responses range from a concept of evil inherent in the finite condition as such to evil as resulting from human errors (through the Fall and subsequent sins). Evil evokes, of course, the strongest reaction among monotheists: Jews, Christians, and Muslims, who consider all human beings created by a free, personal God. Here again the nature and urgency of the crisis have resulted in a variety of responses.

Judaism alone presents several models. According to an archaic retaliation model, God inflicts suffering as a punishment of human sins. Of course, one might wonder, why humans created by a good God should be able to commit sin and thereby attract punishment. Jews and Christians have never ceased struggling with this question. So, many felt compelled to look in a different direction. They argued that the overcoming of evil would be delayed until a final time of righteousness. But why should creation have to pass through more evil in order to achieve a final good? In the face of such major difficulties, two different models emerged. According to the book of Job, humans are not to question God's inscrutable decrees, while the author of the second part of the book of Isaiah, in his description of the messianic Suffering Servant, considers suffering submissively undergone intrinsically redemptive.

Christians adopted all these models and attempted to combine the scriptural positions with the prevailing philosophical ones of Neoplatonism and Stoicism. According to the Neoplatonic interpretation, evil consists in the mere absence of good—*privatio boni*. As John Hick has shown, this solution is suitable for an order of being in which inevitable emanations moving down from the *One* cause serious difficulties in a universe created by God.[4] Although the Neoplatonist *One* is not responsible for all the ills that with absolute necessity emanate from it, a free, good, and omnipotent Creator appears accountable for all that exists. Augustine, who established the Neoplatonist, negative conception of evil in the Christian West, supported the theory by the Greek aesthetics of form. Contrast, for him, including the contrast between good and evil, adds to the perfection of a created form. Needless to say, an aesthetic principle of perfection that requires the simultaneous presence of physical pain and moral evil and that ends with the final damnation of most moral agents hardly corresponds to the theist idea of God's goodness. The God of love preached in the gospel of salvation here makes room for an Olympian Artist. Nor does one soften that grim picture by declaring that the Creator allows moral evil merely as long as one holds God to be capable of freely creating a world that contains less suffering and less moral evil.

Created Autonomy versus Causal Determinism

The positions that in the wake of theological and philosophical controversies came to prevail in much of Western thought under the direct or indirect influence of St. Augustine resulted in the following questionable theses:

1. God creates the intelligent agent free, yet predestines him or her to damnation or salvation.

2. The good exists as an independent value prior to the Creator's choice.
3. God remains unaffected by finite reality.

All three of these theses would in some form find their way into the rationalist assumptions of theodicy formulated in seventeenth- and eighteenth-century philosophy and, to a great extent, are still surviving in theology today.

The controversy over divine predestination did not reach a critical stage until the sixteenth century, after Calvin had denied the exercise of free choice in the order of grace and when Thomists and Molinists initiated an acrimonious dispute on the efficacy of grace. For Bañez and his Thomist followers, God's position as the absolutely universal cause of creation entailed that he was at least responsible for a "negative reprobation" of some, independently of their personal merits and demerits. God causes no evil, but may decide not to create the good that would prevent evil from occurring. Without God's *efficacious grace*, human nature, left to its own fallen and fallible liberty, inevitably sins. To this determinism, Molina and his school, anxious to preserve human responsibility, opposed a free human causality next to divine causality. These conflicting positions share the burden of an impossible task: reconciling total divine causality with full human responsibility for evil.

The second thesis posits the *good* as an ideal *a priori*, preceding God's creative act, and thus imposing upon a moral God the obligation to create a universe that approaches this ideal as closely as a finite composition is able to do. The very necessity that determines God's being leaves no room for either divine freedom or finite contingency. Leibniz, who reformulated the position in a clearly articulated principle, attempted to escape its pantheistic implications by distinguishing God's intrinsic necessity to create the best possible world (which he denied) from the "moral" necessity by which God owed it to his goodness to create the best possible world (which he affirmed). In this rationalist scenario, God contemplates the nonexistent essences of several possible worlds, after which he decides to create the actual world in accordance with his goodness—but he was not intrinsically forced to do so.[5] Even if we leave out of consideration the untenable real distinction between God's goodness and his omnipotence, we must still question Leibniz's interpretation of divine omnipotence. Does it refer to God's power to do "anything at all"? That is hardly meaningful, and Leibniz himself hastens to restrict it to what is logically possible and compossible with God's other attributes. If God is supremely good, he is not able to do evil. We should then restrict our definition of divine omnipotence to God's ability to do anything he wills provided it be *in accordance with his divine nature*.

But even then, the expression "anything he wills" raises further questions. God's "acting" defines his nature; unlike human acting, it serves not as a means to satisfy particular wants or desires by the attainment of goals that lie outside it. A wide gap separates what I *am* from what I attempt to be by acts intended to overcome my experienced weakness. None of this applies to God. Nor am I able to conceive what God's acting implies or does not imply. All that believers in a divine creation can do is look at the concrete, visible result of that divine action, which we call *creation*. But here precisely theodicy ought to follow a procedure opposite to the one it usually follows when it decrees that the world must conform to standards of human rationality that it has *a priori* set up for God. A genuine, religious theodicy *begins* by accepting the world *as it is* (including its unpleasant realities and possibilities) as an expression of God's nature, rather than by dictating *a priori* what a divine expression ought to be like. As we shall see, such an attitude does not condemn theodicy to blind faith, for it must critically examine what it may learn of the divine nature on the basis of this created expression, and it may conceivably conclude that this created expression fails to meet even minimal human standards of goodness. But the believer should do so on the basis of the total evidence (including the one provided in the specifically religious experience of faith) rather than of an *a priori*, narrowly rationalist definition of what God ought to be and therefore ought to do.

Returning, then, to Leibniz's argument, it should be clear that the idea of a divine choice with an antecedent moment of deliberation and a consequent moment of decision, patterned after the model of human persons deliberating about several alternatives, is itself heavily anthropomorphic. Leszek Kolakowski put it well:

> In God himself essence and existence converge and this implies that his will is identical with his essence. God neither obeys rules which are valid regardless of his will nor issues rules according to his whims or as the result of deliberating various options; He is those rules. Unlike

humans, God never faces alternative choices and then freely decides which of them he ought to take; his decisions are necessary aspects of his Being and therefore they could not have been different from what they are; yet they are free in the sense that no superior powers, no norms independent of God, bind him. He is what he does, decides, orders. Consequently we may say neither that the definitions of what is good and true precede God . . . nor that he precedes them.[6]

In addition to these intrinsic difficulties of the expression of God *choosing* the best possible world, there are others inherent in the very concept of "best possible." Bergson pointed them out and dismissed the entire idea in a few lapidary sentences:

> I can, at a stretch, represent something in my mind when I hear of the sum-total of existing things, but in the sum-total of the nonexistent I can see nothing but a string of words. So that here again the objection is based on a pseudo-idea, a verbal entity. But we can go further still: the objection arises from a whole series of arguments implying a radical defect of method. A certain representation is built up a priori, and it is taken for granted that this is the idea of God; from thence are deduced the characteristics that the world ought to show; and if the world does not actually show them, we are told that God does not exist.[7]

Finite being is intrinsically imperfect, and any attempt to measure its perfection depends itself on finite, hence intrinsically imperfect norms. Thus the idea of the best possible world imposes upon the Creator a subjective, human standard.

The most serious problems begin when modern theodicy attempts to square the idea of a perfect Creator with the creation of free agents capable of perpetrating moral evil and inflicting suffering upon fellow creatures. On this issue, the modern assumption leads to the most questionable conclusions. Both theodicy's adversaries and advocates hold a concept of freedom that from the start sets the discussion on the wrong track. Thus Antony Flew argues that for an action to be free it suffices that it not be compulsive—which, for him, entails not that it be unpredictable, but that the person nevertheless *could* have acted differently had he or she chosen to do so. From these premises he concludes that an omnipotent Creator could have created persons who would always (or more often) have acted rightly.[8] In this respect, Flew follows J. L. Mackie's thesis that human beings could have been so constituted that they would freely choose the good. The idea of a God who could not control men's actions leads to what he calls the "paradox of omnipotence."[9] How the idea of a will determined always to choose the good remains compatible with freedom escapes me. Nor do I see how in a theory of predetermined freedom, evil could avoid being ultimately attributable to God.[10]

A finite freedom with a built-in resistance to evil appears to be a most questionable concept. Freedom is more than the power to say *yes* or *no* to preestablished values, in accordance with a divine preference for or aversion from one or another. Its signal characteristic consists not in the power to ratify or refuse values that exist with a moral coefficient attached to them, but in the ability to create values. Freedom can tolerate contingency and a physically restricted field of operation. But to deprive it of its creative power is to replace freedom by causality. Creativity constitutes its very essence. Both theists and atheists admit that freedom may be "given," but not in a way that causally predetermines it. Even a wholly preestablished order of values reduces its scope. Most of us agree on that point when it comes to humanly induced unconscious conditioning (including hypnosis), such as B. F. Skinner proposes for the improvement of society as a whole. But the same objection holds true for any divine "conditioning." Even a divinely preestablished order leaves man none but a negative creativity (as Sartre perceived). Yet, strangely enough, this inauthentic, reduced freedom of choice, the same one secular critics of theodicy reject in predestinationist theologies, is the one they propose as alone compatible with the existence of a good God.

God creates neither values nor strong or weak inclinations to choose them. Humans are creators who depend on divine power for the exercise of their creative spontaneity, but not for their choice. Such a theory need not result in an exclusion of any dependence in freedom, as it has done in some existentialist philosophies. If the free agent fails to recognize the overall *dependence* of his or her freedom—the fact that he is not free to be free—he elevates relative human freedom onto an absolute level, thereby creating a false absolute without moral responsibility. In creating free agents, the Creator has released a power that may turn against him. In

Berdyaev's words, "Evil presupposes freedom and there is no freedom without the freedom of evil, that is to say, there is no freedom in the state of compulsory good."[11]

The real issue concerning freedom is not whether it deserved to be created, but whether God's necessary being is compossible with the unrestricted freedom, which human autonomy requires. Theodicy should be concerned only with the compossibility of the world as it is, not with the possibility of proving the existence of God on the basis of this world's perfection. Symptomatic for the confusion that often occurs between the two is that many modern treatises of theodicy begin with a discussion of Hume's *Dialogues concerning Natural Religion*. Whatever Hume's intention may have been, he did not write an antitheodicy, that is, an argument excluding any possibility of justifying the idea of God as long as evil exists. The *Dialogues* deflate the exaggerated claims of a natural theology, which on the basis of a philosophical speculation concerning order and purpose in the world concludes to the existence of God. Even on those terms we should beware of overstating the case. Does Philo, the most skeptical of the three participants in the *Dialogues*, after having invalidated all arguments in favor of a benevolent Providence, not concede in the end? "In many views of the universe and of its parts, particularly the latter, the beauty and fitness of final causes strike us with such irresistible force, that all objections appear (what I believe they really are) mere cavils and sophisms; nor can we then imagine how it was ever possible for us to repose any weight on them."[12] One may, of course, dismiss this statement as the expression of a thorough skepticism whereby Philo, after having first invalidated the negative positions of the other participants, in the end undermines his own. But we may also read it as an honest attempt to attain "synoptically," that is, by an immediate, total impression, what analytic inference withholds. If this reading were correct, an "illative sense" might provide what a detailed analysis fails to supply, namely, certitude concerning the existence of an intelligent, good Designer.[13]

The implications of Hume's argument so understood would be less restrictive of a philosophical theodicy than much contemporary fideism, which, rightly dissatisfied with the rationalist theodicy, prefers to leave the justification of God in the face of evil *entirely* to faith. The philosopher cannot remain satisfied with such a total abdication of reason: The presence of evil must be *shown* not to exclude the idea of a good Creator. Nor will the philosopher be satisfied with defining "divine goodness" by standards that have nothing in common with our human conception of goodness, an equivocity that, as John Stuart Mill pointed out, would merely result in "an incomprehensible attribute of an incomprehensible substance."[14] The philosopher rightly insists that the idea of an omnipotent, good God be shown to be compatible with the actual existence of evil. Reason modestly yet legitimately demands only to perceive how the idea of a good Creator and a world tainted by evil are not contradictory. Even if theodicy achieves that modest goal, it does not meet the challenge unless it adequately answers the objection of the third of the Augustinian theses: that God remains indifferent to the suffering of his creatures. Medieval Scholasticism in denying any real relation between God and the world (Aristotle's position) placed itself in an unfavorable position for defending the Creator against the charge of supreme indifference. A number of philosophical systems broadly comprehended under the general name of "process philosophy" have attempted to justify a divine participation in the sufferings of his creatures. Despite essential disagreements, these systems share Whitehead's overall vision of the real as a creative process, wherein God develops *with* his creation rather than *above* it. In his words, "He shares with every new creation its actual world."[15] Indeed, only through the creative process does God attain that full actuality to which Whitehead refers as God's "consequent" nature. Rather than being an unchanging, transcendent Prime Mover, God is the actual entity from which each creative development in time "receives that initial aim from which its self-causation starts."[16] Philosophers have interpreted this divine participation in various ways, ranging from an impersonal "creative event," the source of all human good (Wieman), to a creative personalism (Brightman). But only when the idea of a personal God is preserved can process philosophy contribute toward rendering the monotheist position with respect to evil acceptable.

Peter Bertocci in *The Goodness of God* shows a clear appreciation of the importance of safeguarding this personal character on the ground that a force creating persons must itself be personal. But a Creator-Person need not be conceived as self-sufficient, uninhibited by restraints other than those he imposes upon himself. If personhood attains its highest realization in interpersonal communication, the perfection of the divine Creator would likewise be enhanced, rather than weakened, by sharing the creative conditions of finite persons. A divine Person exposes himself to risks analogous to those run by humans in their attempts to create good—what Bertocci rightly calls "creative insecurity."[17] We procreate without ever knowing or controlling what our children will turn out to be. Insecurity inheres in the very nature of creating another free person. Freedom is man's greatest glory. Yet its price is insecurity.

Bertocci supports his bold personalist interpretation of the Absolute by an even more daring thesis. As he reads it, the insecurity of the creative act expresses a fundamental uncertainty in the very nature of the Agent. A refractory element, not a "flaw" in the divine or an impediment imposed upon the divine, but an essential *passivity* that is inherent in the very act whereby the Absolute gives birth to the relative, prevents the Creator from achieving his goals without the cooperation and the possible intrusion of suffering and evil.

A Passive, Suffering God

To the argument developed in the preceding two sections, I would like to add something I dare no longer call *philosophical*. It describes a theological model that, I think, avoids the objections to traditional theodicy mentioned in the preceding pages. Even though it uses some philosophical conclusions drawn in the preceding sections, it is based upon theses that for the philosopher remain unproven hypotheses. It starts, then, from an idea of God, who renders himself passive in the act of creation, thereby changing his divine nature.

The symbols of the Suffering Servant, of God's Son who dies, and of the lost Imam, all lend indirect, though theologically strong, support to the position of a divine person who suffers and dies in the process of bringing salvation. In all three monotheist faiths, mystical and theosophical traditions have taught that with creation, passivity enters God's very nature. For an infinite, perfect Being to give rise to a being other than itself means not adding to itself—as St. Thomas stated, *dantur plura entia, non datur plus esse* ("more beings, but not more Being")—but causing an emptiness within itself wherein "otherness" can subsist. If God is the fullness of Being, then it is only through annihilation (destruction) within the infinite that the finite can be, Maurice Blondel argued. Although finite being remains *within* the infinite, perfect Being, from which it draws its entire sustenance, being *other* than that perfect Being it nevertheless assumes a certain independence. By allowing it to be in some way independent, the infinite Being ceases to wield unlimited power over it, and comes to stand in a relation to it that is no longer exclusively active.

Of course, philosophers who adopt Aristotle's definition of God as pure act exclude all passivity from God as incommensurable with divine perfection. Yet if we assume pure act to include the potential to "re-act" to events and circumstances in a manner that requires the acting subject to move out toward the other than itself in order to return to itself in a new manner, then passivity is not *a priori* excluded. Obviously, the kind of acting whereby the agent loses himself in order to find himself anew does not apply to God *as he is in himself.* God as perfect, infinite Being cannot be called active any more than passive. In creation, however, the two moments of activity and passivity simultaneously emerge. Although the act of creation requires no external support and in this respect may be called entirely "active," in the very "otherness" of created being, God places himself in a position where, in *reacting* to the finite creatures the Creator becomes passive as well as active. Aristotelians avoid this conclusion by asserting that God has no *real* relation to the world. But such a claim, intelligible enough within Aristotle's theory of an uncreated cosmos, is inadequate in a creationist theology.

In such a doctrine, God never stops *reacting* to the creature's initiative. In claiming that God *redeems* what he has created, Jews and Christians affirm God's ever-renewed creative action. Unfortunately, believers often use the concept of redemption for stopping the gaps of ignorance that remain after they have depleted their supply of rational justifications for suffering and evil. Rather than whitewashing evil by such an *argumentum ex ignorantia*—as irrefutable as it is unprovable—the believer should admit that this world contains a great deal of unexplainable suffering, and that creatures endowed with a free will remain capable of causing unqualified evil, an ability of which they all too frequently avail themselves. Rather than using the term "redemption" to make suffering and evil vanish into an invisible realm of goodness, the believer ought to admit that in his redemptive action God *reacts* to *real* suffering and *real* evil. To be effective, the idea of redemption must be integrated with that of creation as one continuous, relation of the Creator to his creatures. Divine activity from that perspective appears as an open-ended, ever-renewed dialogue with creation. At each moment of time, God creatively responds to conditions shaped by creatures.

A divine response, then, counteracts existing evil by creating opportunities for converting evil into good. Christian writers have persistently upheld this divine ability to restore creation to a new innocence. Jacques Maritain, who freely mixed philosophy with theology, wrote, "Each time that a free creature undoes for its part the work that God makes, God remakes to that extent—for the better—this work and leads it to higher ends. Because of the presence of evil everything on earth, from the beginning to the end of time, is in perpetual recasting."[18] Such a reversal of evil to goodness necessarily takes the form of a struggle, an *agon*. In theist theology, God through a predestined person's suffering and death overcomes the power of evil. By thus linking the mystery of evil to the even greater mystery of redemption, theist believers have decidedly left the domain of philosophy and moved into a theological domain that lies entirely beyond philosophical reflection.

The admission of theological doctrines into a universal, philosophical theory ought to be justified more thoroughly than space here allows.[19] One reason that urged me to admit it here as a philosophical hypothesis is that the very standards by which we measure what does and what does not count as "good" depend to some extent upon the acceptance or rejection of a religious (to the believer: *revealed*) hierarchy of values. Any attempt to erect a system of values upon a religiously neutral basis, common to believers and unbelievers, fails precisely in the area where theodicy matters most, namely, in defining what must count as *definitely* good or evil.

Ontological commitments affect moral values. Theories that omit any reference to a *given* norm differ from value systems that at least in part are ruled by a relation to a divine revelation: "The believer, not satisfied with exclusively self-satisfying goods, may value an awareness of God's presence, acquired through much pain and suffering, more highly than a satisfaction of physical needs."[20] Different value systems result in different judgments concerning standards of good and evil.

Nor need a position based upon a religious assessment of values merely be a fideist anticipation of future well-being. For the believer may actually *experience* suffering as redemptive, that is, as endowed with a more than merely negative meaning. It finds unambiguous theological support in the doctrine of redemptive suffering, which, for Jews, Christians, and Muslims, transforms the meaninglessness of suffering into various patterns of meaning and goodness. No writer has pursued the theme of redemptive suffering further than Dostoevsky. Those critics who see no meaning in suffering routinely refer to Ivan Karamazov's charge against a God who tolerates unredeemable suffering, such as the pain of innocent children and animals that lack the capacity to learn from pain. Usually they fail to mention Alyosha's later reply. He admits the full scandal of innocent pain and, like his brother, refuses to accept it. But he assumes this scandal into the even greater one of God's own suffering: when, dying in extreme pain, Christ feels abandoned by his Father and the tragic conflict enters God's own Being. In his intra-divine *theologia crucis*, God is set against God, as in Goethe's dark saying, *Nemo contra Deum nisi Deus ipse* ("No one against God but God himself").[21] This scandal does not "justify" evil, but it makes God a participant in the pain, as several theologies have implied, and mystical ones have explicitly stated.

Some gnostic and theosophical doctrines in the three monotheist religions have daringly introduced the origins of evil into God's inner life. In contrast to orthodox beliefs, they trace the possibility of evil (though not its actuality) to an intradivine division, which has disturbed the harmony of creation. The resulting conflict gave birth to that realm of unrest, which is the physical universe.[22] It is not my intention here to defend such speculations. But before we dismiss them as unworthy of philosophical attention, we ought to consider that major philosophers, beginning with Plato and continuing with Boehme and several nineteenth-century mystics, have persistently turned to mythical and religious interpretations that locate the origin of good and evil in a transcendent source. Even some modern philosophers have attempted to trace the opposition between good and evil to a separation within the Absolute. Thus in Karl Jaspers's memorable treatment of "The Law of the Day and the Passion for the Night," night and day appear as oppositions within the one Absolute. The diurnal law "regulates our existence, demands clarity, consistency, and loyalty, binds us to reason and to the idea, to the One and to ourselves The night functions as the negative desire to transcend finitude, limit, and temporality."[23] Though irreducible to the law of the day, the passion of the night presents an equally essential dimension of human existence. In mythical (and highly controversial) language, such reflections on complementarity within the Absolute articulate what I have described as the "passivity" that enters infinite Being when it gives birth to the finite.

Orthodox monotheist theologies have never accepted the gnostic equation of creation with the Fall. Nor do they accept conflicts "within" the Godhead to account for the existence of evil in creation. Rightly, I think, because gnostic myths and theosophical interpretations lead to theological inconsistencies. But the underlying assumption that the *possibility* of evil cannot be explained unless we trace it back to the divine act of creation rests on a profound insight, no more irrational than God's own participation in human suffering. Still, the philosopher cannot but wonder what such theosophical speculations may contribute to the kind of rational reflection to which he or she is committed. Passivity in God neither explains the actual origin of evil nor justifies its existence. Nor do theosophical doctrines reduce the "mysteriousness" of evil; if anything, they deepen it. What they may accomplish, however, is to extend the boundaries within which theology has conceived of that mystery. Whereas the traditional theistic position attributed the source of evil entirely to the creature, either as a result of sin or as an inevitable effect of finitude, theosophical doctrines force us to consider the divine act of creation itself and the momentous transition it accomplishes in moving from the one to the many.

ESSAY 8

Intimations of Immortality

Some psychologists account for the religious belief in a life after death by a natural resistance man feels to a total destruction of the self. Humans tend to attribute a permanent moral value to selfhood. Does this attitude in any way justify a belief in immortality? I think not. For whatever significance people attach to an afterlife, they rarely conceive it as a somewhat modified continuance of their present existence. Religious immortality is the exact opposite of a ghostlike endurance of life. Though I deny that the desire for mere survival is an adequate foundation for the religious belief in immortality, I do not deny that a desire for being preserved may well play a significant role in that belief, but *on a higher level* than present life offers. Indeed, the American philosopher William E. Hocking defined religion as "an ultimate demand for conscious self-preservation, man's leap as individual and as species, for eternal life in some form."[1] This desire may be all or partly unconscious. The religious dissatisfaction with present life in no way implies a desire of protracting it beyond the grave; it rather is a call for total change: "The soul's hope has not been for more of the same, but for something altogether higher and better."[2]

The very desire of religious eternity understood as unending bliss seems to arise not mainly from fear of annihilation, but from those "peak" experiences in which humans perceive a glimpse of a permanent, qualitatively different form of existence. In ancient Greece at least, a desire to participate in the godly life through Dionysian ecstasy played a significant role in both the belief in and the desire for that life after death, particularly among the initiated in the mysteries.

According to the existentialist philosophers of the recent past, the idea of life after death basically conflicts with the very nature of man's self-understanding and self-realization within the limits of a finite freedom. An eternity of free self-realization would destroy freedom altogether, since an unending succession of possibilities of self-realization is impossible. Human existence implies many possibilities of being human, yet after a certain time they will all be exhausted. In her philosophical novel *Tous les hommes sont mortels*, Simone de Beauvoir shows that an indefinite protraction of life would not only be absurd but also unendurable. Man lives his life as a limited succession stretching from a time of preparation, to maturity, and ending in decline. The finitude of the time for achievement belongs to the very conception of a life's task. The cycle of life may remain incomplete, but it cannot be indefinitely extended. If Plato and Aristotle were around today, they would sadly have survived themselves.

It is on the very transformation of existence in the religious expectation of an afterlife that a philosophical investigation should concentrate. How much discontinuity is compatible with the preservation of *personal identity*? Jacques Maritain simply assumed that even though all images and impulses will vanish after death, our intellectual powers nevertheless remain awake to the soul's substance and, through it, to God.[3] But can the mind preserve its identity when sense perceptions and sense impulses no longer sustain it? Must such a bare state of consciousness not result in a loss of all creative imagination and, in the end, even of memory? H. H. Price envisions life after death as a world of mental pictures in which "imagining replaces perceiving."[4] He assumes that images of organic sensations could provide a substitute to our present life. Yes, it might do so during a few weeks or even years, but not indefinitely. Could personal identity even survive a total disruption of one's habitual environment? Can a person remain the *same* without a body or with another, "spiritualized" body? Prior to a discussion of those problems of identity, we must at least provisionally settle on the meaning of the preliminary question: What is a person and how far can the concept be stretched?

In a well-known analysis of this concept, professor P. F. Strawson concluded that the concept of personhood logically precedes that of a subject of states of consciousness and that of a subject of corporeal attributes, even though it requires both.[5] With regard to survival after death, Strawson concludes, as Morris Schlick and H. H. Price had done before, that the state of a bodiless self can be made empirically intelligible only if we attribute to the person the same components as in the present life with the exception of the bodily senses: "One has simply to think of oneself as having thoughts and memories as at present, visual and auditory experiences largely as at present, even perhaps—though this involves certain complications—some quasi-tactual and organic sensations as at present, whilst (a) having no perception of a body related to one's experience as one's own body is and (b) having no power of initiating changes in the physical condition of the world, such as one at present does with one's hands, shoulders, feet and vocal chords."[6] Strawson concedes that this would be a strictly solitary existence in which the individual is severed from all contact with, or even awareness of, other individuals, and that the existence after death would be that of a *former* person who must exclusively live on memories of the past. As they fade away, must the awareness of self not also recede? His description brings to mind the fate of the dead townspeople in Thornton Wilder's play *Our Town*. They [the living townspeople] gradually lose interest in their past before entering into total silence. Survival on those terms may well seem unattractive, Strawson admits, and the orthodox have done well to insist on the resurrection of the body.[7]

Despite these concessions, Strawson's concept has rightly been attacked. Roland Puccetti charges that it is too broad and lacks two determinations without which it would also apply to animals. The first one is the ability to symbolize, which enables the person to learn language. The second is some sense of responsibility for one's actions, which renders a person a moral agent. According to Puccetti, this moral character in turn requires the existence of sensations and emotions. It would seem true, indeed, that without being confronted with situations in which he or she must make decisions, a person can no longer be called a moral agent. This requires powers to choose and to act, and, some might add, even a similarity of environment.[8] Although I am not entirely convinced that the presence of sensations and emotions is a necessary condition for moral action in any circumstances, I nevertheless share Professor Puccetti's concern about Strawson's seeing without eyes and hearing without ears.

Could a case be made for seeing and hearing without sensuous input? I know of only one serious attempt, made in an entirely different context, that could shed some new light on the problem. The Belgian philosopher Joseph Maréchal, in a remarkable analysis of mystical states, showed how the mystic may experience a vivid awareness of some bodily presence unsupported by sense perception.[9] One cannot dismiss such feelings or the actual sense images by which they are occasionally accompanied by calling them "hallucinations." For the existence of such "hallucinations" is the very problem to be solved. Maréchal shows that a relative independence of the feeling of presence from actual sensations is not only possible, but quite common. No associationist theory can adequately account for those phenomena, since it leaves unexplained the initial transition from mere internal feelings to the awareness of an *external* presence. Complexity and intensity of sensations may assist us afterward in distinguishing the feeling of presence as truly objective from others that only seemed to be objective during the experience. But can consciousness dispense with the body *altogether?* I think not. For even mystical states remain body-oriented. The body alone provides the stable vantage point that directs our experiences, even when we do not directly rely on its sensations. Without a link with the body, the mind would become totally disoriented.

A somewhat similar case could be made about the functioning of memory without the support of the body. The argument was initiated by Bergson, who in *Matière et memoire* argued that the functioning of memory is not dependent on any specific part of the brain and that the psychic state, like the hidden part of an iceberg, is in most cases immensely wider than the cerebral state.[10] We might extend this discussion to the entire relation of mind and body. William James once claimed in an Ingersoll Lecture: "In the production of consciousness by the brain, the terms are of heterogeneous natures altogether and as far as our understanding goes, it is as great a miracle as if we said, Thought is 'spontaneously generated' or 'created out of nothing.'"[11] That statement seems too strong, because the body still has a function to fulfil in transmitting bodily sensations to the mind. Even if no transmission occurs, it still defines my relation to me and to the world.

Spinoza first in modern philosophy asserted the indissoluble union of body and mind. The mind to him is the idea *of the body*. Some distinctness between physiological and mental processes is undeniable. Yet nothing suggests that the mind would ever be able to dispense with the body, as it seems to do in the dualist positions of Plato and Descartes. Even the assumption of a "spiritual" or a "new" body does not guarantee the survival of consciousness. For the intimate union of mind and body suggests that personal identity is linked to a particular mind–body relation. A different body would jeopardize this identity: "It is essential to me not only to have a body, but to have *this* body. It is not only the notion of the body which, through that of the present, is necessarily linked to that of the *for-itself*; the actual existence of *my* body is indispensable to that of my 'consciousness.'"[12] Traditional theories of immortality mostly regard the body as an object in the world through which the mind acquires information that might be acquired in other ways. But the body is not a part of the world: it presents my viewpoint on the world: "When I say that my foot hurts I do not simply mean that it is a cause of pain in the same way as the nail which is cutting into it, differing only in being nearer to me; I do not mean that it is the last of the objects in the external world, after which a more intimate kind of pain should begin, an unlocalized awareness of pain in itself, related to the foot only by some causal connection and within the closed system of experience. I mean that the pain reveals itself as localized, that it is constitutive of the pain-infested space."[13] Theories of the mind–body relation, such as the one from which this quotation was taken, make it hard to conceive how any personal identity could be maintained apart from my present body.

Precisely for reasons of this sort, Christians, Muslims, and many Jews think of an afterlife in terms of reembodiment rather than of an unending extension of life. But before considering the specific difficulties inherent in such a view, we do well to remember that resurrection and immortality are usually not alternatives. Some years ago, the German theologian Oscar Cullmann, in an Ingersoll lecture, stirred up a major sensation with his thesis that the New Testament assumes a dormant period for the dead until the day of resurrection. Even though such an assumption does not deny immortality, it was strongly criticized. The reason why Cullmann's arguments were challenged was not their lack of support in scripture but their conflict with the later, anti-Platonic development of the idea of immortality. Even though the body perishes at death, the mind's essential relation to a bodily existence remains uninterrupted. Thus Thomas Aquinas, against Aristotle's clear denial, declared the mind, even as *form* of the body (*forma corporis*), to be immortal. He thereby established a much closer link between body and mind than the ancients knew. It still remains to be seen whether a body-oriented mind without a body is able to preserve its identity outside its former, fully embodied existence.

Before answering this question, we ought to investigate whether a full reembodiment is possible. Clearly here also difficulties abound, particularly after an extensive period of time. A human body is never an isolated atom or monad. It occupies a particular segment of space and time, in which it communicates with other bodies. How could a new body possibly be related to the same universe at the same time in the same space? Does the universe of risen or spiritualized bodies occupy a space of its own, which allows its bodies to communicate with one another but not with the ones in the present world? This raises the difficult question whether two different spaces could possibly coexist. For two spaces with a common point, such as the "passage" to the underworld or to the island of the dead, or the mirrors separating the realm of the living from that of the dead (as in Cocteau's film *Orphée*), inevitably collapse into one space. Even to describe one space as lying "outside" another is to use a questionable metaphor, since the "outside" belongs to the same space as the inside. What is needed here is a relatedness of autonomous spaces in the same consciousness. William E. Hocking believes this to occur in actual experiences such as the relatedness of the space of my dreams to that of my waking consciousness, or of the aesthetic space within a painting to that of the room in which it hangs. In neither case is there an interval between any single point of one space and any single point of the other. Still the mind easily passes from one to the other. The very nature of concrete freedom requires a transition from the space of an existing world into that of a possible one. Hocking has drawn some far-reaching consequences from this fact:

> In the devising of free deeds within the context of a particular fact, there is a literal sense in which the self is in presence of at least one other space world all the time.... If there were a plurality of such closed systems, the relation between them could never be expressed in terms of the internal processes of any of them. But the mind is essentially such a relating entity or *vinculum*, holding before itself, in contemplating action, a plurality of such closed groups, as if it were itself a most general field in which space-time fields could coexist, a "field of fields," so to speak. Hence the existence of the mind can be *no function of events within* any of its object systems. This being the case, the event of death, involving the body of the self belonging to some one nature system, does not necessarily involve the death of the

self (nor of its body) as already envisaging other worlds independent of the given world.[14]

Hocking's solution leaves a number of questions unanswered, specifically, how any communication would ever be possible between the two worlds. This problem never seems to have worried the defenders of reembodiment or of bodily resurrection. My difficulty with such a concept of unrelated bodies in an independent space is that it seriously weakens the meaning of the term "body." Are we still speaking meaningfully when we surmise that after the destruction of the ordinary, terrestrial body the individual continues to express him- or herself through a "miasmic, subtle body"? To be sure, a strong religious tradition supports the notion of a "spiritualized body." According to some of the Gospel narratives, Jesus's body after his resurrection was not subject to the ordinary laws of physics. He entered when the doors were closed (Jn. 20:19) and had changed so much in appearance as to be unrecognizable or at least to raise doubts about his identity (Lk. 24:16; Mk. 16:12; Jn. 21:12). Other texts, however, emphasize that his body was the same as before his death. He invited his disciples to touch him and to eat with him to prove that he was not a mere ghost (Lk. 24:39–43; Jn. 20:27). Paul first applied to his risen body the name "spiritual body" (*soma pneumatikon*) and assumed that the bodies of the risen on the last day will be of a similar nature.[15]

The very discrepancy of the narratives has led some modern theologians to regard the events described in the resurrection passages as essentially visionary. The term "visionary" does not necessarily refer to the real nature of the apparitions, but their *physical* character. That the distinction was by no means a clear one is indicated by the fact that Paul himself equates his own mere "vision" of the risen Christ with apparitions to the apostles, which he clearly conceives to have been in some way physical. The more "physical" interpretations of the Resurrection tend to stress the continuity between the present and the past. Yet if we pass from Jesus's resurrection after a short period in the tomb, to the concept of resurrection at the end of time, the problem of personal identity returns with full force.

Can we truly consider the risen body identical with the decomposed one? One recent attempt to cope with the difficulty detaches the concept of survival from that of bodily identity. On the basis of a hypothetical excision and subsequent transplantation of one hemisphere of the brain,

Derek Parfit raises the question whether the two individuals in whom the "I" would survive must be considered "identical" with the original person. The answer must clearly be negative, if identity is conceived as the one-to-one bodily relation it is commonly held to be. However, if psychic continuity were taken as a criterion, a person could be said to survive if he shares his memories with one who preceded him. Parfit suggests that, since psychological connectedness is a matter of degree, the appropriateness of the term "I" should be left to the choice of the speaker.[16]

But can a person simply decide which part of his past he will assume and which he will reject? Terence Penelhum strongly argued against such a loose concept of personal identity. What is part of me and what is not can be defined only by the spatial and temporal bounds of the physical body: "That part of us from which we wish to dissociate ourselves is as much a part of us as that with which we wish to identify."[17] Since the resolution of past conflicts in a future state implies a radical change from the present state, a carefully defined notion of identity is all the more required in a discussion of life after death. This requirement is not met by the evidence of some common elements in the *ante mortem* and the *post mortem* person. Penelhum does not claim that a complete assumption of one's earthly past is possible in the afterlife, but that without self-identity the religious notion of immortality becomes meaningless, even though the criteria may be lacking for establishing how much change such an identity would allow.

This conclusion, I believe, touches the heart of the problem and indicates the very nature of the difficulty we face here. Ninian Smart referred to the problem of survival as ultimately an empirical question. It is not *a priori* impossible to *conceive* of the person in such a way that bodily death does not mark the end of the individual, but whether personal continuity can be preserved in any other way than through permanence in the same physical body cannot be *a priori* established. I consider it the prime merit of the empirical position to have drawn attention to the basic deficiency of every *a priori* argument for immortality. Since no adequate empirical evidence is available of actual survival after death, are we not forced to conclude that no conclusive *a priori* argument for immortality can be given? Yet the weakness of the empirical tradition consists in its inability to establish an adequate idea of the self on the forever-shifting ground of personal identity. The fundamental problem of the empirical position in this matter is that it is forced to rule about the continuity of life on the sole basis of phenomena in which a change as substantial as death has, to our knowledge, never occurred. Obviously no present experience could prove that the self *does* survive after death. Even the question whether it *could* survive cannot be decided without a notion of the self that exceeds the actual boundaries of experience.

Our criticism of the empirical notion of the self must not be interpreted as an attempt to reintroduce a purely *a priori* concept of the self, pretailored to be immortal after the fashion of the ancient soul. At most we may be able to establish the positive possibility (i.e., more than the mere absence of contradiction) of life after death. We are wont to identify the self with self-consciousness. But a moment of reflection shows that this identification cannot be consistently maintained. Although the self passes through prolonged periods of unconsciousness, no one would conclude that its existence is therefore suspended. At all times, philosophers have accepted the idea of a "dark side" of consciousness. Leibniz developed this insight into a distinction between perceptions and apperceptions (conscious perceptions).

The existence of an unconscious yet essential part of psychic selfhood gained full acceptance when depth psychology showed the impact of such a greatly unconscious upon conscious conduct. For the unconscious part of the self is obviously more than a storage place of what the mind has forgotten or blocked out. Nor must it be regarded as merely the more "primitive" part of the self in which the instinctual conflicts take place. Primitive it may be in the sense that the activity of the self on this level precedes all conscious acts, but not in the sense in which the "lower" is said to precede the "higher." William E. Hocking has described this deeper self: "What we call *subconsciousness*, so far from being a sort of mental sub-basement, is at the center of selfhood, and the invidious term '*subconsciousness*' is an inept recognition of the fact that the primary springs of selfhood are not habitually at the focus of its outgoing interests." Those who reached for the most intensive experience of the self have at all times believed that in the end they would attain a self extending beyond the bounds of consciousness. The common objection that whatever must be attained through consciousness must be conscious itself is not really pertinent. Although the unconscious as such undoubtedly escapes the direct glance of reflection, it may well manifest itself indirectly, as the achievements of depth psychology have proven.

Not only mystics but also philosophers have considered this *deeper self* worthy of their attention. From a different perspective also, psychologists recognize the existence of a permanent element that allows the mind to retain what flows by and to reconnect what is broken off. Memory enables the mind to unite various experiences undergone at different times. Without it there would be no consciousness. Hume's phenomenalist view, according to which selfhood consists of a variety of phenomena united in a single memory, fails to explain how different phenomena can remain connected in a common memory *in spite of* total interruptions of consciousness. Memory itself, then, is what must be explained and what the empiricist notion of the self takes for granted. How can the self continue to be operative during the interruptions of the stream of consciousness unless we accept a *sub-phenomenal* and also a phenomenal self? To answer that question, William E. Hocking posited two "selves," one conscious of the world it inhabits (the excursive self), the other (the reflective self) transcending the worldly flux. The reflective self is not subject to the lapses of the excursive one: steadfastly it maintains itself through the blackouts of consciousness and bridges the gaps between the intermittent stretches of awareness. The body may be indispensable for keeping this constant identification process united, but it cannot be its ultimate foundation, since the body itself needs to be recognized as remaining identical from one achievement to another.

> Why is this self, upon waking, the *same self*? Is it indeed because of the faithfulness of the physical world it deals with? Is it because this body and these walls are the same as yesterday? But the body and the walls of yesterday are gone: the body is indeed the same, but it is wholly incapable of presenting the self with the knowledge of that fact—it can work in the moment, it cannot retain its own past. It is the self which recognizes its body as the same; the physical constancy would be meaningless were it not for the underlying constancy of memory.[18]

The self, then, surpasses the sum total of conscious phenomena. Indeed the phenomena remain unintelligible until we realize that from a sub-phenomenal source they derive permanence and coherence.

The reflective self depends considerably less upon bodily support than the phenomenal self. The former's activity continues uninterruptedly after a withdrawal from the physical world in sleep, in trance, at moments of intense concentration, sometimes even in daydreams. In those states we notice a strange interference of the unconscious with the conscious self. On such occasions, the self appears to be led beyond the boundaries of its ordinary world and to escape its ruling laws. It becomes expressive rather than reactive, revealing the workings of an inner power instead of those of its bodily world. Could the self ever dispense altogether with this world? To some, the answer to this question comes easily: death to them is no more than a transition to a new world and a new embodiment. Unfortunately Hocking's language leaves the impression that there are two selves rather than two states or conditions of one self.

After considering the difficulties we encountered with the notions of disembodied and reembodied self, I am somewhat less sanguine about this possibility. Even if we granted a relative independence to the unconscious self, some embodiment appears to be an essential requirement for full consciousness. Could the difficulties be avoided by assuming the persistence of remembered bodily determinations without the presence of an actual body? One might conceive the mind as so essentially and definitively determined by the body that after death it still preserves its identity by the memories of its past life. In such a state there would be no question of a "hearing without ears and seeing without eyes." Yet if such memories were to survive at all, they would gradually decrease and, after a while, fade away altogether.

Nor does the distinction between a conscious, totally embodied "self" and a self embodied only in memory prove that the latter can survive death. It can never be *proven*, I think, that one aspect of the self may be preserved after the other dies. On this matter a great deal may be learned from Spinoza's philosophy. By defining the soul as the idea of the body, Spinoza linked the two aspects of the self more intimately than any of his philosophical predecessors. He thereby seemed to exclude a survival of the mind after the death of the body. Nevertheless Spinoza argues in the *Ethics* (5.23): "The human mind cannot be totally destroyed with the death of the body: some of it is eternal and remains." He confirms and explains this in the Scholium to 5.38. The more clear and distinct its knowledge is and the more it thereby loves God, the less it will be exposed to the corruption of death. In a brilliant article, Alan Donagan has shown what these intriguing statements mean.[19] After death, the mind attains some independence of its relation to the body, even though the mind continues to be a formal idea of the body. Yet this idea is no longer mediated through an existing body. Indeed, it loses all contact with the body's modality of existence. Being eternal, any notion of actual time disappears. At this stage it should attain the highest degree of consciousness, namely, the knowledge of all things through their ultimate cause, God. It knows the body only *sub specie aeternitatis*, that is, in the light of eternity as all things forever are in God. Bodiliness survives, but only as "the idea which expresses the essence of this or that human body under the form of eternity" (*Ethics*, 5.21). In this "ideal" survival the mind fully becomes what it was only partially in the present life.

Does that mean that my finite mind continues knowing after death? No, because ideas under the attribute of extension can be known only when, beyond their possible or formal essence, they also are known in their actual existence. Otherwise these contingent ideas remain totally unknown, since their essence is not such that they *must necessarily* exist. The main problem raised by Spinoza is how individuality can be preserved without the actual presence of a physical body. Can individuality survive the loss of an actual embodiment? Some conditions must be fulfilled for individual survival to be possible. To survive, the mind must maintain a permanent relation to an individual body; bodiliness of some sort, then, appears to be an essential condition for preserving personal individuality after death. It would be unwarranted to conclude that the mind can ever function in total independence of a body. All we can claim is that at least some functions appear not to be directly dependent upon the actual presence of all physiological conditions of conscious activity. Yet they presuppose the actual presence of the basic other ones, such as a functional brain, blood supply, and so on. Hence the relative independence of some states of consciousness of an actually present body requires a link with an actual body, at least in the present state of physiological and mental being.

The conclusions of the preceding investigation are very limited and almost entirely negative. Life after death is not impossible—at least for all we know. Yet the final answer on the possibility may only come from empirical evidence. If we know one person who has definitely died and, after a sufficient time to confirm his death, has returned to life as the same person, only then can we safely assert that death has not been the end of his life. I have read that this occurred to a few individuals: Jesus of Nazareth and his personal friend Lazarus. Were the events more than apparitions to Mary of Magdala, his disciples, and groups of believers? I think so, because there were several people involved who shared a meal with the formerly dead ones. Most importantly, Are the reports reliable? To believers they were; to nonbelievers they were not. No scientific research has brought the two groups to agree on the facts. It is not for us to take sides in this dispute of faith.

The preceding philosophical discussion has neither confirmed nor denied an important thesis of most theist religions. Its function has been mainly critical. The result shows that only empirical evidence would confirm the religious doctrine of life after death and on that evidence minds remain divided. The fact that the division between acceptance and denial of the possibility of a life after death runs along lines of faith indicates that religious believers may derive evidence from a source that remains unavailable to nonbelievers or that believers consider the matter part of a package of which there is enough evidence on other matters to take obscure ones for granted, as long as they do not obviously conflict with what is from all physical evidence impossible. In ancient Buddhism, the question is left undecided as being not essential to the main purpose of religion. In Christianity, it is essential and, to my mind, sufficiently established by the reliability of its witnesses. This makes the mystery a matter of faith, not of blind faith, but faith confirmed by the word of those who gave their lives for it.

PART III

Phenomenology of Religion

In the twentieth century, phenomenology extended the scope of philosophical reflection. It did so by means of a philosophical principle that had been well known in medieval thought but had since been forgotten in modern subjectivism. The principle stated that consciousness is by nature intentional, *that is, ideally intends its object. Thinking thereby becomes thinking of. Yet, being an object of consciousness, it remains a mere psychic phenomenon (object of psychology), until the mind separates the ideal meanings of a phenomenon from the psychic conditions that made its appearance possible and concentrates exclusively on the ideal object itself. In doing so, one removes any empiricist obstacles from a philosophical study of religion and avoids narrow rationalist boundaries that leave little of religion worth investigating. In short, phenomenology has reopened the field of philosophy to a study of religious meanings by freeing the entrance to the ideal meanings of religion from rationalist and empiricist impediments.*

In essay 9, I investigate the effects this new approach might have upon the philosophy of religion in general. In essay 10, I perform a similar clearance around the dominant question of religious truth. In essays 11 and 12, I apply the method of descriptive phenomenology to the fields of religious art and ritual on materials provided by art history and by comparative religion. In the three final essays (part IV), I discuss a subject that is unique to religion. Indeed the religious consciousness culminates in it, and yet it does not belong to its very essence: it is not true that all forms of religious consciousness ought to be mystical, but only that the mystical consciousness plunges its roots in the religious one.

ESSAY 9

Phenomenology of Religion

Limits and Possibilities

Edmund Husserl, the father of phenomenological philosophy, never submitted religion to a sustained phenomenological analysis. He left a good many notes and fragments on the philosophical significance of religion. In an early article, "Husserl's Thought on God and Faith," published in *Philosophy and Phenomenological Research* (1969), I attempted to order them into a coherent theory. In retrospect, I feel that my project failed, for some of the statements conflicted with others. Still, the fragments of Husserl's thought played a significant role in preparing a phenomenological theory of religion, all the more so since their author showed a lively interest in the subject, as appears from an answer to his disciple Roman Ingarden, who asked him what he considered the most fundamental problem in philosophy. Husserl responded: "The problem of God, of course."

Why, then, did he neglect to treat systematically a question that he considered so important? Most likely because he considered religion the *final* problem of philosophy, which had to wait until all others had been adequately defined. He may have thought of a philosophical study of religion as a task to be done after all others had been dealt with. Nevertheless, he considered the problem of God of primary importance. In his archives, I found a note probably addressed to himself: "All forms must first be shown in their full universality, the totality must first be disclosed in its complete system of particular forms . . . before teleology [of religion] can be shown to be that which ultimately makes it possible and thereby to realize all being in its concrete, individual totality" (Husserl Archives, Ms. E III 9, p. 65). For that reason, the scientific understanding of religion is a question to be discussed after we have attained "a clear understanding of the mental process involved in [the formation of] religious symbols" (Husserl Archives, Ms. E III 9, p. 30). Husserl never refers to the problem of God as a causal one. Causality for him (in the limited, modern sense) belongs "to the system of the constituted intentional world, and has no meaning except in this world."[1]

After a period of intense interest in the phenomenological study of religion that had started with Max Scheler and Gerardus van der Leeuw and concluded with Mircea Eliade and Henri Duméry, a silence of exhaustion has fallen over the subject. The decline might be because those who had excelled in phenomenological description, especially van der Leeuw and Eliade, had sidestepped the ontological problems involved in this field, which are meant to surpass the level of generalized ethnological observations. This may surprise, since even Husserl's contemporaries had known that a phenomenological description of religion first requires a philosophical justification of the method. As early as 1926, Jean Héring, a young French scholar, had been aware of some of the methodological issues in his *Phénoménologie et philosophie religieuse*.[2] So had Max Scheler in a memorable analysis of the religious act in *On the Eternal in Man* (1921). Still, neither Scheler nor Héring had sufficiently recognized the complexity of the symbolic expressions through which the religious act intends its object. Are we truly justified in attributing the common name *religion* to the endless variety of mythologies, rituals, and dogmatic beliefs we so casually collect under the name *religion*? Or do they merely display a vague family resemblance between intentional acts that fulfill essentially different functions? These questions were seldom raised, and ethnologists remained skeptical of the phenomenological results.

Gerardus van der Leeuw mentions the foundational question in the penultimate chapter of his classic *Religion in Essence and Manifestation*, but fails to answer it: "Phenomenology consists in a systematic discussion of what *appears*. Religion, however, is an ultimate expression that evades our observation, a revelation which in its very essence is and remains concealed. But how shall I deal with what is ever elusive and hidden? How can I pursue phenomenology when there is no phenomenon?"[3] So far as I know, he never answered these questions. Since then, one phenomenologist, it must be said, went to the heart of the problem, namely, the role played by what Kant had called the *transcendental ego*, that is, the self acting as creative subject in the formation of symbolic theories, images, and practices. The French philosopher Henri Duméry explored the philosophical foundations of the phenomenology of religion. Outside a small academic circle in France, his work never received the attention it deserved. The neglect may partly be due to problems Duméry created for himself by capping his transcendental phenomenology with a Neoplatonic theology of the Absolute, thereby alienating orthodox theologians and orthodox Husserlians. Equally responsible may have been the highly technical vocabulary in which the author couched his ideas.

Duméry justified his strange excursion into the extra-phenomenological domain of the "religious intuition" by drawing attention to the fact that, in the case of religion, the phenomenological intuition, as Husserl had described it, even in a phenomenological study requires a number of preliminary distinctions between what is taken for granted and what needs to be proven. The first one, the so-called *eidetic reduction*, is known to all phenomenological philosophers. The mind ought to "bracket" all contingent, psychic elements from the appearing phenomena in consciousness in order to concentrate exclusively on the ideal qualities. Yet on the second reduction, called *transcendental* or also *phenomenological*, even phenomenologists do not agree. It requires the phenomenologist to abstain from any reference to the phenomenal content in order to concentrate exclusively on its relation to the constitutive self. A third, *egological* reduction considers the phenomena as not merely related to but as *produced by* the transcendental ego. Here begins what later was to be called the *idealism* of Husserl's phenomenology.

The problem was that, after all these reductions, Husserl had provided no unifying factor to relink what his method had divided. Philosophers in the Platonic tradition and also monotheist believers have always assumed that all things and ideas must come together in an ultimate unity, an absolute *One*. Since the phenomenological description of religion attains no such ultimate absolute, Duméry added a fourth, *henological* (referring to 'ἕν, "one") reduction to the three others established by Husserl. He thereby attempted to ground the transcendental ego in a not further definable absolute principle of unity. Plotinus's *One* served that purpose. But most of his followers identified this unknowable One with the monotheist idea of

God. The phenomenological theory thereby became an *itinerary of the mind to God*—much to the displeasure of traditional phenomenologists. With this interpretation, phenomenology turned into a particular type of metaphysics, which Husserl had been anxious to avoid. Moreover, what justified the philosopher to call this One beyond all categories of knowledge to be the God of religion? The absence of any natural content forced Duméry to stress the need of a revelation. Only a revelation renders the mind capable of knowing the One. Obviously, at this point we are leaving philosophy and entering theology. In a later edition of his *La Foi n'est pas un cri* (1957) ("Faith is not a scream"), Duméry admits that the notion of revelation surpasses all natural determinations of language. Still, he adds, God is the source of our speaking. He therefore may also reveal himself in human language.

Duméry's critics were not convinced by these arguments and argued that the henological reduction had eliminated the very subject of his investigation. Was it necessary? I agree with Eugen Fink (one of Husserl's most reliable interpreters) that the descriptive analysis of such phenomenologists as Eliade, van der Leeuw, and the entire Dutch school required the support of some metaphysical foundation. Has Duméry provided it? Most phenomenologists found the preceding arguments less than persuasive. Let us look at other attempts to support descriptive phenomenology. According to Husserl, the phenomenological analysis, if adequately performed, results in a *Wesensschau*, an essential *intuition*. How would this be possible in the case of religion, where the intended "object" lies beyond experience? Precisely for that reason, Max Scheler concluded that God becomes directly accessible to humans only in acts of devotion and worship. In prayer alone does the believer know God through an immediate, albeit merely symbolic, intuition. The God of religion is present exclusively in the religious act, not in metaphysical thinking.[4] Only in the act of faith or in a reflective retracing of that act does the phenomenologist gain access to a transcendent object. For Scheler, then, an intuition of what the religious act intends is possible only in faith.

Van der Leeuw attempted to solve the same problem by distinguishing *"religion-as-experience,"* which he limited to a search for the meaning of life in its totality, from *"religion-as-transcendent"* exclusively given in a divine revelation. Phenomenology would be able to deal only with the former while having to abstain from the latter. This answer remains inadequate even by the norms of van der Leeuw's own practice: his study constantly refers to "revealed" texts. As indeed it should, for without a reflection on what the believer himself regards as the driving motives of his faith, namely, revelation and a divinely granted grace, phenomenology never comes to grips with the real act. Living religion centers on a nucleus, which believers consider to be *given*. To exclude that nucleus from phenomenological reflection means to abandon a crucial part of what determines the religious attitude. Van der Leeuw's distinction shows a reluctance, which Karl Barth later made into a theological principle, to subject the core of his own Christian faith to the same scrutiny he applies to other religions.

If one thus separates the experience of a revealed religion from the revelation that informs it, the problems concerning the religious act become insoluble from the start. Must we not rather assume that the experience of a religion in some way contains its object as *intentionally immanent* in it? To prove that this is possible, a number of philosophers, especially those influenced by Blondel, Maréchal, and Rahner, attempted to show that not only religious but all mental acts are intrinsically related to a transcendent ground of meaning and value. According to their view, all human striving implicitly intends a self-transcending end and is moved by a transcendent impulse. (Please note that the term *transcendent* as used here by no means implies that the ultimate principle of metaphysics and religion is *only* transcendent, but that the aspect of transcendence is pertinent to the relation here discussed. Also note, the term *transcendent* is, since Kant, to be distinguished from *transcendental*, which refers to the essence of an act or being.)

Returning to the question raised by Scheler and van der Leeuw, we wonder, Can the phenomenologist truly grasp the meaning of the religious act without actively sharing the believer's faith? Obviously, phenomenological analysis does not coincide with faith. One originates in a critical, the other in a passive attitude. Nevertheless, does the very capacity of understanding the inner meaning of the act not *presuppose* that even the critical observer in some way "imitates" the act of faith? In earlier writings, I have argued for a qualified version of Scheler's thesis.[5] The phenomenologist must in some way enter into the believer's act, through present or past faith, or at least through an actual acquaintance with acts and experiences analogous with the ones the observer attempts to analyze. A mere description from without, accompanied by some *general* theory about religious attitudes and feelings, never yields the kind of intuitive insight a phenomenological analysis seeks. A philosopher deprived of any empathy with religion is incapable of successfully analyzing its acts, meanings, and symbols. A correct phenomenological description of faith also requires a substantial acquaintance with the self-interpretation inherent in the act.

Finally, I shall attempt to uncover the unique dialectic between the essentially receptive attitude, which the religious act adopts toward a transcendent revelation, and the active role the believer plays in creating the symbols, theories, and norms within which he or she incorporates that revelation. An investigation of the self's religious creativity demands a move from phenomenological description to phenomenological philosophy similar to the one Husserl introduced with his transcendental reduction. Unlike the eidetic reduction, the transcendental one relates the phenomena to a transcendental ego. This transcendental reduction has remained controversial in the phenomenological movement: some, such as Eugen Fink, have strongly asserted its necessity, while others have rejected it as a slide into idealism that basically conflicted with Husserl's original project.

However one may judge these controversies, a phenomenological study of religion cannot but admit the active part the meaning-giving mind plays in the presentation of doctrines, institutions, and social structures of a particular faith. A monotheist religion—such as Judaism, Christianity, and Islam—derives most of its theoretical and practical norms from what its adherents claim to be a divine revelation contained in canonical scriptures. Yet these scriptures bear signs of the personal identities and idiosyncrasies, cultural backgrounds, and of the varying degrees of imaginative and intellectual powers of their individual writers. Their cosmological and social views, and a good number of their religious conceptions, rituals, and customs, depend on those of the surrounding culture. Because of this obviously human contribution to any act of religious symbolization, secular thinkers have attributed the entire process to a mere projection of their authors. To do so, however, is to ignore the dominant awareness of a fundamental passivity believers uphold in this symbolic creativity with respect to what they believe to be a transcendent source. Even to believers who are fully conscious of man's creative role in any symbolic expression, religion is neither a "projection," as Feuerbach claimed, that is, an attribution of idealized human qualities to an imaginary deity, nor an "illusion" in the Freudian sense of wishes unsupported by any possible realization. The more the philosopher succeeds in tracing conceptions, structures, even categories to the creative activity of the mind, the more the religious intentionality appears to be fundamentally given. Unless phenomenology takes account of the irreducible transcendence of the religious intentionality of the act, the phenomenological reduction misses the specifically religious quality of the act. Indeed, the quality of fundamental *givenness* that adheres to the object of the religious act constitutes its specific difference. Whereas other acts *bring* their object to givenness, the religious act accepts the a priori givenness of its object.

Hence the interpreter must pay careful attention to the subtle dialectic between the projective and the passive qualities of the religious act. In this act, as in all others, the *transcendental ego* provides the meaning-giving elements of the act. Yet its intentionality is *given*. The transcendental ego projects the meaning over the various areas of consciousness: the imaginative, the rational, and the spiritual. Yet this *projection* must not be understood as referring to an exclusively human activity of the mind: "Consciousness is projective, because it is expressive: it cannot fail to express itself on various levels of representation."[6]

To be sure, this transcendent intentionality of the religious act is culturally transmitted from one generation to another. Yet *what it transmits* surpasses mere tradition. The alleged revelation may include "facts," historical or legendary, to which historical religions in particular attach a vital significance. Thus Christian faith could not survive if a man called Jesus had never lived. But the *fact* of Jesus does not become religiously meaningful until the believer assumes it within a religious intentionality, that is, accepts it as transcendently given. Many witnessed the events described in the Gospels, yet did not consider them religiously meaningful as *signs* pointing beyond the events. To the believer, the ability to *see* this symbolic *surplus* appears as given. This intimate cooperation of divine inspiration and human expression leads to a number of paradoxical conclusions.

The phenomenology of religion has provoked questions about the truth of religion, which phenomenological descriptions do not answer. The question reminds me of a discussion that took place at the Yale Department of Religious Studies and Department of Philosophy after a splendid lecture by Mircea Eliade. At the end, an old teacher in both disciplines raised the question: "That was very beautiful, sir. But is it true?" In the next essay, I shall discuss the question of truth in the phenomenology of religion.

ESSAY 10

Phenomenology and Religious Truth

If one thing distinguishes traditional conceptions of truth from modern philosophical ones, it is the absence, or secondary role, of epistemological concerns. Despite their substantial differences, early religious traditions agree in stressing the ontological and moral qualities of truth more than the purely cognitive ones. Truth refers to *Being* before it refers to *knowledge*. In Sanskrit, the mother tongue of Indo-European languages, *truth* is *satya* and *being* is *sat*. Gandhi based his lifelong quest of truth upon the quality of *right-being*. In 1932, he formulated it as follows: "Nothing is or exists in reality except Truth. That is why *Sat* or Truth is perhaps the more important name of God. In fact, it is more correct to say that 'Truth is God' than to say that 'God is Truth.'"[1] The proper ways to acquire ontological truth are devotion and fidelity: the path of truth is the path of devotion (*bhakti*).[2] From this identity of true being and right conduct may have stemmed the later theory of truth as correspondence. At any rate, originally the nature of truth consisted in an *ontological* state of *Being*. *Knowing* the truth, then, requires *being in* the truth.

The religious nature of truth was later confirmed by its divine origin. From the start, religion assumed that the Absolute is expressive, that God *speaks*. Christianity and Islam took this doctrine to its farthest extreme: the former proclaimed that God's Word is God and the latter that the Word of God is the self-manifestation of God. Thus divine truth became the ground and principal analogate of *all* truth. How in the West's modern age rationality gradually detached truth from its religious origin is a story I shall tell in the early part of this essay. In the second part I shall investigate whether a concept of religious truth could still be justified by the modern concept of truth.

Truth within Religion

Even if we restrict the discussion to the Western religious notion of truth stretching from late antiquity to the early modern epoch, the canonical writings of monotheist religion, such as the Hebrew Bible, the Christian New Testament, and the Muslim Quran, we see that Jewish and early Christian thinkers turned to Greek philosophy for translating the religious concepts of the Bible. A pioneer in adjusting pagan Greek philosophy to biblical language was unquestionably Philo, the first-century Jewish philosopher of Alexandria. For him, Plato's thought confirmed the philosophical truth of the Bible. In the second and third centuries, some Christian theologians in Alexandria (especially Clement and Origen) viewed Christian faith as the only true *gnosis*. In fact, however, the Christian notion of *gnosis* consisted neither in a rationalization of faith nor in an extension of philosophical understanding, but in the self-understanding *of* faith. Initially the gnostic Christian was one who had intellectually *appropriated* what he believed. He was not, or not primarily, a person who, besides being Christian, had been educated in philosophy. Christians steadfastly believed that the act of faith contains its own explanation. Alexandrian and Cappadocian Church Fathers ruled out the kind of opposition between *faith* and understanding that later was to trouble much of modern thought.

Nevertheless, the Latin West had misgivings about mixing worldly wisdom with revealed truth, even where the interpretation of faith as the supreme mode of understanding was at stake. Tertullian bluntly opposed faith to philosophical insight (*credo quia absurdum*). Full acceptance came with Augustine—and not without reservations. After a Neoplatonic period, the newly baptized Augustine rejected philosophical learning as a temptation of *impia superbia*. Yet he soon came to see that any search for truth is *intrinsically* good and virtuous.[3] Cicero's *Hortensius* spurred him on toward a quest of eternal wisdom (*Confessions* 2.4). However, Augustine excluded certain subjects from his virtuous search, branding their pursuit as mere *curiositas*. Yet he all the more stressed that a divine, revelatory quality was inherent in all genuine truth.[4]

A major innovation in his conception of religious truth consisted in what we now call its *interior* quality. Whereas originally religious understanding had come with the faithful acceptance of the Bible, the gospel, or the Quran, all believers were convinced that God interiorly teaches each individual soul, but always in consonance with the objective testimony of scripture and tradition. As Augustine wrote, the divine teacher educates the believer not only in the truth of scripture but also in profane learning (*De magistro*, nos. 38–46). In his doctrine of the Interior Master, Augustine achieved a new synthesis of faith and understanding. What for early theologians had essentially consisted in an explication of scripture now becomes an illumination *simultaneously* subjective and objective. With the internalization of divine truth came the mandate to explore it interiorly, otherwise even divine Wisdom might degenerate into an undue intervention of reason. In this life, the quest of divine truth is limited to a *seeking* of faith (intellectus *quaerens* fidem). Augustine always accompanied his daring speculations about the interpretation of the Bible by a note of healthy skepticism concerning their ultimate validity.

With Anselm of Canterbury, the quest for truth takes a new turn. His "faith seeking understanding," despite its Augustinian tone, moved in a different direction. There is no ground to question his loyalty to Augustine, which he explicitly professes in the preface to his *Monologium*. Augustine had written: "There are those things that are first believed and afterward understood. Of such a character is that which cannot be understood of divine things except by those who are pure of heart" (*De diversis questionibus*, nos. 8, 83). Anselm echoes: "Right order requires that we *believe* the deep matters of the Christian faith before presuming rationally to discuss them."[5] Still, the very revelation in which we believe urges us to reflect on its implications and to draw appropriate conclusions from them. One such conclusion consists in the *necessary* nature of God's Being. Inasmuch as God is necessary in his entire Being, all divine activity proceeds from an inner necessity. On the basis of this principle, Anselm develops a logic of immanence and transcendence that encompasses even the historical events of Christ's life.

In applying God's inner necessity even to historical contingencies, Anselm goes well beyond the limits of what a human explanation of revealed truth would be. Thus he defines God's choice after the Fall as *demanding* a satisfaction. Since such fundamental assumptions concerning divine freedom are neither stated nor implied in the sacred text, Anselm's theory can no longer be called an analysis of scripture. Indeed, it contains the seeds of future rationalism.[6] Still, throughout it, Anselm's rationality remains a *devout* one that never deviates from the principle stated in the *Proslogion*: *Quaero credere ut intelligam, non autem intelligere ut credam* ("I seek to believe in order to understand, not to understand in order to believe"). Faith remains the basic presupposition of all genuine understanding. Yet a trend was set, and the full rationalism that emerged with Abelard was far less pious. No theological knowledge of scripture was needed, he thought, to investigate the truth of religious mysteries. Logic alone sufficed to understand even such recondite dogmas as the Eucharist or the Trinity. The reception of Aristotle's systematic works made the study of theology something it had never been before, namely, a *science* in the Aristotelian sense. With it came the epistemic distinction between two orders of knowledge: a philosophical and a theological.

At the very beginning of the *Summa Theologiae* (article 2), Thomas Aquinas raises the question: Is sacred doctrine a science? Of particular interest is the Aristotelian definition by which he supports his affirmative answer, namely, that "science" proceeds from self-evident principles. Principles "known by the natural light of reason" here appear on an equal footing with principles "established by the light of a higher science, namely, the science of God and the blessed." To us, such an equation may appear surprising, for it proves by means of what has to be proven. Need not the so-called science of God and the blessed itself be first established as a science? Thomas takes the "first principles" of sacred doctrine for granted. A little later he fully admits that they are *articuli fidei* ("articles of faith"), hence grounded in a divine revelation: "As other sciences do not argue in proof of their principles but argue from their principles to demonstrate other truths in these sciences, so this doctrine does not argue in proof of its principles, which are the articles of faith, but from them it goes on to prove something else" (*Summa Theologiae* I, q. 1, a. 8). The higher "science" then turns out to be revelation—an application of Aristotle's text that its author would have found surprising. Thomas, concerned only about the formal procedure from principles to conclusions, unhesitatingly transplants the method from science to faith.

Such a scientific definition of religious truth differed too obviously from the one advocated by Augustine, and the preceding Greek-Christian tradition did not long remain unchallenged. The Paris condemnations of 1277 and the Nominalist theology that had led to them profoundly shook the Thomist position. Still, in one respect Thomas's "scientific" presentation of religious truth may not be as far removed from the Augustinian tradition as it seems. The articles of faith remain "external" principles until an "interior light induces the mind to assent." The light of faith provides the formal element that converts the objective data of faith into religious principles.[7] For Aquinas as for Augustine, what ultimately determines the act of faith is God's own internal witness. Truth about God can come only from God, and in faith human beings respond to God's witness. Aquinas moves within a well-established tradition: religious truth derives its constitutive evidence from a divine illumination. The external object of belief (the "principles") reveals itself as *true* only within the act of faith.

Nominalism soon undid the synthesis of faith and reason that Thomas had achieved. Henceforth, religious truth, though still possessing the internal evidence of experience, could no longer count on the concomitant support of reason. Henceforth, there would be two separate conceptions of truth. The one of reason eventually found its basis in the harmony of mind and nature; the one of theology rested exclusively on an authority beyond nature. Most theologians began to adopt a different procedure: they attempted to establish the *truth about religion*, despite the fact that faith possessed its own internal truth based on revelation. The former gave birth to an intellectual exercise that had never existed before: proofs for the existence of God based on reason alone. Of course, Anselm and even Augustine had construed some rational formulation of the mind's ascent to God. But neither they nor any orthodox theologian had ever done so independently of *faith*, which had provided the idea of God in the first place.

The purport of the arguments had been to prove, independently of any internal religious evidence, the existence of a particular being called God. The "truth" of religion thereby emerged from a process of reasoning from the finite and contingent to the necessity of an infinite, necessary principle. Even if the proof had succeeded in establishing the existence of such a principle *beyond* the world—a most difficult task, indeed—it still had to establish that this principle coincided with the God of faith.

Aquinas, no more than Maimonides or Avicenna, had ever faced this challenge, for they started by accepting the God of faith, and then proceeded to show that to do so is not irrational. Once the finite's need of the infinite was established, they did not hesitate to identify this infinite with their religious idea of God: from a theological reflection on faith they already knew that the God in whom they believed must be infinite and necessary. Since the authors beforehand knew the outcome of their arguments, they were anxious to reach the conclusion, and were often careless in their logic of getting there. But in principle their method was unobjectionable.

Truth about Religion

In contrast with this theological method, philosophers pretended, by a process of reasoning on the nature of the phenomenal world, to arrive at firm conclusions on the existence and nature of God. But an argument that concludes to a transcendent ground of being is not sufficient for attaining the idea of God as religious faith has traditionally conceived it, namely, as Creator and goal of the universe. The idea of transcendent Being implies no conclusion concerning the existence of God, as Christians and other believing theists knew him. A philosophical study of Being may state the problem; it does not provide the solution. In the so-called arguments for the existence of God, modern thought reveals its skeptical attitude toward religious truth. It assumes that there is no specifically *religious* truth inherent in religion itself, yet that reason has allotted religion a specific field of learning, the truth of which lies within the competence of reason. The rules directing the arguments did not originate in religion's native land; they were a creation of the modern mind and a rationalist epistemology.

By the middle of the eighteenth century, the rationalist interpretation of religious truth began to show its serious deficiency. The synthesis of faith and rational knowledge was faulty or, rather, there was no synthesis. Religion added nothing to the body of rational knowledge. Rational knowledge is not open to additions derived from a different source than reason. A revelation, then, particularly a historical one, is an indigestible item to purely rational knowledge. Lessing's objections against the use of historical events to establish theories of eternal truth are well known. It became also obvious that faith had nothing to gain by adopting an idea of truth so foreign to its origins and so impoverishing in its effects.

Soon a revolt against this theological rationalism began. The leading figure in the theological *reconquista* was the Berlin theologian Friedrich Schleiermacher. His attempt to keep religion *as feeling* outside the battlefield should not be considered an abandonment of religious truth-claims, as his Kantian colleagues at the university thought. His efforts to rescue the proper identity of religion aimed at nothing less than at regaining a firm foothold for a truth proper to religion. The term "feeling," so loosely used in Schleiermacher's early work, signals in fact an attempt to escape from the kind of scientific objectivity and philosophical rationality to which truth-claims had come to be reserved. What Schleiermacher really pursued was a mode of consciousness that anteceded the rationalist subject/object split. Once this split between faith and reason has entered the foundation of religious truth, the proper place of religious truth ceases to exist. Whether the term *feeling* even in Schleiermacher's unique vocabulary was appropriate for defining the new ground of truth may be questioned. But to him is due the lasting credit of having broken with the rationalist tradition.

The reinstatement of the notion of religious truth as total, inner experience proposed by Schleiermacher's followers held a particular attractiveness to believers of the Romantic epoch. Yet many had forgotten that formerly that experience had been linked to a *revealed* message. Over the years that link had become much looser. What for Augustine had been an inner enlightenment that *accompanied* a revealed message had become *separated* from its original content. Yet a religion of experience detached from any content obviously endangered the truth of religion as much as rationalist theology had ever done. A vague moral or sentimental sympathy was not sufficient to preserve the integrity of religious truth.

The question, then, arises: Can any statement be made concerning the truth *about* religion, which does not derive from or is intrinsically linked to the *internal* truth of religion? Modern philosophical theories of truth were to a major extent developed for the purpose of securing a foundation for scientific practice. This does not *a priori* render them unfit for discussing the specific nature of religious truth. The basic *models* of truth used in those theories predate the scientific concerns of the late Middle Ages. Some may even have grown out of religious soil. Yet we must not hope to "justify" religious truth by scientific models of truth alone.

In the next pages, I intend briefly to test the aptitude of the main models of truth current in modern philosophy for justifying the truth of religion. If the nature of religious truth proved to be incompatible with all existing models, the critical believer would have serious grounds for questioning the existence of a religious truth in modern thought. Yet in doing so, we ought to keep in mind that the rejection of a genuine truth claim may be due to a mistaken *application* of it rather than to the model itself. A further question to consider is whether a religious truth claim is fit to be *integrated* with other truth claims (e.g., scientific ones). If religion were to have no more than claims totally isolated from all others, we would have a serious problem with its own claims.

The Correspondence Theory

The correspondence between idea and reality has from the beginning played a vital role in the philosophical arguments of the existence of God. Yet after philosophy took the critical turn, it found nothing but a nest of troubles concerning the neat division philosophy used to make a purely "mental" concept and a purely "real" object. Precisely the insurmountable difficulties inherent in the unproven assumption of a harmony between the mind and the world led to Kant's radical reversal of the correspondence theory. After his "Copernican revolution," the line that distinguished correspondence from coherence became hard to draw. Thus Edmund Husserl in his basically Kantian *Logical Investigations* asserts about the relation between ideas and things: "The connection of things, to which the thought-experiences [*Denkerlebnisse*]—the real or the possible—are intentionally related, and, on the other hand, the connection of truths, in which the unity of things [*die sachliche Einheit*] comes to objective validity as that which it is—*both are given together and cannot be separated* from each other."[8]

The famous "things themselves" (*die Sachen selbst*), to which Husserl's philosophy claims to return, proved to be as ideal as the reality to which they refer. The very notion of intentionality—the relation between the mind and its object—is interpreted as an immanent *relatedness*: the object is constituted by an act of consciousness. The intuition of truth in the end, then, is the outcome of a process in which the mind *brings* an object to an ideal presence. Both the intentional act and the object belong to the same ideal realm. We cannot but regard the appeal to "the facts," which some contemporary critics of religion continue to make, as patently uncritical. No facts are perceivable without an ideal process of interpretation that converts loose phenomena into objects. To perceive a complex of data as a fact always includes seeing it from a mental perspective. In the case of religion, which deals with the ultimate structure of the real, interpretation plays a particularly significant part. It is quite common for two persons, confronted with the same state of affairs, for one to see it *as* religious, for the other as not religious, and to do so without in the least contradicting each other on the nature of the observed phenomena. Both may agree on a *basic* (physical) interpretation, but one may require an additional, symbolic meaning, which the other rejects or considers unnecessary. Basic interpretations suffice for practical, scientific work and, in most cases, even for measuring social exchanges. Symbolic interpretations alone shed a different light on all aspects of the real.

A philosophical evaluation of the "truth of religion" on the basis of a correspondence theory of truth, then, requires taking into account not only the legitimacy of separate levels of interpretation but, in addition, the possible conflict between an interpretation made on one level with those made on another level. Nevertheless, solid reasons urge us to continue speaking of correspondences between religious and other truths. For truth in religion always contains a *relation* to what ultimately *is*: it includes a conversion, both moral and ontological, toward being in its very roots and origins, contrary to appearance and deception.

Coherence

Most theories of truth, implicitly or explicitly, refer to coherence as a criterion of truth. They particularly do so in the case of religious truth. Some philosophers, disheartened by the demands of an empirical verification, saw in the modern version of the coherence theory an escape from their troubles. Linguistic theories, such as the ones found in Wittgenstein's *Philosophical Investigations*, would legitimate any discourse in its own right, provided it *consistently* apply the rules of coherence. Undoubtedly, the coherence theory has protected the realm of religious meaning against undue intrusions. Each particular system, each "significant whole" (as Harold Joachim defined it in *The Nature of Truth*), obeys laws of its own that differ from those of other significant wholes.[9] An internal articulation organically integrates the separate elements into a unity of meaning. In the case of religion, the recognition of this relative autonomy becomes particularly significant, for it withholds us from applying criteria normative in some to other significant wholes, to which they do not apply.

Nevertheless, the notion of coherence requires several qualifications, if religious truth is still to relate to other forms of meaning. Coherence easily turns into closedness, which would isolate it from comparing some with other coherent systems and finding out whether they are compatible. To make genuine truth-claims, a system must be coherent not only within itself but also in relation to other coherent systems. This requires at the very least that principles inherent in what may be called "basic" interpretations do not contradict those active in the more remote systems of interpretation. To claim that discourses of religion and of physics substantially differ is not sufficient to exclude *a priori* any possible conflict. That religion has staked out its own circle of discourse does not dispense it from having to enter into dialogue with other realms of meaning and to show that their claims are compatible or not incompatible. This is particularly important with respect to the physical sciences. Even such standards as verifiability and falsifiability should not be dismissed as not pertinent to religion's "higher" realm. In dispensing religious truth from the rule to submit to universal criteria, we rescue it from outside criticism only to drown it in total meaninglessness. If religious truth were not to share some basic assumptions with other areas of truth, the term "truth" would cease to have meaning at all.

Closing religious doctrines off from other realms of thought may create worse problems than open conflicts. Precisely the failure to harmonize its doctrines with the scientific worldview has rendered religion improbable to many of our educated contemporaries as not deserving any serious consideration. C. D. Broad, although he agreed with the claim that nothing in modern science "refutes" the belief in miracles and in an afterlife, nevertheless dismissed both for being totally out of tune with the scientific worldview: "There is literally nothing but a few pinches of philosophical fluff to be put in the opposite scale to this vast coherent mass of ascertained facts."[10] A preposterous conclusion, to be sure—but one made possible by the increasing "hermetization" of religious discourse.

Facing social, psychological, and scientific pressures that modern believers feel unable to integrate with their faith, they tend to disconnect their unexamined religious beliefs from the rest of their convictions, as islands of truth isolated from the mainland of modern culture. Yet such a strategy draws a line, beyond which even the most hallowed "revelation" becomes highly improbable. Taken by itself, the theory of coherence proves insufficient to account for the most characteristic quality of religious truth—namely, that it originated *outside* the system, within which it is bound to live.

Disclosure

The correspondence and coherence models remain relevant for understanding the truth of religion. But the more they reflected the subjective turn of modern thought, the more they moved away from what religion has traditionally understood to be the essence of its truth. We noticed how hard it was to accommodate the idea of revelation in theories for which the norms of correspondence and coherence are restricted by observational limits. The disclosure theory appears untainted by modern subjectivism and proved therefore more obviously suited to express the nature of *religious* truth. In recent discussions, that religious model of truth has moved again to the center of the philosophical attention. It is not new: its origins may be traced to the beginnings of Western thought. We find it in Plato and before him in Parmenides's famous poem about being. Signs of it even appear in the dark recesses of Greek myths. In its modern form it reasserts the priority of *ontological* over epistemic truth. "Truth," Heidegger states, does not possess its original seat in a proposition but in a disclosure "through which openness essentially unfolds." Allowing things to be, to disclose themselves in the open, is the very essence of freedom. Though the source of disclosure is freedom, its focus is not on the human subject, but on the openness within which Being itself appears.[11]

The idea of disclosure is definitely congenial with the nature of religious truth. Indeed, it originated in religion. Yet it is not without problems.

How can a theory so obviously dependent upon the ancient idea of illumination meet the modern critical demand that truth *justify* itself? *Disclosure* may be the concept in which religion manifests its truth to itself, but how will it respond to the requirements of critical philosophy? Since the days of Heidegger and Gabriel Marcel, the theory of disclosure has gone a long way in justifying itself, not, to be sure, by the critical method, but by freeing the internal illumination of Being from the epistemic criteria of the positive sciences. In this respect we may compare it with the aesthetic consciousness, the truth of which surpasses the critical demands of factual accuracy.

Hans-Georg Gadamer defined the issue as follows: "Our task demands that we recognize in it an experience of truth which must not only be critically justified, but which itself is a mode of philosophizing."[12] Its "critical justification" (the term is misleading in this context!) here consists in being a particular "mode of philosophizing," whereby we retrace in philosophical *reflection* what we are actually doing in *religious practice*, rather than in providing the kind of *a priori* framework, as philosophy does for the positive sciences. The purpose of this immanent reflection is to uncover the radiation that the metaphysical idea of Being sheds on all objects of knowledge. Religious truth discloses the ontological significance of reality.

Things seen in this light become ontological symbols conveying a *Seinszuwachs*—an increase in density of Being. The term eminently applies to the truth disclosed in religious symbols. Precisely the ontological nature of religious symbols discloses their characteristic truth. Something of this nature was also, I believe, what Hegel had in mind, when he called the characteristic of the Christian religion to be *truth*, that is, endowed with a capacity for expressing the deepest dimension of Being: "[Christian doctrine] is not merely something subjective but is also an absolute, objective content that is in and for itself, and has the characteristic of truth."[13] Rather than submitting this disclosure to antecedent criteria, Hegel subjects the critique of religion to the higher authority of religion's self-disclosure. Moreover, in disclosing its own truth, religion also discloses the ultimate truth of all things: "The absoluteness of religious truth is due to the fact that its disclosure includes all reality and that it implies its own necessity" (*Lectures on the Philosophy of Religion I*, 319).

Next, however, Hegel adds that the truth of religion is fully disclosed only when religion itself loses its representational form and becomes philosophy. The *justification* of religious truth—which formerly had mostly consisted in a critical *reflection upon* an already established truth—now comes to consist in religion constituting its own truth, not in theology but in philosophy. Is Hegel not withdrawing with one hand what he had given with the other? In reclaiming an ontological ultimacy for religious disclosure, however, Hegel supports the position of the mystics who, almost unanimously, assert that religious disclosure contains an ontological richness unparalleled by any other mode of truth.

Theologians and some philosophers were quick in adhibiting the theory of disclosure to their own interpretation of religious truth. Understandably so, since the term *disclosure* was returning an indigenous religious idea to its native, religious habitat. Religious symbols uniquely disclose a fullness of being. Of course, critical philosophers still found themselves stranded with the arduous task of *justifying* this ontological manifestation without directly appealing to any *supernatural* revelation. Many chose to ignore this difficult issue and were satisfied with *describing* the unique disclosure that occurs in religious symbols without taking a position on their natural or supernatural origin. To them it was sufficient that through religious symbolism, all contents and relations came to stand in a new light. Even as we suddenly perceive a picture, without changing its configuration, by merely transforming our interpretation of a few lines or colors into a recognizable image of another object, so a religious disclosure conveys to an ordinary reality a metaphorical and symbolic quality.

The disclosure of faith excludes the kind of objective, impartial justification on which philosophy insists for legitimating its truth, but requires an actual participation in the religious content that philosophy cannot, and should not, reproduce. Phenomenologists experienced this when, in their attempts to justify religious disclosure, they ran into Husserl's *epoché*—the bracketing of all existential elements required in bringing the phenomenon to its pure "essential" appearance. This kind of abstraction from all existential elements is not possible in the justification of truth as disclosure, which dominates all religious truth. How, then, can phenomenology preserve the *transcendent* nature of what the religious act intends? The *doxic* modality (i.e., the modality of belief essential to faith) affects not only the *real* (empirical) experience of the act but also the *ideal* conditions of its object. The religious act intends its object as transcending the immanence of the experience. One may well wonder, then, whether the phenomenological method, restricted as it is to the *ideal immanence* of that object, suffices for *justifying the truth* of its disclosure. Unlike other acts of consciousness, faith never brings its intentional object to full immanence. It experiences its object as lying *beyond attainment*, and its only immanence in the experience consists in the very awareness of a lasting transcendence.

Two prominent students of the phenomenology of religion, Gerardus van der Leeuw and Max Scheler, therefore concluded that the religious act and its intentional object cannot be understood unless one shares the faith that conditions them—that is, unless one *accepts* the transcendence of its object.[14] Clearly, if this implies the need to convert philosophy into faith, philosophy would cease to *justify* religious disclosure altogether. Yet, according to another, milder interpretation, an adequate philosophical evaluation of religious disclosure requires only that the critic be *in some way* directly acquainted with the actual experience. This acquaintance need not consist in an active participation in the faith on which one reflects; it may be no more than the memory of an actual faith, or even no specific faith at all, but only a personal acquaintance with the religious experience in general.

ESSAY 11

The Enigma of Religious Art

The Spanish-American philosopher George Santayana considered art and religion to be basically identical. Although that position appears more and more untenable in modern culture, the two had undoubtedly remained united during the longest period of human civilization. Throughout the early eras of culture, art had formed an essential part of that symbolic integration of life to which we now, in retrospect, give the name "religion." To the archaic mind, all aesthetic activities had, next to other meanings, a religious significance. Distinctions appeared only *within* one, sacred sphere. The much-heralded distinction between the sacred and the profane is by no means a primary one: it concludes a long social evolution. Yet even after distinctions have become firmly entrenched and the sacred no longer determines all aspects of life, aesthetic and religious activities remain intimately linked. The religious community prays in song, moves in dance, and acts in drama. The artist, on his part, remains aware of the sacred allegiance to which he owes much of his inspiration and, often, his livelihood. The notion of sacred art becomes problematic only after a society has become at least partly secularized. Even then, ancient myths survive in poetry and drama. Everywhere we still recognize the continuing inspiration of religious symbols. But is that sufficient to call all art religious? Is it sufficient even to maintain the possibility of religious art in the traditional sense?

In answering those questions we must consider the claim often heard that all art is implicitly religious, and attempt to define more precisely the quality that renders aesthetic achievements explicitly sacred. My initial assumption (which I shall try to prove) is that authentic art at all times, including our own, retains an affinity with the sacred. This thesis does not imply that at all times all cultures produce genuinely sacred art. Yet in the presence of great art, as in the religious experience, humans confront what appears to them most intensely real. In both instances, the mind overcomes the opposition that divides objective knowledge from subjective desire. Like the religious experience, the aesthetic one is accompanied by a heightened awareness of being in the presence of what *truly counts* and a desire to let the experience continue. With Goethe we feel moved to exclaim: *Verweile doch, du bist so schön*! F. David Martin, who devoted a thoughtful study to the subject, describes the similarity as follows: "Both are intimate and ultimate; both are attuned to the call of Being; both are reverential in attitude to things; both give enduring value and serenity to existence; and thus both are profoundly regenerative."[1] To this participative experience, Martin attributes a religious quality, yet to me, that seems a little premature.

If they would totally coincide, as they undoubtedly did at one time, we might be satisfied with Goethe's maxim: *Wer Wissenschaft und Kunst besitzt, der hat auch Religion* ("Who possesses science and art also has religion"). Yet the two are no longer identical and have been distinct, if not separate, for centuries. Are they distinct, as R. G. Collingwood claimed, in that art asserts nothing? Unquestionably, much as the artist strives for veracity of perception, in one sense, at least, existential *reality as such* is of no concern to the viewer or listener. It matters little whether Mont Sainte-Victoire *really is* as Cézanne painted it (Is that even a meaningful question?) or whether someone exactly like Coleridge's Ancient Mariner ever lived. Even in portraits, expressiveness aesthetically prevails over exact physical resemblance. The only reality the artist and the educated perceiver care about is the reality of the appearance, which is not the real as such. One might therefore be tempted to consider the aesthetic attitude as noncommittal with respect to reality. Yet to do so without basic qualifications would be to abandon the ontological meaning of art altogether, and to give in to an aestheticist deviation.[2] Great art has always been ontologically meaningful: if it ceases to be significant concerning the deeper issues of existence, it has strayed from its original course. Ever since art no longer coincided with religion, its ontological vision has ceased to express the transcendence of Being. To be sure, the aesthetic consciousness possesses a transcendence of its own. It sets up ideals that surpass the givenness of the present. It opens up a realm of possibility in which freedom finds its vital space. Yet this transcendence remains purely ideal. Ernst Bloch, the rhapsode of an aesthetic utopia, refers to it as a *Vor-schein*, a "fore-glow" or "fore-show" of full reality.[3]

While expressing the inner entelechy of the present, art anticipates the future. It moves beyond what exists and creates an emptiness for freedom, in which Being may reveal itself. However, art manifests no more than the *immanent* presence of being. To assert its transcendence it must await further word. "Further word" because the ascent from an aesthetic to a religious level requires the assistance of words. How then can the artist create works that are genuinely *religious*, that is, explicitly manifesting a religious reality? The representation of a so-called religious scene or object is by no means sufficient for this purpose. Any religious claim made for paintings of a Madonna by artists such as Rafael or Parmegianino remains hazardous. Though they do not exclude a religious interpretation, their work does not require one: it is predominantly aesthetic. What distinguishes genuine religious art—say, Angelico's paintings or Bach's oratorios—from other masterworks dealing with similar subjects and yet not qualifying as unambiguously religious?

Before presenting my view, I must dispose of a popular answer. Religious art can definitely not be described as an expression of the artist's religious commitment. Aside from the fact that any theory that posits the work of art as "expressing" a previously completed feeling fails to account for the intrinsic quality of the aesthetic creation. In this particular instance the theory conflicts even with commonly known facts. Some religious artists were genuinely pious persons. Such was clearly the case with Fra Angelico and Bach. But what about Perugino, whose libertine opinions about the Christian belief in immortality contrasted so strikingly with the meditative piety of his work? Or the worldly Matisse, the creator of the religiously moving paintings in the chapel of Vance? Of course, the existence of authentic religious sentiment was never a monopoly of church affiliation—today even less than in the past. Yet my claim goes considerably further. Not the quality of the artist's preceding feelings determines the religious nature of his work, but his ability to probe and articulate the religious attitude in the creative process itself. Such an exploration undoubtedly requires some previous acquaintance with the religious attitude, but it is by no means necessary that the artist himself be religiously committed when he or she takes up brush, pen, or chisel.[4] The specific feelings expressed in the work of art are both articulated *and constituted* in the creative process itself. Besides, no religious person would accept the equation of religion with feelings, pious or other. Feelings, however uplifting, are clearly distinct from the religious vision the artist pursues. To be sure, no artist creates genuinely religious art unless he or she is seriously acquainted with the religion he or she represents. But an acquaintance of this nature, however intensive, is clearly insufficient for the creation of religious *art*. Many devout souls write, sing, or paint what they are unable to contain within themselves. But only aesthetic sensitivity is able to convert those pious expectations into artistic creations.

It hardly needs saying that a definition of religious art by its effect—the ability to evoke pious feelings—is even less adequate. Aside from the practical difficulty of distinguishing such feelings from related ones, such as the sublime, the noble, the morally uplifting, and so on, we must face the fact that what religiously inspires one person may fail to do so in others. Hence the religious effect is not sufficient to consider a work of art religious. The effect often depends on the setting in which it appears, rather than on the work itself. Many believers are religiously affected by art associated with the cult. Thus they may be piously moved by the converted lyrics of a German drinking song known in its sacred version as "A Mighty Fortress Is Our God." An identical composition sounds sacred when played on an organ in a church and "profane" when performed on a piano in a salon. A definition by association inevitably fails, because different cultures use different sounds and images to evoke the sacred.

For all those reasons I must reiterate the crucial yet insufficiently recognized principle that art no longer becomes religious in modern culture as it did in ancient times. The difference results not merely or primarily from the fact that different aesthetic standards are used by different cultures; it affects the very *essence* of art. To the archaic mind, art belongs mainly to the area of what is more significant and powerful than ordinary reality. The notion of the "sacred" was not yet distinct from the profane at its earliest stage. Whether the cave drawings of Altamira were magical, religious, or artistic is a moot question, since such distinctions did not yet exist. The distinction between the more and the less significant presupposes the existence of the sacred as a *distinct sphere* of being. Only at this later stage religion proper (for which archaic culture has neither word nor concept) originates. Religious symbols gradually assume a religious quality that distinguishes them from other symbolic forms. If those who claim that all primitive art is religious mean that primitive artists felt the need to create an explicitly religious work of art, they antecede the course of history: the sacred as a distinct sphere did not exist.

The religious artist of our times faces an even greater problem in expressing what has come to be recognized as ultimately inexpressible. He or she must rely on representations that contemporaries explicitly *recognize* as religious symbols. The difficulty is that such symbols differ from one culture to another. If the artist creates beyond the limits of his own established culture, recognition often requires a verbal initiation. Words alone can denote *explicitly* what surpasses visible or nonverbally articulated auditory signs. In a secular culture, the recognition of religious art as such has become increasingly dependent on an initiation, which in earlier times would have been superfluous to people belonging to the same culture. To fellow members of a religious tradition, religious meaning may be conveyed directly through aesthetic symbols. Images evoke the well-known message without words. Primitive Christians recognized the emblem of the fish as a symbol of Christ as easily as educated Christians today identify the half-naked old man with book and lion as St. Jerome. Yet to the outsider, such symbolic reminders of a lost verbal initiation remain cryptic. Only a Buddhist or a student of Buddhist culture directly perceives the Buddha in the position of the hand of a sitting male, or a Bodhisattva in the oval-shaped flame around the body.[5] Still we must remember that conventional symbols alone do not suffice to render a work of art genuinely religious. An alabaster vase may have saved many a painting of a female nude from moral censorship. But more is needed to convert it into a *religious* portrait of Mary Magdalen. Symbols or words (e.g., the title of an instrumental composition) may be indispensable to all to achieve a transition from the implicitly to the explicitly sacred.

If an artist confines his works to a particular religion, as most artists in the past did, his works are likely to appear religious only to those acquainted with the religious doctrines within which it originated. Few symbols are by *nature* religious, even though their existence has been a common assumption in much art criticism. To be sure, certain symbols occur more readily to the religious mind than others. Thus, light, expanding spaces, and silence quite often suggest the presence of a mysterious reality. Yet they may not be exclusively religious. Even symbols at one time introduced for their religious power may lose their expressiveness and freeze into mere artistic conventions, no more aesthetically significant than the allegorical symbols (alabaster vase, book, and lion) that clutter religious iconography. On the other hand, the repeated use of a particular symbol in a religious setting may reinforce its religious expressiveness.

It is safe to assert, I believe, that religious art always, in one way or other, tends to display the inadequacy of the aesthetic form with respect to its transcendent content. This inadequacy may be conveyed in a number of ways. One of the simplest and oldest modes of expressing the transcendence of content over form consists in the adoption of outsized proportions. The colossal masses of Egyptian pyramids evoke a superhuman world. So do Mexican temples, Babylonian reliefs, and large statues of Buddha.[6] The presence of the inexpressible may also be suggested by the fragmentary character of the work. The unfinished easily evokes the idea that the subject exceeds the artist's creative power. Ernst Bloch even ascribes the incompleteness of such masterpieces as Beethoven's late quartets, Goethe's *Faust*, a number of Michelangelo's sculptures, and some of Leonardo's paintings to an unusual awareness of an eschatological distance that divides the idea from the artist. Even technically "finished" religious works often display suggestions of incompleteness: they tend to remain open-ended. This is one reason why Renaissance sculpture and architecture, so complete in their self-contained perfection, often suggest an ideal world, yet overall, Renaissance art impress us as less religious than Gothic or Romanesque works of art.

Members of one religion tend to judge the symbolic expressions of another cult by their own standards. Thus the more elementary style of "archaic" Greek sculpture appears to modern viewers more religiously inspired than the classical beauty of the fifth century. Modern Westerners are probably right in claiming that the empty space characteristic of Chinese landscape paintings radiates infinity. In the famous Japanese Oxcart pictures, form progressively vanishes, leaving the viewer in the last one with nothing but a blank meditation on Nirvana. Even in architecture this effect of transcendent emptiness has been pursued and obtained. When the visitor to the Borobudur temple in Java, after ascending along an endless repetition of Buddha statues, finally emerges at the top plateau, nothing awaits him but open space.

Inadequacy is also conveyed by the distorted figures of Grünewald's *Crucifixion* and by the elongated bodies of van der Weyden and El Greco (in whose work it became reduced to a purely formal principle). Even indeterminateness and ambiguity may be religiously expressive. The vine mosaics on the vaults of Santa Constanza in Rome might be merely decorative designs or devalued pagan symbols. But to one who considers them to be Christian (which they probably are),[7] their indeterminate character provides them with a religious force and richness seldom found in more precisely defined symbols. Is it not their very discreteness that makes the fishes and vines of primitive Christian art religiously more inspiring than the rigidly defined allegories of later times? The Baroque vault surpasses its architectonic function altogether, and, along the receding lines, frescoes of religious apotheoses (most spectacularly in the Gesù and in San Ignazio in Rome) soar into a groundless beyond. The elliptic form of some Baroque churches suggests a circle breaking through its own enclosure. All the preceding forms evoke transcendence in a negative way, that is, by displaying their inadequacy.

Yet there are also positive symbols of the divine. One of them, so universally known that it seems to be almost a natural symbol of the divine, is light. We find it in reliefs of the monotheist Egyptian king Akhenaton, in statuary of the Iranian religion of Ahura-Mazda, in the sun and moon pyramids of Teotihuacan, in Byzantine mosaics and in Baroque *chiaroscuro* paintings. The contrast between divine light and profane darkness abounds in the Bible, where the very word for God's glory, *kavod*, suggests effulgent light. To the alleged writer of the first letter of Saint John and of the fourth Gospel, "God is light" (1 Jn. 1:5), and Christ "the light coming into the world" (Jn. 1:9), while Paul addresses his Christians as "children of light and day." The first and the last hymns of the liturgical office are odes to the rising and the setting sun: *Lucis Creator Optime* ("Great Creator of the light") and *Te lucis ante terminum* ("before light vanishes"). In our artistic tradition, the specific use of the light motif is mostly derived from Neoplatonic sources. For Plotinus, light alone refracts the spiritual in the material world. After Pseudo-Dionysius had adapted the religious light symbolism to Christian theology, it came to determine the entire course of Christian art. Mosaics reflecting light in chipped stones proved to be a particularly appropriate medium for celebrating God's majesty. Italian primitives still imitated the golden background of Byzantine mosaics in their early paintings. Caravaggio flooded his sacred figures with light in the midst of darkness. But it was Rembrandt who used the new technique to its greatest religious effect. With him, light, like marble under the hand of the Baroque sculptor, ceased to be a physical entity; it became a spiritual expression.

Neoplatonic spirituality transformed representations of the entire world into religious symbols. They confront us in the frontal position of its figures—their immobility, lack of perspective, and absence of individual resemblance: by all those characteristics religious artists attempted to overcome the transitory, contingent world and to capture the permanent essence of a God-filled, spiritual universe.[8] Byzantine images, more powerfully as abstract symbols than as physical representations, through simplicity of design, purity of lines, and quiet harmony, majestically evoke a celestial cosmos. We find similar tendencies in the static, depersonalized representations of Buddha statues. Whether in the hieratic mode of Siam or in the simple one of Ceylon, the Enlightened One always appears as having overcome individual personhood.[9]

Of course, the idea of God's transcendence causes a constant tension in religious art, which periodically explodes in iconoclastic movements. They left a permanent mark upon the religious aesthetics of Judaism and Islam. Apprehensive of expressing the invisible in visible forms, these radically monotheist faiths prefer to renounce iconography and instead to concentrate on the word and the more abstract forms of music and architecture. In Christianity, strong faith in the Incarnation always prevailed over the dissatisfaction with existing forms. Thus after the iconoclasm of the Isaurian emperors, in the ninth century the Fourth Council of Constantinople decreed: "It conforms to reason and the oldest tradition that the icons, since they refer to the principals themselves, in a derivative way be honored and adored, even as the sacred book of the holy gospels and the image of the precious cross are venerated."[10]

In this instance, victory led to a total restoration. The iconoclasm of sixteenth-century Calvinist theology in the Low Countries left more permanent effects. It spurred the development of a secular art. Yet even the radical revolution did not mark the end of religious iconography in reformed regions, but steered the religious imagination to explore new possibilities. Driven out of the church, iconic art went into book and print, where it was less likely to become an object of "idolatrous" veneration and more subject to the close supervision of the written word. The more literalist exegesis following in the wake of the *sola scriptura* principle favored philological information over mystical inspiration and, in religious iconography, replaced mannerism by naturalism. In such great religious masters as Rembrandt it inspired an unprecedented search for inner truth. In other artists, the search of pious interiority soon secularized into psychology. Still, in Rembrandt's work, psychological truth itself became in fact expressive of a deeper religious inwardness.[11] In his last years, the Dutch master had become so intimately familiar with the biblical scenes on which he daily meditated that he often dispensed with the stories altogether and directly represented their impact upon the witnesses.

Few of the principles exposed in the preceding pages still apply to modern art. The secularization of our age makes it questionable whether much of today's art may still be called religious, even in that minimal sense in which all authentic art is "potentially religious." In his study of modern art, Karsten Harries explains why: "Man has given up his attempts to discover meaning in the world of objects. If there is to be meaning, it must have its foundation in something beyond that world. But it is no longer possible to give definite content to this transcendence."[12] The link with any reality outside the work of art has gradually been severed. What we witness now is the exact opposite of what happened in Baroque culture—the last religious one in the West—when the attempt of form to reach beyond itself was often more important than its inner consistency. Even the heaviest marble and the darkest color came to life in efforts to move *beyond* artistic representation. Baroque art expanded in time and in space: it told a story.[13]

When Cézanne replaced contour lines by color patches, he thereby isolated the object and even parts of it into opaque realities; he reversed that narrative principle in painting and isolated the object, thereby ending the Renaissance relatedness to the viewer. Similar changes transformed sculpture, architecture, and music: the artistic representation of the new era became detached from the viewer and the listener, and came to be enclosed in the object's own inner space. Not how things look to the *viewer*, or how music sounds to the *listener*, defines the new artistic creation, but how forms and tone combinations appear in relation to each other. Pictorial objects continue to appear within a particular perspective, of course, but not one that is readily accessible to the viewer. Tones are received with specific expectations of harmony, but the composer makes no effort to meet the receiver's expectations. He or she follows other, less euphonic rules.

Eventually, the work of art came to stand by itself, independent of the viewer and ceased to refer beyond its own space and time. We find ourselves in a *presence* without history and without world, and, of course, without reference to a religious beyond. Things simply *are what they are*, indifferent to the observer, self-contained in an unprecedented solitude. In architecture and in sculpture, the self-sufficiency of the work of art often took the form of a new emphasis on the material of the construction, the specific qualities of brick, stone, or wood, often at the price of its former aptitude to receive and orient visitors or of any reference to a reality outside the work of art. In religious buildings, worshippers now frequently find themselves in churches with neither front nor center, where a multitude of vectors intersect at various places. In such a directionless space, each person is left to discover his own Orient, to create his own perspective, and to explore his own feelings. The new spatial construction, it is sometimes claimed, allows a person to find his or her own perspective instead of having the architect enforce one upon the visitor. Nothing in this space refers beyond what is actually given. The tendency of postmodern art consists in an attempt to restore the immediacy of the work of art lost in tradition, and in giving artist and viewer total freedom of interpretation.

It is as if artists, cautious to avoid the pitfall of replacing an overt subjectivity by a hidden one, have consistently attempted to do without the subjective filter of the psyche altogether and to reduce the artistic representation to a pure, naked object. In so-called minimal art, expression has made place for sheer presence. Only pure form survives. Of course, the bothersome question continues to nag the artist of whether form can ever be "pure," whether absolute object-hood can be realized. Is form itself not a mental construction? When the modern art critic Fried writes "presentness is grace," does he not return his objective art to that more subjective realm from which the artist had attempted to retrieve it?[14]

Whatever the answer may be, we are reaching here an advanced stage of what Ortega y Gasset in his 1925 essay of that name called "the dehumanization of art."[15] Even a "subject" in the traditional sense of the word disappears. Paintings now become entitled "Study 1, 2, 3, . . ." The title of Frank Stella's well-known painting summarizes the entire trend: "What you see is what you see." The work of art has ceased to refer to the mind of its creator and to the outside world. In this achievement, the aesthetics of subjectivity of the modern age seems to have come to an end. But what is there to succeed it?

We have lived through an unprecedented explosion of symbolic creativity. In novelty and in fertility, the past century's cultural scene resembles the "big bang" of creation. It has liberated all symbolic structures from the established, given order and has taken it upon itself to convey order and meaning through a self-centered symbolic production. But it has lost the coherence with life characteristic of earlier ages. Symbolic creations have become autonomous but, inevitably, also fragmentary. For a while, the divisive quality of the new trend remained hidden behind the heroic posture of its maker, who in the guise of aesthetic *genius* had declared himself absolute. Today that once transcendent subject has lost confidence in the cultural effectiveness of its own projections and incapable of restoring new life to an exhausted civilization. We are left with a universe of fragments. Each symbolic structure (literary, artistic, social, political) tends to become a small universe of its own, valiantly striving toward a maximum of independence. Nor can we genuinely "share" these "universes" as a common possession. The reader, viewer, or hearer is invited to recreate the artist's private world into a private world of his own. Aesthetic criticism no longer considers it its task to bridge the gap between the hearer or viewer and the artist, but rather to expand the number of private possibilities by creating new ones of his own making.

Does this self-related aesthetic theory still have any chance of inspiring genuine religious art? The impact of such powerful abstractionist painters as Matisse, Rothko, and Kandinsky leaves no doubt that it does. Nonetheless it would be confusing to call their work religious in the same sense as Duccio's or van der Weyden's painting. Whereas a religious interpretation remains *a possibility* in modern art, in religious art of the past it was a *necessity*. Postmodern art creates an openness in which a religious meaning may be discovered, yet it does not impose such a meaning. The despair we recognize in many postexpressionist works by such masters of modern agony as Arshile Gorky, Francis Bacon, Willem de Kooning, and

Germaine Richier undoubtedly raises *questions* of ultimate meaning. But their visions of doom were mostly inspired by the artist's own despair about the possibility of any answer. Their images of insufficiency may invite the viewer to an inner vision along the same lines, but it does not enforce any liberating vision. The great religious artists of the past did more than questioning, they suggested a single perspective. Religious art of the past left no absolute freedom of interpretation. To enter into Bach's oratorios or Van der Weyden's *Deposition*, even a secular person had no choice but temporarily to adopt the artist's vision. For a brief moment, the artist forces the viewer to share his own religious worldview.

Is this to say that no decisively sacred art exists in our time? To see the absurdity of such a conclusion, it suffices to think of Matisse's chapel in Vance, of some of Manzù's sculptures, of most of Chagall's and Rouault's paintings, or of Messiaen's and Penderecki's sacred compositions. Those works demand an unambiguously religious interpretation, if one is to enter their meaning at all. Nor can they be dismissed as cultural leftovers from an earlier age: their creators were pioneers in modern art. Still, though the endurance of their work is beyond doubt, they can hardly be considered representative of their time. More attuned to the climate of our age are the postexpressionist artists we discussed above. Particularly interesting are those ambivalent abstractionists who attempted to create religious art, as Barnett Newman in his *Stations of the Cross* or Rothko in his Rothko Chapel in Houston, Texas. In them the religious ambiguity of modern art stands fully exposed, and with it the need of the support of language. Without the titles, one might not recognize their works as religious. They reflect a situation in which our contemporaries have lost the direct experience of the sacred. Rarely do they attain more than a sense of absence, a silence, or, at best, an inner space in which a sacred reality *may* become manifest again.

ESSAY 12

Ritual

The Sacralization of Time

Of all the burdens man has to carry through life, I wonder whether any weighs heavier than the transient nature of all experience. All life inevitably moves toward decline and death. The continuous passage of time allows no phase of human existence ever to reach a definitive meaning. Transitoriness and oblivion mark life as a whole and each one of its segments. In his theological anthropology, *De hominis opificio* ("On the Creation of Man"), the fourth-century Cappadocian bishop Gregory of Nyssa describes existence in time as an imperfect condition that, after the Fall, was introduced into the plan of creation to forestall the inevitable punishment of the human race's instant destruction. At the end of the world, however, time will be abolished. The futility of a life in time continues to oppress our contemporaries as much as Gregory's and the countless generations that preceded him. Nietzsche said it well. That what *was* no longer *is*, and that what *is* will soon no longer be, is the condition from which man most urgently desires to be saved: "To redeem those who lived in the past and to re-create all 'it was' into a 'thus I willed it'—that alone should I call salvation."[1] Through the idea of an eternal return, Nietzsche attempted to salvage something stable from the all-dissolving impermanence of time. With others, I doubt whether he succeeded. Only in utopian dreams have humans ever envisioned the return of an ideal age in which the efforts of history will at last be crowned with an enduring new beginning. As Virgil sang in his *Fourth Eclogue*, "Then shall a second Tiphys be, and a second

Argo will sail with chosen heroes: new wars shall arise, and again a mighty Achilles be sent to Troy."[2]

Even historical faiths, such as Judaism and Christianity, which consecrate the passage of time by assigning to each event a permanent significance, postulated at the end of history a return to the beginning. *Endzeit ist Urzeit* ("the final time is the original time"). Nor have the secular dreams of our own age abandoned the eschatological hope of ever arresting the motion of time. Marx's vision of the future, however far removed from a sacred age, still recalls that fullness of time in which human efforts will at last reach completion. Meanwhile, men and women of all ages have felt the need to order and structure the flux of time by recapturing, again and again, the founding events of the beginning. By recalling the past in archetypical gestures interpreted through sacred words, they hope to convey at least a permanent form to the continuous indefiniteness of the present. What is it that gives ritual, particularly when interpreted by myth, this mysterious power to regain, even in the midst of time, the awareness of an irreversible present? Which bond links the ancient narrative to the enduring gesture?

Whether myth follows rite, as reflection follows deed, or whether the two were originally united in a single act, the rite always resists the shifts and changes of the mythical narrative. The ritual gesture is to be understood through its own structured movement, not as an allegorical reenactment of an ancient tale. Some religions even appear to have detached ritual from myth altogether. Roman religion has too often been misunderstood as an unimaginative imitation of Greek mythology. A more correct view is that because of their practical attitude, Romans *deliberately* demythologized rites.[3] Where the myth survived, it was the ritual that revived it in the living present.

Rather than commemorating an event of the past, the rite's "real and thoroughly effective action"[4] recaptures the event itself. Jewish and Christian celebrations have always insisted on the actual effectiveness of their ancient rites. The ritual creates a new temporality in which the succession of the rite conveys a permanence of life. Tearing itself loose from the uniform fabric of time-measured-by-space, it boldly reaches back to a more primitive experience of duration. The essentially mental process of time reluctantly submits to the homogeneous measuring by space. The inner time experience never ceases resisting the spatial projections of ordinary and scientific concepts of time, imposed by the bodily need to move within a spatial world. Time refuses to be numbered, to be counted, and, above all, to be homogenized by a one-dimensional "standard."

To be freed from the constrictions of a spatially determined temporality, humans perform gestures that have neither past nor future. The ritual allows them to express duration in motions that, although spatial, nevertheless break through the monotonous *continuity* of a spatio-temporal succession. To be sure, time is successive by nature, and remains so even in the ritual, but there it ceases to be irreversible. The more attuned the mind becomes to the experience of inner time, the more each moment differs from all others and the freer the mind feels to move forward and backward across the continuous flatness of spatio-temporality. In the ritual, neither clock nor calendar measures duration, but only memory does through the awareness of a constancy that underlies duration. It is in this realm of recollection, of inward gathering, that ritual takes place. The sacred deed recaptures the primeval time of a god, hero, or ancestor: "Ritual abolishes profane, chronological time and recovers the sacred time of myth, which enables one to become contemporary with the exploits that a god, hero, or ancestor performed '*in illo tempore*.'"[5]

The simplicity of this description hides an amazing instant transformation. With one stroke, the time of ritual has reversed the direction of ordinary duration. At the ground of man's awareness of the sacred lies the primordial assumption that some experiences of time and of space differ from others. For also a sacred place must be segregated from the surrounding space (*templum* is said to be derived from τὲμνειν, "to cut") where sacred rituals are to take place. The mind refuses to be satisfied with the physical notions of place and duration. In the sacred notion of a time without end spent in a place without restrictions, I find the ground of a belief in immortality, which has played such a powerful role in protecting humans against despair. Some have thought this belief to be grounded in the steady experience of the seasonal cycles, a constant reminder that not all is lost when decay and death set in. But the religious calendar never coincides with the rhythms of nature.[6]

In distinguishing reversible (essential) from irreversible (contingent) time, man first expresses the need to overcome his inability to retain the meaningful moments in an essentially transitory life. Some anthropologists and sociologists used to attribute to the ritual an essentially social function. Such was Durkheim's well-known thesis, which still appears in many variations today. It is undoubtedly true that in ritual, individual and society interpenetrate one another. Nevertheless, rites have a more fundamental meaning: they transform the realm of the externally defined *societas* into the more internal *communitas*.[7]

What distinguishes sacred time is not that it stays with the present, but that it may be recalled from the past. The past has always been the gate to whatever permanence humans may attain in life. Memory freezes the flux of becoming into definitiveness. For Plato, the eternal can only be *remembered*, while ancient Christian language refers to the awareness of God as *memoria Dei*. Ritual temporarily *restores* the past: it does so by formalizing and schematizing the gestures of ordinary life. Ritual eating, drinking, and dancing differ from the common performances of those activities. Rites *symbolize* joyful and sad occasions, but never turn joyful or sad themselves. They express love without passion, austerity without hardship, and sorrow without grief. Rites articulate everyday forms of life; they stylize them, yet never merge with them.[8]

The rite derives its force precisely from the fact that it is free of the ambiguity inherent in the ordinary deed. All attempts to bring the cult down to "everyday life" are therefore ill-directed: they destroy the metaphorical quality essential to their sacred meaning. Ritual presents the *ideal* deed, the one the gods or heroes performed before the confusion of historical time. The ideal deed never ought to return to that intricate net of half-formed intentions and never completed acts that reduce our daily lives to permanent indefiniteness. In ordinary life, before the act is completed, the initial impulse has become caught in a web of uncontrollable contingencies that preclude the full emergence of its intended meaning. The agent's intention may have been simple and pure. Yet even if the agent knows his mind and intends to express it in his action, the expression seldom unambiguously reveals the original intention. As soon as the deed enters the outer world, it irresistibly moves away from its original simplicity into the murky, unpredictable world of causes and effects. In the ritual act, the deed coincides with its ideal image. The conditions were clearly established and the time was predetermined.[9]

This brings us to the most difficult aspect of ritual. How can a rite that moves in time *redeem* temporality? The answer lies in the different time conjuncture of ritual performances. Each ritual act moves in its own, ideal time, while the time of an ordinary act merges with that of other acts, and together all these times constitute our common time experience. The rite resists synchronization with other experiences. As an immovable ideal model, the rite protects order against the ever-invading chaos. Its foundation lies beyond the succession of time—*in illo tempore:* in the primeval time of a single event. The link with that event is particularly strong in historical faiths. In most religions, founding events lie buried in the mist of an unknown past, but Judaism, Christianity, and Islam *re-present* these founding acts as having been performed at a specific moment of history. Often the faithful may not succeed in justifying the date of that moment, but this has never prevented them from insisting it occurred as a unique event in common time. They may use a great deal of imagination in their attempts to the place it in history, as Catholic theologians used to do in supporting Christ's institution of the sacrament of confession that is never mentioned in the Gospels. Without in some way *re-presenting* the event, however legendary it may be, a religion easily evaporates into a purely interior attitude of which the origin is celebrated but not renewed.

Through its rites, Christian faith claims to reactivate the historical deeds of its founder. The Eucharist makes Christ's saving death into an ever-renewable sacrificial rite. Early in the past century, Dom Odo Casel aroused a major controversy by his insistence on the reality of the ritually reenacted sacrificial death of Christ in every Eucharistic celebration. His opponents objected that what is essentially a historical fact cannot be repeated. Yet if this were to be an absolute principle, it would undermine the meaning of many religious rituals. Founding deeds are never merely historical. In some way, they surpass history in reaching men and women of all ages. It is precisely this aspect that the ritual *re-presents* forever anew. To interpret rites, then, as mere commemorations of a primordial event goes against the fundamental meaning of a genuine ritual. The life of Christ remains significant to Christians only as long as that life continues to be a ritually renewable event. Such a return in time is certainly what the Christmas liturgy intends when the choir in Catholic churches at the opening of the Midnight Mass intones the words of Psalm 2: *Dominus dixit ad me: Filius meus es tu, ego hodie genui te* ("The Lord spoke to me: Today I have begotten you"). Similarly the Easter rite does not "commemorate" the resurrection of Christ: it *re-presents* it, year after year. In the words of the *Exultet* hymn during the Easter night, *Haec nox est, in qua destructis vinculis mortis, Christus ab inferis victor ascendit* ("This is the night in which Christ broke the chains of death and rose victorious from the nether world").

The historical nature of the events recalled in an ever-renewed ritual gives them a uniquely inclusive character. Historical facts are inextricably linked to other *historical* facts. In re-presenting one salvific event as *historical*, the Church inevitably recalls the entire history surrounding it, all the way to the present, since the fabric of history is continuous. Thus Benjamin Britten composed a Christian opera about the rape of the pre-Christian Lucrecia, and Paul Claudel exclaimed in *La ville*:

*Rien n'a pu ou ne peut
Être qui ne soit à ce moment même; toutes
Choses sont présentes pour moi.*

―――

Nothing could or can be that no longer is at this moment: all things are present to me.[10]

The symbolism of the ritual assumes that no part of the past is entirely gone. The danger of this interpretation is, of course, that by casting the founding event within the course of history, the ritual becomes part of the transience the rite was attempting to overcome. The ritual, although oriented toward a past event, does more than commemorate an ancient gesture. The celebration is a creative act in its own right: it constitutes a new meaning. It is as new as it is old.

Nor is its pattern of return modeled after the succession of the seasons. It may incorporate the basic rhythms of nature, as spring enters into the celebration of Easter. Yet they are not the meaning-giving element. Developed religions have never fully trusted the all-too-natural periodicity of nature and have used symbols that in some way surpass the automatic repetition of seasons. Not without reason, Judaism has transformed its ancient agrarian holidays into historical commemorations, while still preserving enough of the early celebrations to be recognizable in the new rites.

The secularization of the modern age has radically changed attitudes toward the ritual. Time no longer holds the sacred meaning that men of former ages attributed to it. The fragmentation of the symbolic world (see essay 2) has steadily weakened the modern ability to regard any act as moving beyond the closed circuit of ordinary, homogeneous time.

Moreover, the historical awareness of the modern age has obstructed a proper understanding of the return of the past in ritual behavior. The Romantics of the late eighteenth century looked upon the past as definitively completed and therefore unrepeatable. The ruins of Pompeii and the medieval castles of Scotland fascinated people precisely *because* they were anachronistic witnesses of an irreversible past. In the intense awareness of the past as past, our contemporaries started concentrating exclusively on the question, *What exactly happened?* The transpositions of historical events into the present, so popular in medieval mystery plays, have become quaint relics of another age, interesting only as documents of an unrepeatable past. When the possibility of recapturing the past became questioned, the attempt to overcome time through ritual lost much of its significance to the modern mind.

The past was definitively closed, and only one dimension of time remained open: the future. The epoch that discovered history was also the first to grant priority to the future over the past and in some instances even over the present. Belief in progress and effective action to realize it replaced the search for meaning through ritual replay of the past. This epochal reversal created major problems for the religious consciousness of the modern age. In Judaism the actual sacrifice of animals, deemed too crude for modern sensitivity, disappeared, as it had done in all other modern religions. Yet its memory remained vividly present in the Yom Kippur liturgy. In recent times, however, Reform Judaism has also removed the recitation of this atonement rite from the ceremonial readings. Richard Rubenstein feared an increase of anguish, such as once occurred during and after Dutch Calvinism, when ritual atonement and oral confession ceased to be available.[11] All of us will have to face the consequences of a temporality exclusively conceived as a commitment to the future—a most unsettling prospect of modern life!

Unlike our ancestors, we have come to view life-in-time as a planned career. One critic of modernity spells out the disastrous effects of such a one-sided approach to the future: "Futurity means endless striving, restlessness, and a mounting incapacity for repose. It is precisely this aspect of modernization that is perceived as dehumanizing in non-Western cultures. There have also been strong rebellions against it within Western society."[12] It is, of course, well known that we in North America have taken this turn toward the future more radically than any other nation in the past or present: "The American lives on the very edge of the now, always ready to leap toward the future" (Octavio Paz). Less known is the high price we pay for living a life that consists primarily of hard work performed in the present on promises forever postponed to the future. Everything is in transition. Our actions are mostly functional, measured by their effectiveness in obtaining the practical goals they pursue, rarely by any intrinsic meaning. Even some churches have forgotten the sacred gestures and are busy replacing the "antiquated" rite by bare, functional moves. With the sense of the past has vanished the feeling of living in a meaningful present. It had been the ritual's task to preserve both.

While churches are increasingly losing the sense of ritual action, our contemporaries look for it in other places. One such place has, of course, always been the theater. In the ancient drama, man directly confronted the sacred powers of life and death. The *catharsis* that, according to Aristotle, followed from participating in dramatic performances was the very effect that ritual achieves. Yet when the tragedy lost its religious meaning, the enduring time of the ancient gods and heroes made room for the transient heroes of the day, and the theater's moral effectiveness became severely reduced. Already a world of distance separates Aeschylus's sacred simplicity from Euripides's psychic complexity.[13] Modern playwrights and spectators have largely lost the conscious link with the ancient rite. They have come to view the stage as an arena of psychological projection that assists us in unraveling our individual problems in the privacy of a dark theater. Unwittingly our contemporaries still look for the ritual catharsis, which men and women of a former age sought in rites or in ritual drama. Today we still witness an unprecedented need for dramatic projection. A daytime television soap opera may have little else in common with a sophisticated production of a Shakespeare play, but both express similar concerns about the meaningfulness of life. As in other instances, literature attempts to substitute what the religious cult no longer provides, but rarely does theater or book succeed in touching the fundamental issues of human existence.

PART IV

Mysticism

The Silence of Faith

---

*Part IV deals exclusively with religious mysticism, especially in its relation to philosophy. I have interchangeably used the terms "mysticism" and "spiritual experience," not as if there were no difference between the ecstatic experiences of the mystic and the spiritual ones common among devout persons. Yet the two are intrinsically related and, in some way, contiguous. Even the reading of mystical texts evokes in most devout persons what William James referred to as "the echo of the call." I shall not distinguish "natural" experiences from allegedly "supernatural" ones, as if the latter depended exclusively on an exceptional grace and the former on the mind's "natural" resources. To the religious mystic, nature and grace appear simultaneously. Philosophy then should not start dividing what the actual experience perceives as united. Moreover, the concept of "mere nature" (*natura pura*) born in late medieval Scholasticism remains questionable in philosophy.*

In essay 14, I argue that philosophy began with religious concepts, of which ancient Eastern cultures have preserved the original meaning even today. This is particularly the case in Vedantic Hinduism and in some philosophical schools of Buddhism. In the monotheist religions of the West, however, an ethical element soon became dominant. Eventually, Western philosophy was to split from religion altogether, and sanctity came to depend on conduct rather than on contemplation. Nevertheless, the passive experience at the origin of religion endured and at present appears to resume an increasing significance in monotheist religion. The British-Austrian Friedrich von Hügel considered the intuitive-emotional element essential in all forms of religion.

Essay 15 presents a philosophical justification of mystical religion on the basis of the intimate natural union of spiritual beings with the supreme Spirit. Nowhere did I find the nature of this union better described than in the writings of Nicholas of Cusa, the fifteenth-century mathematician and philosopher, especially in his treatise De visione Dei *(On the Vision of God).*

ESSAY 13

Is a Natural Desire of God Possible?

To the modern mind, the idea of a natural "desire of seeing God"—a common expression in the modern age—appears highly problematic. When I first heard the question at the head of this essay, I did not even know what it meant. How could philosophy justify what by modern definition falls outside its field of knowledge? The religious idea of God, the alleged source of this desire, originates not in philosophy but in what believers refer to as a "revelation" of some sort. Nonetheless, until the fifteenth century, most Christian, Jewish, and Muslim believers accepted the existence of such a desire. Why has what once appeared so obvious become so questionable? The difference is due to a different conception of philosophy than the one that prevails today.

Thinkers of the late antiquity would have found it hard to conceive of nature without a transcendent first cause supporting it. Even the ancients had rarely done so. This dependence did not include a divine act of *creation*: the cosmos had no beginning; just like the gods, it was everlasting. Nor did Plato conceive this causal dependence as being merely efficient. The dependence of changing appearances on a foundation of unchangeable ideal forms consisted in what was later to be called a *formal causality*.

Christian philosophers, however, accepted the Hebrew representation of a divine Creator who *created* the world by his word. They may have considered their interpretation confirmed by the fact that also for Aristotle the dependence of the lower spheres upon the Prime Mover was unquestionably one of *efficient* causality. Hence the turn of the created mind to God came to be conceived in terms of an *effect* of the Prime Mover, who by a universal Eros attracts all beings to himself without ever moving. If we possessed only this one presentation of Aristotle's thought in the *Physics*, we might still mistake his "theology" as being no more than a figurative representation of celestial mechanics. Yet in his treatise *De anima*, Aristotle describes the principle active in all thinking as "divine": The mind is able to move to actual cognition only under the impact of an always active principle of cognition. W. D. Ross, the translator of Aristotle's *Metaphysics*, wonders with Aristotle: "Does not this transition from potential to actual knowledge imply that there is something in us that actually knows already, some element that is cut off from ordinary consciousness, so that we are not aware of this pre-existing knowledge, but which is nevertheless in some sort of communication with the ordinary consciousness or passive reason and leads this on to knowledge?"[1]

In the *Nicomachean Ethics* 10.7, 1177b, Aristotle even claims more directly that in the present life the highest state of existence is the contemplative one—which surpasses a merely human capacity: "Such a life would be too high for man; for it is not insofar as he is a human person that he will achieve it, but insofar as something divine is present in him; and by so much as this is superior to our composite nature is its activity superior to that which is the exercise of the other kind of virtue. If reason is divine, then the life lived by contemplative principles is divine in comparison with human life." This consideration also affected the natural end of man. If that end had been no more than the effect of an efficient causality, it would have been finite, whereas early Christian thought had conceived of the person's ultimate end as a permanent life in the immediate presence of God.

A natural desire of God is possible only if the mind is in some respect connatural with the divine. It presupposes, as Augustine wrote, that the mind had already found God before seeking him. Nature cannot desire what lies totally beyond its capacity. In the same vein, Thomas Aquinas continued that the highest knowledge consists in knowing what God knows, namely, God's own Being: *Intelligere deum est finis omnis intellectualis substantiae* ("To know God is the purpose of each intelligent being") (*Summa contra Gentiles* 3.25; cf. also 3.52). In his analysis of this question in St. Thomas, Georges Cottier, O.P., writes, "The natural desire has its source in the metaphysical nature of the intellect: its object is *Being* in its full extent, however much a knowledge that attains the first Being only through inferior analogates may fall short of this ideal; by nature it spontaneously moves toward the perfect knowledge of its object, namely, the knowledge of the cause of being."[2] By the same token, Thomas and his medieval followers believed that humans may also pursue a natural, finite end. In the *Summa contra Gentiles* 3.25, Aquinas treats the theme from two different, yet related, points of view. On the one hand, he posits that each being seeks to realize the full potential of its nature. Truth and goodness are perfections that a spiritual being naturally desires, even though its limited capacity prohibits it from ever fully attaining them. The desire (*appetitus*), then, is natural, even though its full realization lies beyond the potential of human nature. The natural ideal of intellectual creatures consists in acquiring the highest knowledge. In the same article, St. Thomas claims that all creatures seek the kind of similitude with the Creator that corresponds to their nature.

In the ethical domain also, Aquinas agreed with Aristotle's natural virtues: he considered them subordinate to theological virtues, yet indispensable for attaining man's ultimate end as revealed in the Gospels. Beyond each limited good or object of knowledge, the mind implicitly pursues an unlimited one. He likewise considered all natural pursuits to be accompanied by a natural desire of the infinite good. This desire cannot remain unfulfilled, even though the human mind is incapable of satisfying it by its own force. Still, the mind cannot *demand* the satisfaction of a desire the fulfillment of which lies entirely beyond its capacity. The desire for seeing God, then, may be called "natural" only to the extent that it seeks its fulfillment in a general, not in a theologically specific, way. The transcendent goal inherent in all spiritual activity anticipates that this goal is attainable, even though its full attainment may exceed the capacities of human nature. The desire in some way anticipates an attainment of what never ceases to surpass our capacity of fully attaining it. To the extent that the person remains conscious of the dynamism that drives this desire, he or she experiences some measure of fulfillment. Hence, for Bonaventure, Aquinas, and Scotus, philosophy and theology had a mystical dimension, insofar as the desire for spiritual knowledge is driven by a transcendent dynamism. The natural desire of God becomes intrinsically transformed into a "supernatural one" of divine origin. Yet it is only in striving for the realization of this desire that humans become conscious of the supernatural impulse that impelled it.

In 1270, the theologians of the University of Paris declared Thomas's synthesis unorthodox. They regarded the Aristotelian concept of nature as being fundamentally estranged from God. Divine ordinations surpass reason and are unrelated to human expectations. If this Nominalist theology of the late Middle Ages had prevailed, it would have permanently separated the natural from the "supernatural" and eliminated any natural support of religious mysticism. However, there were exceptions to the Nominalist trend: Nicholas of Cusa, the fifteenth-century philosopher and theologian, reunited what Nominalism had divided. He did so by means of an entirely new synthesis of philosophy and theology. Human nature shared some divine qualities. Even after the Fall, the human mind had remained an *imago Dei*, forever longing and looking for its divine prototype. Thus, the goal of all intellectual acts consists in the mind's attempts to rejoin its divine origin. All desire to know is a desire to know oneself and hence includes a desire to know one's divine model. In *De filiatione dei* (*On the Sonship of God*), Nicholas describes the road of knowledge as naturally headed toward a union with God: "Therein is that supreme intellectual joy, when the intellect beholds that its beginning, middle, and end surpass even the highest power of conception although it beholds them in the proper object of the intellect, that is, in pure truth."[3]

Thus, all search of understanding, according to Cusanus, is motivated by an implicit desire to comprehend God. Finite objects are no more than "symbolic signs" of the true. No genuine knowledge is ever intrinsically secular. Human nature can be understood only as a dynamic tendency toward *theosis* (deification): "God, who is in all things, shines forth in mind when the mind, as a living image of God, turns to its own Exemplar and assimilates itself thereto with all its effort."[4] In *Idiota de sapientia* (*The Layman on Wisdom*), Cusanus argues that God's eternal wisdom attracts the mind by granting it a foretaste (*praegustatio*) of what she (wisdom) will achieve and thereby arouses a marvelous desire for her. Since this wisdom constitutes the very life of spiritual understanding, she incites us to seek the source of this life. Without that foretaste, the mind would not seek its source. It might not even know that it had received it, if indeed it had done so. The mind is moved to it as to its own life.[5] While seeking its own unity (the norm by which it measures all things), the mind finds it in that Principle in which all things are one.[6] In its search for unity and self-identity, the mind expresses a fundamental desire for *union with God*. Only against the mystery of God's perfect Being does the mind grasp both its unity and its distinctness. In God's mirror, the mind recognizes itself.[7] The drive toward union with God propels the entire progress of thought. The intellect reaches its destination only when it becomes divinized.

Later thinkers in the Platonic tradition, including Ficino, Malebranche, Berkeley, Rosmini, and to some extent also such non-Platonists as Newman and Maine de Biran, continued to conceive of the intellect as moved by an implicit desire of God, while Scholasticism increasingly separated nature from the supernatural as if it were a wholly distinct domain of being. This led to the well-known controversies about the existence of a *desiderium naturale* (natural desire).

Most commentators agree that a natural desire may be aroused (*elicited*) by some *knowledge* of God's existence. Yet a strong disagreement divides them about the *vision* of God as object of that "natural desire." Some propose that an innate natural desire is formally directed at a *vision* of God as God is in himself. They rule out the existence of a state of "pure nature" independent of man's supernatural destiny. Such has been the position of Henri de Lubac, Hans Urs von Balthasar, and John Milbank. Others, among whom Sylvester of Ferrara comes closest to Aquinas, argue that even an innate desire can be no more than a desire to know the ultimate cause of reality. Such a desire stems from the mind's natural desire to extend its knowledge as far as possible. The position assumes a state of pure nature at the root of this (purely) natural desire of God.[8] The alleged foundational desire of *seeing* God consists in the desire of an intellect that cannot be satisfied before resting in the infinite, but in a manner totally proportionate to its nature.

Most of the Scholastic commentaries, whatever their internal differences, end up with a dualism of two states and two natures. Aquinas's position is ambiguous. The idea of a natural desire has mostly disappeared from modern philosophy. The main cause is the gradual narrowing of the field. Philosophy has come to define itself as reflection on reality as it presents itself to our *observation* or calculation. The idea of religious transcendence thereby withdrew to a field to which philosophy claims to have no access. Recently, however, it appears that it may be regaining its former place in modern thought, and with it the legitimacy of the idea of a natural desire. Several philosophers have accepted that no philosophical discourse about reality can succeed without a discussion of what defines its limits and hence also its efforts to surpass them. According to Heidegger, philosophy's first task consists in exploring the transcendent horizon of the known. At times he even compared the philosophical investigation with Eckhart's mystical explorations.[9] Also in Jaspers's philosophy, the notion of *Transzendenz* occupies a central position. Existence, for him, must be defined through its relation to what surpasses it. Neither Heidegger nor Balthasar gave the term *transcendence* an overtly religious meaning.

Contemporary Christian philosophers, especially Maurice Blondel and Karl Rahner, have attached a religious significance to this horizon. Still, aware of other, nonreligious interpretations of the term, they abstained from asserting that it forms the basis of a philosophical *desire of seeing God*. Is an equation of a transcendent moment in all cognition with the God of religion still philosophically justified? The answer depends on the answer to the question of whether philosophy has any authority in passing judgment about religious truth. If it does, as we concluded earlier (essay 10), then "a natural desire of seeing God" is possible. Yet only experience can inform us about its actual existence.

The German phenomenologist Max Scheler did argue that such a desire actually exists since, in his judgment, it lies at the ground of the affirmation of God's existence: "Only a real being with the essential character of divinity can be the cause of man's religious propensity, which is the propensity to execute in a real sense acts of that class whose acts, though finite experience cannot fulfill them, nevertheless demand fulfillment."[10] Note that Scheler does not claim that God exists because the desire for God has to be *satisfied*, but because the very *existence* of that desire presupposes a divine reality. Nevertheless, Scheler's argument, in my opinion, still goes too far. The fact that the mind's intellectual dynamism surpasses the immediate object of knowledge and desire does not necessarily lead to any conclusion about the *nature* of its transcendent object.

Karl Rahner is more cautious in establishing the religious nature of the idea of transcendence. For him, all knowledge presupposes a "pre-apprehension" (*Vorgriff*) of *absolute being*: "The pre-apprehension of this *being* is not an *a priori* knowledge of an object, but the *a priori* horizon against which the perception of an object appears. It constitutes the very condition for an *a posteriori* appearance."[11] The idea of infinite *Being* that functions as the horizon against which we know all beings, cannot but be transcendent. To the objection that a purely negative concept of the infinite might suffice for functioning as a horizon, Rahner responds that the *priority* of the infinite horizon with respect to the cognition of the finite requires that the horizon *actually* exists. Already Descartes had responded in a somewhat similar way to the objections leveled against his claim that in all real affirmations of a finite reality, the infinite has a priority over the finite (*Third Meditation*). For Descartes, the background of an *existing* infinity is a necessary condition for the mind to recognize the finite as finite.

The question remains, however, whether an infinite horizon implies that an infinite being corresponding to the idea of God exists. In itself the idea of *being* is neither finite nor infinite: it is indefinite. Logically, a pantheistic or a panentheistic answer would be equally possible. In my opinion, the metaphor of a transcendent horizon establishes no more than that a desire of God is *possible*. The purpose of this discussion was merely to provide a foundation for the existence of a religious mysticism.

Many of our contemporaries would not know what to make of a desire of what has become totally alien to them. Even religious men and women living in secular cultures might find the idea of a personal God genuinely puzzling. At the time when the idea of a natural desire of God was formulated, the West recognized monotheism as the only philosophically legitimate form of deity. That condition has ceased to exist today. Equally vanished, however, is the rationalist *a priori* opposition to the idea of God, on the ground that what cannot be strictly proven by reason or direct experience deserves no place in philosophy. Nothing entitles philosophy to restrict its investigation to what can be established by scientific truth or logical argument. Philosophy has ceased to be the science of "reason alone." Philosophy now consists primarily in a reflection upon experience, from whatever sources experience may draw its content. In a secular atmosphere of modern culture, the mind's religious desire would seldom be explicit, as it may have been in the past. Only mystically gifted, committed religious individuals appear to have a full awareness of what I have described here in abstract philosophical terms. Others will have to be satisfied with what Aquinas formulated as a desire of a *beatitudo in communi*, a general idea of beatitude.

Where does this leave us with respect to the possibility and nature of religious mysticism? It shows that the mind is open to the highest object of human desire and that the most intimate union with it may be strongly desired.

ESSAY 14

Mysticism and Philosophy

Mystical Elements in Philosophy

The link between philosophy and contemplation was strong in ancient Greek philosophy, probably never more so than during the Hellenistic period. Inspired by Plato and Aristotle, Plotinus and later Neoplatonist philosophers considered contemplation the goal of philosophical reflection. Plato repeatedly reminded his readers of philosophy's origin in mystical Orphic and Pythagorean cults. His theory of the Ideas, ideal prototypes of reality, prepared a philosophical theology. Plotinus, Proclus, and a number of Neoplatonists interpreted this doctrine as expressing the soul's nostalgia for the ideal world where it was born. Their language continued referring to ancient myths and cultic representations, not to suggest a return to the ancient religion, but to confirm the link with philosophy's mystical sources.

Essay 13 concluded that for Aristotle no less than for Plato, in the act of contemplation the soul participates in a divine activity and thereby shares in a divine reality. Aristotle's idea of the soul's attraction by the unmoved mover, more even than Plato's nostalgia for an ideal world, inspired Christian and Muslim believers to consider divine attraction the source of all thinking. Christians later justified this mystical desire by the idea that the soul as an image of God naturally looks for its divine prototype.

For medieval thinkers—Jewish, Muslim, and Christian—theology was the primary subject of thought. Ancient Greek philosophy had prepared and confirmed its mystical orientation. Yet Judaic and Christian theologies overdetermined Greek thought, as appears in God's answer to Moses's question about the origin of the mysterious voice he heard near the burning bush: "I am who I am."[1] This revelation induced philosophy to identify God with the metaphysical idea of Being.

Seldom before the fifteenth century did Christians consider philosophy an end in itself. During the Renaissance, this subordination of philosophy to theology considerably weakened, while the emphasis on philosophy's own mystical qualities grew, particularly among Italian Neoplatonists such as Marsilio Ficino, later also in England, with the Cambridge Platonists and Bishop Berkeley, and in France, with Malebranche. They all regarded philosophy independently of theology, [as] an itinerary of the mind to God. Yet not before the twentieth century did Scholastic philosophers regard the study of mysticism a subject worthy of philosophical attention. At that point, most believing philosophers and even some nonbelievers started taking the mystical element of philosophy seriously. Bertrand Russell, in his *Mysticism and Logic* (1921), declared that scientists needed mystical inspiration as much as they needed science for their work.

The most amazing return of philosophy toward mysticism in the late modern age was undoubtedly Ludwig Wittgenstein's *Tractatus Logico-Philosophicus* (1921). Many have interpreted the final statement, "What we cannot speak about we must pass over in silence," as the conclusion of a logical positivist closing the book on any discussion of "higher things," such as religion. Yet the author's "silence" of words and meanings turned out to be very eloquent on "showings." Indeed, it opened an entirely new view of the world, not by explaining *how* the world is (science will do that) but *that it is*. His insight originates not in the discovery of new *meaning*: the world as a whole has neither meaning nor value for Wittgenstein; it simply is what it is. Yet the mere existence of a world devoid of meaning opens the mind to the only insights that really matter in life, such as time and eternity, life and death. For that reason the final statement of the *Tractatus*, "What we cannot speak about we must pass over in silence," far from embracing a positivist dogmatism, rejects it for closing the mind to all that is worth human attention.

Still, the term *mystical*, which the Austrian philosopher used to describe the philosophical ignorance of matters most significant in human existence, cannot but sound strange to anyone who has actually read religious mystics. Nevertheless, something in the statement sounds familiar. William James, in his remarkable *Varieties of Religious Experience*, ranked *ineffability* first among the characteristics of the mystical consciousness. Nor did James primarily write about ecstatic emotional moments, with which we all too easily identify mystical states; he included those cognitive moments present at the heart of most religious experiences.

If all mysticism must in some way be cognitive, we may wonder about the content of the so-called mystical enlightenment. The religious mystic may call it divine. Yet the word *God* first appears in Wittgenstein's *Tractatus* one page before the last, where he writes: "God does not reveal himself *in* the world" (6.432). God is beyond the world and yet is the totality of all relations *within* the world. God is not the many, yet neither is God different from the many. So we end up referring to God in negative terms: God is infinite, unlike any and all finite beings. We only "know" God in our *relation* to him. There all these abstract negations become meaningless, and yet they present all that the mystic claims to know. The experiences occur in time, yet the mystic experiences them as a single moment of a timeless present. We cannot even imagine what that "still point" beyond time would be. The German philosopher Robert Spaemann illustrates it by quoting two well-known "quietist mystics" of the eighteenth century: Fénelon and his penitent Madame Guyon. The former wrote in well-chosen words: "To enclose oneself in *the present moment* is one of the most important rules of spiritual life"; Madame Guyon: "Through losing hope one recovers peace."[2] Their attitudes reflect what, for Wittgenstein, experience without fear and without hope means: "If we take eternity to mean not infinite temporal duration but timelessness, then eternal life belongs to those who live in the present" (*Tractatus*, 6.4311).[3]

Before moving to descriptions by traditional mystics, I want to draw attention to one other twentieth-century philosopher who referred philosophy to mysticism. In his later years (1955), Heidegger published two short texts in which he likens the philosopher's waiting for a manifestation of *Being* to the mystic's expectant quiet. Both treatises refer to Eckhart's term *Gelassenheit* ("resignation," "composure," or "waiting in patience"). The German philosopher was not the first to link philosophy to a mystical waiting for enlightenment. Indeed, more than Heidegger, whose attitude to religion had for many years been ambivalent, Vedantic Hinduism and later Buddhist philosophy have always derived wisdom and insight from the same religious source.

Mysticism without Philosophy

If mysticism is to be expressed in mainly negative terms, can there be a *mystical* theology? It seems not. Nevertheless, most religious mystics have recorded their experiences within the doctrinal structures of the faith from which they drew their inspiration. Yet they seldom make doctrinal assertions. Their intense *personal* confrontation with the divine mystery appears to move them beyond dogmatic principles. Even within the same religious tradition, diverse and often conflicting mystical currents emerge. In the fifteenth century, a serious controversy originated on the question whether the mystical experience consists in spiritual knowledge (hence, in a theology) or in an act of loving union with God. For Eckhart, the spiritual ascent ends in a total darkness, negative theology, where even the distinctions among the divine Persons of the Trinity disappear. For other mystics (Ruusbroec being the most articulate one), the soul ascends to the divine light and partakes in the life of the Godhead moving into the intra-Trinitarian relations. Here the Father is the silence in which the Word originates, while the Spirit seals their creative union. The soul follows them even further into the divine effusion of creation. Thus Ruusbroec's Trinitarian mysticism proceeds by the dogmas of an explicitly Christian theology. I shall return to it in the next essay.

During the Renaissance and Reformation, as the significance of theology weakened, that of affective mysticism grew. After the fundamental *caesura* of Nominalist theology, which severed philosophy from piety, mystical literature came to consist in reports on feelings and devotion. Speculation about God's nature became rare among the devout, who had grown increasingly cautious in avoiding ecclesiastic censorship. In those circumstances, a new piety emerged in Western Christianity, which gave rise to the *Imitation of Christ* and similar dogmatically sober writings. Mysticism came to be described as an exceptional state of affective piety granted to some, yet withheld from most. This was the time when the subdued piety of Quietists and Pietists came to dominate entire communities and even universities. Luther, however strongly he had opposed Gabriel Biel and other Nominalist theologians, twice published a mystical treatise, the *Theologia germanica*, written by a late medieval anonymous author, who explicitly stated that the divine light, the uncreated and the created one, illuminates and transforms the soul—a position that contradicts Luther's own theological thesis that grace yields no more than a *forensic* justification. Calvin interpreted the entire order of nature as resulting from a divine decree and is subject to a positive divine law. Still for him also, spiritual experiences continue expressing man's natural desire of God. God's image in the soul, although wiped out by sin, has left a residue, which in the elect the Lord restores to "full integrity" (*Institutes*, I, 15, 4). From these sources, a reformed spirituality developed that, particularly in the Low Countries, flourished into a new religious humanism.

Finally, we should not forget that during and after this speculatively low season in the West, the Greek East, inspired by the older inheritance of Maximus the Confessor (580–662) and by the works of the mysterious Dionysius (sixth century?), developed a cosmic mysticism, which the West had missed altogether. In the nineteenth and twentieth centuries, the great Russian thinkers Soloviev, Lossky, and Florensky nurtured these seeds into a unique political mysticism, which continued feeding the spiritually starved Russians during years of atheist governments. Contrary to what happened in the previous period, when philosophy had been mainly a preparation to theology, during the modern epoch, philosophy and science came to be recognized as the summit of intellectual life.

The most creative period of mysticism in the modern West was the transitional time of the Baroque culture in the late sixteenth and seventeenth century. Teresa of Avila may well have been the first mystic who consistently analyzed the stages of mystical development and the nature of their effects upon the human faculties. Her confessor, John of the Cross, partly on the basis of her writings, concluded that the supreme mystical experience occurs in the "substance of the soul." However rudimentary his and her psychology may now appear, they nevertheless described the specific role of the mystical experience in religion. Teresa describes her visions as *intuitions* of an unmediated consciousness. This was, of course, the kind of cognition that Kant was to declare inaccessible to the human mind. Jacques Maritain qualified this Kantian verdict by limiting the mystical intuition to an immediate awareness of God's presence, which differed from the normal awareness of another person's presence induced by sensuous stimuli. Conceptual knowledge, Maritain admitted, excludes such an intuition, but a *connatural knowledge* would at least make it possible. His argument rests on a theological thesis. Sanctifying grace makes the faithful *consortes divinae naturae* ("participants in God's nature"), as Catholic doctrine defines it. By this argument, however, most religious persons would be potential mystics.[4]

The philosopher may accept or reject this argument: it contains no contradictions, but neither does it prove the actual presence of mystical knowledge. It remains purely theological, that is, justified within a system that neither is nor pretends to be universal in its claims. Elsewhere Maritain has written on a "fruitive experience of the absolute" that requires no connatural knowledge through grace yet is attainable even by the mind's natural forces.[5] This distinction between a mysticism of grace and a natural one rests on a fundamental split between nature and the supernatural, which renders a philosophical discussion of mysticism very difficult if not impossible. The psychological studies of Joseph Maréchal avoid those excursions into Christian theology without, however, reducing mysticism to a "natural" phenomenon.[6] The merit of Maréchal's extraordinary analyses consists in that he admits a link between certain psychic dispositions and uncommon religious experiences. Mystical states confront philosophy with unprecedented problems. Yet it had become clear that one could no longer dismiss them as pathological phenomena.

Phenomenological psychology also started an unprejudiced study of religious mysticism. Much of the discussion here depends on the notion of *selfhood* or *soul*. While reflecting on the religious belief in some form of immortality, the American philosopher William Ernest Hocking[7] assumed the existence of two "selves": the *excursive self* is conscious of the world in which it lives; the *reflective self* surpasses this worldly self and is the source of *self*-consciousness. I have discussed Hocking's theory in essay 8. Here I would merely add that the reflective self transforms space and time from *a priori* forms of perception (Kant) into intuitive vistas of an inner realm with mysterious rhythms and successions. From archaic depths, the imagination (if it has not been eclipsed during the experience) may evoke visions known in fragments by the dreaming consciousness, yet normally not by the waking mind.[8] In privileged instances, the *intellectual intuition*, exorcized by Kant's critique, reasserts its rights, and the mind may *perceive* as directly as it ordinarily does through the senses. The intellectual visions described by John of the Cross and Ignatius of Loyola are truly *visions* in that they may belong to the order of perception, even though all sensorial input and, in some cases, all images have disappeared. Does all this not support William James's observation that the ordinary, rational consciousness is only one kind of consciousness, while all around it, "separated by the flimsiest of screen," there are forms of consciousness of a completely different nature?

That the concept of soul is originally religious Edward B. Tylor tried to show by the primitive awareness of a ghost-soul that is able to wander while the body remains stationary. Although Tylor's simplistically rationalist interpretations of the primitive mind have been rejected, on one crucial issue he was undoubtedly right: the idea of soul has emerged as a religious notion. In the Greek mystery cult, the soul was above all a subject of ecstasy, first in this life and, after death, in an afterlife.[9] According to the classical scholar Erwin Rohde, the ecstatic quality of the soul is what may have led to a belief in its immortality.[10] Even in developed religious cultures, the soul has preserved this numinous quality. Thus much in India's Vedantic writings may be interpreted as an attempt to penetrate to that point of the soul where Atman (the individual self) *becomes* Brahman (the absolute, yet also my truest self): *Tat tvam asi* ("That is what you are"). The Bhagavad Gita describes the Atman in the sacred terms of "marvelous,"[11] "indestructible," "immutable," "incomprehensible."

Christian theology regards the soul as created and is therefore more reserved, at least in its orthodox expressions. Yet by no means did it "desacralize" psychology. The concept of the soul as image of God determines the development of Christian mysticism as much as the notion of the Atman determines Vedantic visions. The divine "character" of the redeemed soul, as presented by Paul, was developed into a Christian psychology by the Cappadocian theologians in the East and by Augustine in the West. The difference between the ordinary self and the mystical self is a common distinction in mystical literature. According to Ruusbroec, in the mystical self reason is suspended and the mind is emptied of all objects: "Here our reason and every activity characterized by the making of distinctions must give way, for our powers now become simply one in love, grow silent, and incline toward the Father's face, since this revelation of the Father raises the soul above reason to a state of imageless bareness. There the soul is simple, spotless, and pure, empty of everything. In this pure emptiness the Father reveals a divine resplendence, which neither reason nor the senses, neither rational observation nor distinctions can attain."[12]

Metaphors of isolation, secrecy, height, and depth suggest the difference between the two levels of soul. Plotinus speaks of the innermost sanctuary in which there are no images,[13] Teresa of the inner castle, Catherine of Siena of the interior home of the heart, Eckhart of the little castle, Tauler of the ground of the soul, the author of *The Cloud of Unknowing* of the closed house. In these secret dwellings, John of the Cross asserts, the mystical transformation occurs: "When God himself visits it [the soul] . . . it is in total darkness and in concealment from the enemy that the soul receives these spiritual favors of God. The reason for this is that, as his Majesty dwells substantially in the soul, where neither angel nor devil can attain to an understanding of the intimate and secret communications which take place there between the soul and God. These communications, since the Lord Himself works them, are divine and sovereign, for they are all *substantial* touches of divine union between the soul and God."[14]

Repeatedly John of the Cross insists that those touches occur "in the substance" of the soul, not in its faculties, and consequently that they have neither form nor figure.[15] He seems to use the term "touches" to denote an experience unrelated to sensation yet analogous to it by its directly intuitive character. The sense of touch was probably selected because of its greater intimacy. John Tauler equally stresses the discontinuity with ordinary thought: "This inner ground of the soul is only known to very few people . . . it has nothing to do with thinking or reasoning."[16] Yet it is precisely in this darkness of the substance of the soul that the Enlightenment of God's presence illuminates the soul. Pseudo-Dionysius powerfully describes the paradox: "Into this dark beyond all light, we pray to come and, unseeing and unknowing, to see and to know Him, who is beyond seeing and beyond knowing precisely by not seeing, by not knowing."[17]

In the following excerpt from his autobiography, Ignatius describes what he experienced near the Cardoner River:

> As he sat there, the eyes of his understanding began to open. Without having any vision he understood—knew—many matters both spiritual and pertaining to the Faith and the realm of letters and that with such clearness that they seemed utterly new to him. There is no possibility of setting out in detail everything he then understood. The most that he can say is that he was given so great an enlightening of his mind

that if one were to put together all the helps he has received from God and all the things he has ever learned, they would not be equal to what he received in that single illumination. He was left with his understanding so enlightened that he seemed to be another man with another mind than the one that was his before.[18]

John of the Cross calls an experience such as the one here described an *intellectual apprehension,* because it imprints upon the mind a form "without images, figure of natural fancy or imagination."[19] Teresa sharpens the distinction where she writes that "the Lord Himself in an *intellectual vision so clear that it seemed almost imaginary,* laid Himself in my arms."[20] John claims that intellectual visions take place "in the substance of the soul," and by various other expressions he refers to this substance at the end of *The Dark Night,* such as "His Majesty dwells substantially in the soul" and "substantial touches of divine union between the soul and God."[21] Clearly the term *substance* alone appeared appropriate for that coincidence of being and knowing.

Whatever else this enlightenment may contain, it includes a unique and direct awareness of the self. This direct character is all the more remarkable since it is described entirely in negative terms. One attentive philosophical reader of Christian mystics writes: "The soul empties itself absolutely of every specific operation and of all multiplicity, and knows negatively by means of the void and the annihilation of every act and of every object of thought coming from outside—the soul knows negatively—but nakedly, without veils—that metaphysical marvel, that absolute, that perfection of every act and of every perfection, which is to exist, which is the soul's own substantial existence."[22] The mystical message about the nature of selfhood is that the self is *essentially* more than a mere self, that a sacred character belongs to its nature as much as the act through which it is immanent to itself, and that a failure on the mind's part to become aware of this character reduces the self to *less* than itself. The direct awareness of a self transcending the fluxes and periodic discontinuities of the ordinary forms of self-consciousness constitutes a significant experience on which philosophy has not yet sufficiently reflected.

ESSAY 15

Justifying the Mystical Experience

The Cognitive Nature of Mysticism

In essay 14, I raised the question whether there can be a *theory* of mysticism. If mysticism is no more than a blinding or overwhelming experience, the answer is obviously negative. Yet if the mystical experience includes a cognitive element, an enlightenment of some kind, a theory cannot be *a priori* excluded. One philosopher who had no doubt that such was indeed the case was Nicholas of Cusa (mostly referred to as Cusanus) (1400–1464), bishop of Brixen (now Bressanone) and cardinal of the Roman Church. He wrote what may still be the strongest defense of the metaphysical significance of mysticism. The Benedictine monks of Tegernsee, in whose monastery the cardinal often resided, had requested him to write an introduction on the nature of mystical prayer. Jasper Hopkins, the eminent translator of Cusanus's works into English, considers *De visione dei* (*On the Vision of God*) (1453) the cardinal's response to that request.

In addressing the "beloved brothers" of his favorite abbey, he stressed the "experiential" (i.e., experimental) nature of his work on the subject and asserted that even learning about mysticism is a mystical experience. In essay 14, we saw how William James intimated that all mysticism, even the "dark contemplation" of the sixth-century Dionysius, consists in the first place in an act of cognition. By accepting this position, Cusanus clearly joined those who, with Jean Gerson, chancellor of the University of Paris, called the mystical union a cognitive and not a merely affective act. Gerson's opponents had wondered, How could what surpasses all understanding be cognitive? Their adversaries answered, How could one love without knowing what to love? Cusanus's conclusion was, as was Gerson's, attacked for having misunderstood Dionysius's dark contemplation.[1]

According to Cusanus, an intellectual apprehension always precedes unitive love. What makes the mystical apprehension "dark" is that its knowledge at its highest point overcomes all distinctions and becomes a conscious *not-knowing*. Negative theology does not suspend all cognitive activity, since the mind *knowingly* enters the realm of darkness. Once it has done so, its negative insight rallies all mental powers, the affective and the cognitive, into a single comprehensive experience. In the prologue and first four chapters of *De visione Dei*, Cusanus personally addresses the abbot and brothers of the Tegernsee monastery and introduces his theory with an aesthetic experiment: "If I attempt to introduce you by human means unto divine things, I am forced to do so through a likeness. I have found no image more suitable to our purpose than the image of a person whose face, through subtle activity, is such that it seems to behold everything around it. There are in existence many of such painted faces, e.g., the one depicted by the preeminent painter Rogier [Van der Weyden] in his priceless painting in the town hall of Brussels."[2] Nicholas promises to send the brothers a similar painting with the figure of an *all-seeing* individual, which he calls the "icon of God." He recommends hanging it on the wall and inviting the brothers to stand around and observe it. Independently of the place from which they look at it, each will have the impression that he alone is being looked at *by* the figure. If one walks from one side to the other, the icon's gaze will accompany him, without moving. The same will happen to one who walks in the opposite direction. This image will give the monks an idea of how God sees the entire world in his absolute sight. Later, Nicholas will describe this divine *seeing* as an act of creation: to be seen by God is to be created.

What then does Cusanus mean by his promise to conduct his readers "simplicissimo atque *communissimo modo . . . experimentaliter in sacratissimam obscuritatem*" (#1) ("by way of experiencing and through very simple and common means into a most sacred darkness")? By choosing the aesthetic experience of the icon whose glance always confronts the viewer, the cardinal symbolically awakens the soul's implicit awareness that theological seeing consists in being seen by God. Moreover, the glance the all-seeing One casts on the viewer is, in addition to being creative of him, an act of love. This love, he implies, elicits and, indeed, constitutes my requiting love. The intense mystical nature of Cusanus's thought had also appeared in some of his earlier works. In *De quaerendo Deum* (*On Seeking God*) (1445), for instance, having described the ascent of the soul to a union with God, he concludes with the following exhortation: "Turn to him; enter ever more deeply into yourself, leaving all that is without, so that you may be found on that road whereby one reaches God and so that you may, after all this, truly grasp him." Here, as in the latter part of *De visione Dei* (especially in the final address to Christ), the more affective tone considerably varies from that of the purely theoretical works, such as *On Learned Ignorance*. In fact, all Cusanus's works confirm his mystical theory. Even the common cognitive drive results in an encounter with the One, in whom all distinctions and methods collapse.

But, he insists, intellectual insight will become a mystical awareness of God only if grace transforms the mind's active striving into one of passive contemplation. Not before the mind reaches that point of passivity does it attain the end of its thought.[3] The soul's natural desire of God remains unfulfilled until it comes to participate in God's own nature (*theosis*). Although God's essence remains beyond comprehension, the union with God consists in "a clear vision from face to face." In *De filiatione Dei* (*On the Sonship of God*) (#69), Cusanus even states that only in God does the mind attain its ultimate, appropriate object and its innermost truth. Since the mind is the living likeness of God, it will know itself only when it intuits itself in God, that is, "when God himself is in the intellect" (#86).

Nicholas's information of the mystical life mainly depended on three earlier spiritual thinkers: Pseudo-Dionysius, Meister Eckhart, and (probably) the fifteenth-century Flemish theologian Denys, called the Carthusian. The thought of Dionysius, the sixth-century Neoplatonist, may well have been the most archaic layer of Cusanus's spiritual theology. Nowhere does that appear more clearly than in *De deo abscondito* (*On the Hidden God*).[4] Yet Dionysius's short *Mystical Theology* remains a one-sided work that at the dark summit of mystical life surpasses the central Christian mystery of the Trinity. Cusanus read Dionysius's treatise, however, as it had been received and interpreted by a long Christian tradition, which included the scholastic Albert and his followers at the University of Cologne, Cusanus's alma mater.

Even more decisive than Dionysius's influence was that of Eckhart. The Rhineland mystic was, of course, committed to a more radical Neoplatonism than Albert and his followers had been.[5] According to the Dominican's religious vision, all spiritual creatures in their primordial being are images of the Father. They display a unique *similarity* with God. Yet beyond being an image, the human mind partly coincides with God's own nature. Mystical life, then, for Eckhart consists in bringing the mind's created likeness to a full identity with God's uncreated Image. Ultimately, Eckhart calls for a gradual "de-creation" of the spiritual creature. Yet at that point emerges a tension that had lain dormant in Neoplatonic theology since early Christian theologians had first adopted it. For if God remains above all names and the creature *qua creature* (that is, in all respects except the mind's divine core) totally differs from divine nature, in the final stage of mystical consciousness the soul surpasses its created likeness of the divine Image by a dark identity with God. The participation in the life of the divine Trinity, which in orthodox writers had been the highest stage of mystical contemplation, for Eckhart as for Dionysius, still belonged to an intermediate stage of mystical consciousness to be surpassed by the soul at the end of her spiritual ascent.[6] The mind's being an image of God concludes in a negative, supra-Trinitarian dark vision, wherein the outgoing move of the soul toward differentiation becomes entirely counteracted by the ingoing move toward the undifferentiated Absolute.

Precisely on this issue, Ruusbroec, in other respects so close to the German Meister, chose not to follow him. For the Flemish mystic, a dynamic rhythm of ingoing and outflowing from God into creation and back into divine unity corresponded to an intradivine movement symbolized by the dynamic relation of divine persons, in which the Father generates the Son, and both cause the effusion of the Spirit over all creation. This divine dynamism of exodus from and return to God cannot be surpassed: it is God's own life. For Ruusbroec, the mysterious darkness of the mystical vision resides not "beyond the Father," as Eckhart had claimed; it *is* the Father. There is no evidence that Cusanus ever read Ruusbroec. But in the critical annotations written in his Eckhart manuscript (present in his library in Kues), he obviously moves away from the Rhineland mystic toward Ruusbroec. Nor ought this move surprise us when we remember that Nicholas had become acquainted with Denys, a Flemish Carthusian, who had accompanied him on a papal inspection journey through the Low Countries. The Carthusian's entire work had been a commentary on Ruusbroec. He constantly refers to Ruusbroec as "doctor divinus," "alter Dionysius," and claims to be his disciple.[7]

In tracing the origins of Cusanus's Trinitarian theology, one ought not to overlook the earlier and possibly even more decisive impact of Raymundus Lullus, a Spanish mystic of the thirteenth century.[8] It may well have been in his work that Cusanus encountered the correlative concepts of *complicatio-explicatio* (enfolding-unfolding) that were to play such a central role in his description of the ingoing and outgoing divine rhythm. He considered them perfect instruments for developing a mystical theology along the lines of *The Vision of God*. God remains the same in the *explication* of the creatures as he is in the *complication* of his all-containing Self. God's "unfolding" into creation is as much an expression of the divine essence as his "enfolding" into Himself. For that reason the mystical ascent to the nameless, *enfolded* One must be balanced by a descent toward his *unfolded* being in the multiplicity of creation. *De visione Dei* reflects this dual motion: "When I find you to be a power that unfolds, I go out. When I find you to be a power that both enfolds and unfolds, I both go in and go out. From creatures I go in unto you, who are Creator—go in from the effects unto the Cause. I go out from you, who are Creator—go out from the Cause unto the effects" (#47). This participation of the soul in the divine motions belongs to the core of Cusanus's spiritual doctrine.

Neoplatonic Philosophy

Cusanus, even as the Rhenish and Flemish mystics, proposes an inverted analogy of being in which, contrary to the Thomist one, the Infinite functions as necessary principle for interpreting the nature of finite being. Indeed, for him, the being of the finite creature is the *Being* of God. In *De dato patris luminum* (*On the Gift of the Father of Lights*) (1445–46),[9] Cusanus declares God to be the very ground and measure of created being. God's supreme gift—his *datum optimum*—consists in his total self-communication. To God's total *giving*, responds the creature's total *being given*. The essence of the creature as it is in God totally coincides with the creature as it is in itself: *Neque est alius mundus qui apud patrem aeternus et alius per descensum a patre est factus* ("Nor does the world as it is with the Eternal Father differ from the one that is made by a descent from the Father") (*De dato patris luminum*, 106).

In *De visione Dei*, the unity between creature and God appears in the figure of seeing. Cusanus returns to the image with which this essay started: God's seeing is God's creative Being. By returning God's glance, the creature contributes to God's Being. The very notion of *vision* is, of course, thoroughly Neoplatonic. It is the root metaphor in Plotinus and also in Proclus and Dionysius. Moreover, in Plotinus's *Nous* (Mind), the second hypostasis in his triad, in which intelligence and intelligibility coincide, makes the soul aspire at a state in which *seeing* consists in *being seen*. If God creates, then all created being is so intrinsically dependent on God that its root remains within God as part of God's self-unfolding essence: "For you are present where speaking, seeing, hearing, tasting, touching, reasoning, knowing, and understanding are the same and where seeing coincides with being seen, hearing with being heard, tasting with being tasted, touching with being touched, speaking with hearing, and creating with speaking. If I were to see just as I am seeable, I would not be a creature" (#41).

At this point, the original metaphor of the all-seeing image of Christ assumes a properly mystical character. Of course, an innocuous reading would be that, since all distinctions collapse in God, we may, in a supereminent way, refer to God as *seeing*, even as we freely use other human attributes. But Cusanus means something far more specific. For God to *see*, he claims, implies constituting a multiplicity in being: "Your seeing is your creating; and you do not see anything other than yourself but are your own object.... If so, then how is it that you create things that are other than yourself? For you seem to create yourself, even as you see yourself" (#50). In this passage, God's seeing of the creature appears to be a creating of God himself. Now in the case of God, *seeing-as-creating* must be understood as a double metaphor, twice removed from the "seeing" of the creatures. Insofar as human *seeing* refers to what is outside oneself, God's seeing must be metaphorical, since God owes his Being not to "seeing" outside himself, while creatures owe theirs to God's internal seeing.[10]

But God's *seeing-as-creating* causes more problems when Cusanus describes God's creating as compelled by his very nature. The difficulty is not that God thereby is in all things, as Cusanus asserts in the next sentence. But for God's *Being* fully to be equated with his creative activity means that God's essence requires *otherness* in order to be divine. This may be a sound thesis in Plotinus's theory, where Mind and Psyche *necessarily emanate* from the One. But Cusanus deviates from the Christian doctrine that God "freely" creates, that is, is not compelled by intrinsic necessity, where he writes, "Your creating is your Being." Still, the cardinal intended no discrepancy from Christian doctrine, as appears from his qualification "while nevertheless remaining *free* of them [meaning: all things He creates]" (#50).

Then what did he mean? Obviously he refers to creation conceived in such a way that human consciousness makes a difference to God's own Being—a thesis that reminds of Eckhart's dark saying that the eye with which I see God is the eye with which God sees himself. It means that, if God creates intelligent beings, their reflective glance at their Creator opens up a new dimension in God: it enables God to *see* himself through the eyes of the creatures. Once the believer accepts the fact of creation (on whatever grounds), he is forced to conceive of God as seeing all of creation *and* himself through the eyes of intelligent creatures. Cusanus is clearly aware of the difficulty that the idea of God's depending on a source *beyond* himself would constitute. So he hastens to add that God views all things in their divine source: "You appear to me to see all things in yourself, as would a power in viewing itself" (#49). God's "seeing," then, refers to all created forms as immanent in the Creator. Cusanus calls God the *forma formarum*, the invisible source of all the visible. If God had created no intelligent beings, the predicate "seeing" would not apply to God at all, not even in a metaphorical sense. Yet given the *fact* of creation, it refers to an attribute that God owes to his creative act. To exist as form of forms adds neither to God's perfection nor to his being. Nevertheless, the Perfect Being would not have this particular mode of being if God had not created spiritual beings.

The problem of otherness recurs in still another form. Why should Cusanus refer to God's relation to creatures by a metaphor of distance (*seeing*) to be aware of what is immanent within himself? I suspect that Cusanus's preference for the visual metaphor is rooted in the ancient equation of *form* with *essential being*. In *De dato patris luminum*, Cusanus grants full theological significance to the Western concept of *form*. For Cusanus, as for Eckhart, it is through its *form* or essence that a creature participates in God's Being. But when Cusanus refers to God as *forma formarum* or *absolute form*, he shifts *being* away from referring to existence toward essence. For Aquinas, the highest perfection consists in individual existence, which the essence does not include. For Cusanus, on the contrary, the highest perfection consists in what, for Thomas, would be no more than the *esse commune*, the most comprehensive concept that includes all generic and specific qualities.[11] In the Neoplatonic tradition, *Being* remains entirely on the side of *form*, in the Aristotelian-Thomist one, on *existence*. To Thomas, a real distinction between essence and existence appeared indispensable for safeguarding the contingent nature of created being, a contingency that would have been missing in a conception of reality wherein all forms would be by nature *necessary*, as they are in Platonism old and new. For Cusanus, as for all who had undergone the impact of nominalist theology, formal perfection had lost its intrinsic necessity, since all forms had become dependent on the unlimited and inscrutable power of an omnipotent Creator. This allowed the cardinal to embrace the form-essentialism of Platonic and Neoplatonic philosophies.

In favoring a Platonic ontology, Cusanus followed the trend of the early modern age, when the complete works of Plato and Plotinus came to be translated in the West. But his choice may have been inspired by the greater potential for mystical expression of a philosophy that allowed him to replace the predominantly efficient/causal relation of Thomism by a more immanent, formal one. Of course, with this return to Neoplatonism also returned the problems for keeping the Christian doctrine of creation sufficiently distinct from the Platonic one, according to which creatures necessarily *emanate* from God's essence.[12]

Thus far, Cusanus has given a justification of the mystical experience, yet one that is *philosophical* only for those who consider the idea of creation by a personal God a necessary assumption of any philosophical interpretation of reality. That this is by no means the case is obvious in the Asian religions of Hinduism and Buddhism, and in the Memphite theology of ancient Egyptian religion. Nor was there a creation story in ancient Greek literature other than a few allusions to Prometheus molding clay into persons. Hence what Cusanus presents as philosophical is by no means a necessary thesis on the origin of things. There was an irrefutable alternative: the world may have had no beginning. The monotheist concept of creation has commonly understood the thesis that things have a beginning a necessary assumption of the thesis that all things intrinsically depend on an absolute Being. Yet even Aquinas admitted that reason cannot prove that the world had a beginning. It was Cusanus's good right, then, to argue against the traditional interpretation of creation, as long as he maintained the essential principle, namely, that all things intrinsically depend on a divine Creator.

In the final part of *De visione Dei*, the only explicitly theological one, Nicholas, in mostly Neoplatonic terminology, articulates *how* the individual soul becomes united with God. This final book of *De visione Dei*, far from being an appendix, supports the argument of the entire work. The theological meaning of God conceived as *Love* here becomes the key concept of Cusanus's argument. God as loving is Father, God as lovable is the Word or Son, and God as love itself is the Spirit that unites Father and Son. As incarnated Word, the Son mediates between God and human nature (#86). In this reconstruction of Trinitarian theology, Christ's humanity realizes the union between God and man. The distance between Christ's humanity and the divine Word remains as great as it is in other human beings. Yet Christ's total openness to the divine nature singles him out for a unique role in the sanctification of human nature.

A mystical participation in God's life requires a union with Christ's humanity *through love and faith*. In faith, the mind accepts the message that the God-filled life is uniquely present in Christ. Cusanus refers to the intellect "in its highest degree" (#99) as the only appropriate place for receiving the divine Word. He thereby answered the question of the monks of Tegernsee: "Through the Word of God the intellect is perfected and grows and is made progressively more capable of receiving the Word and of becoming more conformed and similar to the Word" (#108). By its very nature, the intellect is called to this "supernatural" destiny, yet only by subjecting itself in faith to the Word of God will it realize its natural perfection.

In this final part appears what may still have remained dubious in earlier sections, namely, that Cusanus's mysticism, although highly cerebral, is more than an intellectual exercise. The cognitive ascent of faith has taken the mind to a height that knowing alone will never scale. Only love of God may take that final step: *Per fidem accedit intellectus ad verbum, per dilectionem unitur ei* (#109) ("Through faith the intellect approaches unto the Word; through love, it is united therewith"). Throughout, the cardinal assumes that love accomplishes an identity of nature between the lover and the beloved. Thus Christ perfects "all who love [him]" (#109) by raising them to his own state. At this point also the role of the Spirit, which had remained hidden in the preceding dialectic, appears with full clarity. Whenever a mind loves, the Spirit propels it: "Your Spirit cannot be lacking to any spirit, because it is the Spirit of spirits and the Motion of motions" (#111). This final consideration should also dispose of the objection that Cusanus's theory of the mystical vision remains essentially a philosophical one achieved by the mind's own efforts (*experimentaliter*). Grace, that is for Cusanus the Holy Spirit, drives the mind in its quest of God. To follow him here would have been a giant step into Christian theology, which, of course, was not my task in this book. I realize that with this final section on theology I have already passed beyond the limits of philosophy.

NOTES

PREFACE

I want to thank Edith Cardoen for her kindness as I pursued publication for this book on Louis's behalf. Dupré shared the original manuscript for *Thinking the Unknowable* with Cyril O'Regan and me in late 2018. Because of his failing health and death, he was unable to finalize some elements of the work, including the notes and the preambles to parts I, II, and IV. The preambles presented here reflect Dupré's original manuscript. Every reasonable effort has been made to provide complete citation information wherever possible.

1. Louis Dupré passed away on January 11, 2022, at the age of ninety-six.

2. Paul J. Levesque, "Symbol as the Primary Religious Category in the Thought of Louis Dupré: Foundation for Contemporary Sacramentology" (PhD diss., Katholieke Universiteit Leuven, 1995), 226–53. This evolution is also terrain covered in Louis Dupré, *Passage to Modernity* (New Haven, CT: Yale University Press, 1993), and Dupré, *The Enlightenment and the Intellectual Development of Modern Culture* (New Haven, CT: Yale University Press, 2004). The presentation of these themes in this book takes on a more urgent and compelling tone, as when he writes, "Technology has become the very face of reality" (typescript, essay 2).

3. In Peter J. Casarella, *Word as Bread: Language and Theology in Nicholas of Cusa* (Münster: Aschendorff, 2017), I also made an attempt, under the influence and guidance of Dupré, to explore this theme.

4. Ernesto Grassi, "Italian Humanism and Heidegger's Thesis of the End of Philosophy," *Philosophy & Rhetoric* 13, no. 2 (1980): 79–98.

5. Louis Dupré, *Metaphysics and Culture* (Milwaukee: Marquette University Press, 1994), 31.

6. Dupré, *Metaphysics and Culture*, 31.

7. For a condensed version of Buckley's argument, see Michael J. Buckley, S.J., "Modernity and the Satanic Face of God," in *Christian Spirituality and the Culture of Modernity: The Thought of Louis Dupré*, ed. Peter J. Casarella and George P. Schner, S.J. (Grand Rapids, MI: Eerdmans, 1998), 100–122.

8. Here would be the place to investigate Dupré's interpretation of Søren Kierkegaard, but thought of the Dane surprisingly plays no important role in the essays prepared for this book. See Peter J. Casarella, "'Modern Forms Filled with Traditional Spiritual Content': On Louis Dupré's Contribution to Christian Theology," in *Christian Spirituality and the Culture of Modernity*, ed. Peter J. Casarella and George P. Schner, S.J. (Grand Rapids, MI: Eerdmans, 1998), 297–99.

9. This is also similar to Cusanus's "seeing as creating" in *De visione Dei*, a topic that returns in essay 15.

10. Alfred North Whitehead, *Process and Reality*, corrected ed. (London: The Free Press, 1978), 344–45.

11. Whitehead, *Process and Reality*, 346.

12. Dupré cites William E. Hocking, *The Meaning of Immortality in Human Experience* (New York: Harper, 1957), 233–34.

13. Louis Dupré, "Husserl's Intentions of Experience," in *A Dubious Heritage* (New York: Paulist, 1977), 75–93. Scheler actually is mentioned only briefly at the beginning of "Husserl's Intentions of Experience," which does, however, support a thesis of Scheler's that Husserl's reduction of the idea of God does not stand on its own as a proof of the existence of God.

14. Jean-Luc Marion, Étant donné: Essai d'une phénoménologie de la donation (Paris: Presses universitaires de France, 1997); published in English as *Being Given: Toward a Phenomenology of Givenness*, trans. Jeffrey L. Kosky (Stanford, CA: Stanford University Press, 2002). See also Louis Dupré, "Alternatives to the Cogito," *Review of Metaphysics* 60, no. 4 (1987): 687–716, for his reading of the work of Michel Henry.

15. See Robert A. Orsi, *Between Heaven and Earth: The New Religious Worlds People Make and the Scholars Who Study Them* (Princeton, NJ: Princeton University Press, 2005), and Thomas A. Tweed, *Crossings and Dwellings: A Theory of Religion* (Cambridge, MA: Harvard University Press, 2006).

16. Claude Romano, *Event and Time* (New York: Fordham University Press, 2014), 192–99.

17. Dupré is more open to the post-Romantic account of seeing the form in the theology of Hans Urs von Balthasar, but even here he maintains a critical distance. See Casarella, "Modern Forms Filled with Traditional Spiritual Content," 301–2.

18. Hans-Georg Gadamer, *Truth and Method* (New York: Crossroad, 1985), 134; original German, *Wahrheit und Methode* (Tübingen: Mohr, 1960), 144.

19. See essay 8, and Hans Urs von Balthasar, *Theodramatik*, Vol. 1, *Prolegomena* (Einsiedeln: Johannes, 1973), 76–77.

20. Louis Dupré, "On the Natural Desire of Seeing God," *Radical Orthodoxy: Theology, Philosophy, Politics* 1, nos. 1 & 2 (2012): 92–93.

21. One of Cusanus's last works was *De apice theoriae* ("From the Summit of Contemplation").

22. Louis Dupré, *A Passage to Modernity: Hermeneutics of Nature and Culture* (New Haven, CT: Yale University Press, 1993), 253.

23. On the new "poetics" of creation, see Louis Dupré, *Symbols of the Sacred* (Grand Rapids, MI: Eerdmans, 2000), 125.

ESSAY 1

1. Alfred North Whitehead, *Science and the Modern World* (New York: Macmillan, 1959), 156.

2. Alfred North Whitehead, *Process and Reality* (New York: Harper and Row, 1960), 315.

3. Henri Duméry, *Le problème de Dieu* (Paris: Desclée, 1957), 15 (emphasis original).

4. Johannes Hessen, *Religionsphilosophie* (Munich: Reinhardt, 1955), 2:299.

5. Hegel, *Lectures on the Philosophy of Religion*, ed. and trans. Peter G. Hodgson (Berkeley: University of California Press, 1984), 1:366. Also, Emil Fackenheim, *The Religious Dimension in Hegel's Thought* (Bloomington: Indiana University Press, 1968).

6. Hegel, *Encyclopädie der philosophischen Wissenschaften*, ed. F. Nicolin and O. Pöggeler (Hamburg: Meiner, 1959), para. 51, additionally, 78.

7. Karl Heim, *Glauben und Denken* (Berlin: Furche Verlag, 1941), 316.

8. Karl Rahner, *Hörer des Wortes* (Munich: Kösel, 1963) 138; Rahner, *Hearers of the Word* (New York: Herder and Herder, 1969), 112.

9. Rahner, *Hörer des Wortes*, 176; Rahner, *Hearers of the Word*, 143 (my emphasis). See also Karl Rahner, *Spirit in the World*, trans. William Dÿch, S.J. (New York: Herder and Herder, 1967), 184.

10. Blondel's thesis appears in *L'action* (1893) and in *Lettre sur les exigences de la pensée contemporaine en matière d'apologétique* (1896). The method is further explained in Henri Duméry, *Blondel et la religion* (Paris: PUF, 1960), and in Louis Dupré, "Blondel's Reflection on Experience," in *A Dubious Heritage* (New York: Paulist Press, 1977), 94–107.

11. Wilhelm Windelband, "Das Heilige," in *Präluden* (1903), 357 (emphasis most likely added).

12. Martin Heidegger, *Einführung in die Metaphysik/An Introduction to Metaphysics*, trans. Ralph Manheim (New York: Doubleday, 1950), 6–7.

13. Alfred North Whitehead, *Religion in the Making* (New York: Meridian Books, 1960), 83.

14. Otto Karrer, *Das Religiöse in der Menscheit und das Christentum* (Freiburg: Herder, 1934), 134ff.

15. Albert Chapelle, *Hegel et la religion* (Paris: Editions Universitaires, 1963), 1:212–13.

ESSAY 2

An earlier version of this chapter was originally published as "The Modern Idea of Culture: Its Opposition to Its Classical and Christian Origins," in *Ebraismo, Ellenismo, Christianesimo II*, edited by Marco Olivetti, Archivo di Filosofia 53 (CEDAM, 1985), 469–83.

1. Max Wildiers, *The Theologian and His Universe* (New York: Seabury, 1982), 19–35.
2. Tullio Gregory, *Anima mundi: La filosofia di Gulielmo da Conches e la scuola di Chartres* (Florence: G. C. Sansoni, 1955).
3. Hannah Arendt, *The Human Condition* (Chicago: University of Chicago Press, 1958), 305.
4. Francis Bacon, preface to *The Great Instauration*, in Hans Jonas, *The Phenomenon of Life* (Chicago: University of Chicago Press, 1982), 11.
5. Jacques Ellul, *The Technological Society* (New York: Alfred Knopf, 1964).
6. Jonas, *Phenomenon of Life*, 210.
7. Plato, *Timaeus* 30c–d.
8. Lars Thunberg, *Microcosm and Mediator: The Theological Anthropology of Maximus the Confessor* (Lund, 1965).
9. Wildiers, *Theologian and His Universe*, 43.
10. Francis Bacon, *Works*, Vol. 3, *The Advancement of Learning*, ed. James Spedding and Robert L. Ellis (Cambridge: Cambridge University Press, 2013), 349.
11. Max Horkheimer, *The Eclipse of Reason* (New York: Seabury Press, 1974), 93.
12. Immanuel Kant, *Religion within the Limits of Reason Alone* (New York: Harper & Brothers, 1960), 79, 3–10.

ESSAY 3

An earlier version of this chapter was originally published as "The Broken Mirror: The Fragmentation of the Symbolic World," *Stanford Literature Review* (Spring–Fall 1988): 7–24.

Notes to Pages 23–32   165

1. Michel Foucault, *The Order of Things* (New York: Vintage Books, 1973), 28–29.

2. St. Bonaventure, *In Hexaemeron* 12:14.

3. Nancy Struever, *The Language of History in the Renaissance* (Princeton: Princeton University Press, 1970), 47 (Struever's italics).

4. Giovanni Francesco Pico della Mirandola, as quoted by Ernesto Grassi, in *Rhetoric as Philosophy* (Philadelphia: Pennsylvania State University Press, 1980), 60.

5. Nikolaus von Kues, *Idiota de mente*, in Vol. 2 of *Philosophisch-Theologische Werke*, ed. and trans. Renate Steiger (Hamburg: Meiner, 2002), chap. 5, 48.

6. Nikolaus von Kues, *De Beryllo*, in Vol. 3 of *Philosophisch-Theologische Werke*, ed. and trans. Karl Bormann (Hamburg: Meiner, 2002). I cite this reference with reservations. I found it in an English translation in Nancy Struever's *The Language of History in the Renaissance*, but not in my Latin edition of *De Beryllo*.

7. Hans Blumenberg, *Die Genesis der kopernikanischen Welt* (Frankfurt: Suhrkamp, 1975), 238–40.

8. J. Dagens, *Bérulle et les origines de la restauration catholique* (Paris: Desclée De Brouwer, 1952), 22. Cf. P. H. Michel, *The Cosmology of Giordano Bruno*, trans. R. E. W. Madison (Ithaca, NY: Cornell University Press, 1973), 226.

9. Giordano Bruno, *De l'infinito, universo e mondi*, in *Dialoghi italiani*, ed. Giovanni Gentile (Florence: Sansoni, n.d.), 343–537.

10. Giordano Bruno, *Spaccio de la bestia trionfante*, in Gentile, ed., *Dialoghi italiani*, 547–831.

11. Hans Blumenberg, *The Legitimacy of the Modern Age*, trans. Robert M. Wallace (Boston: MIT Press, 1983), 591.

12. Foucault, *The Order of Things*, 48–49.

13. Frank Kermode, *The Sense of an Ending: Studies in the Theory of Fiction* (Oxford: Oxford University Press, 1966), 138.

14. Fredric Jameson, *Marxism and Form* (Princeton, NJ: Princeton University Press, 1971), 173.

15. The prime example of a "novel" laden with metaphysics, aesthetic theory, theology, and a few other forms of learning remains Robert Musil, *The Man without Qualities*.

16. A master of such self-contained literature (which easily becomes tedious!) was, of course, Nabokov. To read his *Pale Fire* requires, beyond a general knowledge of the cultural universe expressed in the English language, a mental dictionary containing the various elements of the novel itself; they

refer exclusively to each other.

17. Henri Lefèbvre, *Introduction à la modernité* (Paris: Paris Éd. de Minuit, 1962), 175–76.

18. Ernest Renan, *Cahiers de jeunesse 1845–1846* (Paris: Calmann-Lévy, 1906), 105.

19. T. S. Eliot, *The Waste Land*, n.p.

ESSAY 4

An earlier version of this chapter was originally published as "On the Intellectual Sources of Modern Atheism," in *Religion and the Rise of Modern Culture* (Notre Dame, IN: University of Notre Dame Press, 2008), 41–56.

1. Étienne Gilson, *God and Philosophy* (New Haven, CT: Yale University Press, 1941), 106.

2. John Locke, *Letters*, in *The Works of John Locke*, Vol. 10 (London: Thomas Tegg, 1823); reissued by Scientia Verlag Aalen (1963).

3. John Locke, *Essay on Human Understanding*, Vol. 4, 18, 2 (emphasis added); probably from Locke, *An Essay Concerning Human Understanding*, 27th ed. (London: Balne Printer, 1836).

4. John Edwards, *Some Thoughts Concerning the Several Causes and Occasions of Atheism, Especially in the Present Age, with Some Brief Reflections on Socinianism and on a Late Book Entitled: The Reasonableness of Christianity as Delivered in the Scriptures* (London: Printed for J. Robinson . . . , 1695).

5. Locke, *Works*, 4:188.

6. Thomas Woolston, *Discourses on the Miracles of Our Saviour* (London, 1727–1729). Locke, *Works*, Vol. 4 (emphasis added); Voltaire, *Elémens de philosophie de Newton* (1738), in *Oeuvres* (Paris: De l'imprimerie de la société littéraire-typographique, 1785), Vol. 63, pt. 1, chap. 6, p. 303.

7. Voltaire, *Elémens de philosophie de Newton* (1738), in *Oeuvres*, Vol. 63, pt. 1, chap. 6.

8. Ernst Cassirer, *The Philosophy of the Enlightenment*, trans. Fritz C. A. Koeln and James P. Pettegrove (Princeton, NJ: Princeton University Press, 1951), 164 (emphasis added).

9. Jean Le Rond d'Alembert, "Discours préliminaire," in *Encyclopédie de Diderot* (1751), ed. Picaret, 15.

10. Voltaire, *Elémens de philosophie de Newton*.

11. Rene Descartes, *Méditations*, in *The Philosophical Writings of Descartes*, trans. John Cottingham (Cambridge: Cambridge University Press, 1984), 2:33.

12. Denis Diderot, *Lettre sur les aveugles*, in *Oeuvres Complètes* (Paris: Le Club Français du Livre, 1969), 2:198–99; trans. Derek Coltman, in Diderot, *Selected Writings* (New York: Macmillan, 1966), 22–23.

13. Julien Offray de La Mettrie, *L'homme machine* (*Man a Machine*) (La Salle, IL: Open Court, 1993[1912]), 50–51 (French), 122 (English).

14. David Hume, *The Natural History of Religion*: Introduction. Since so many editions of this work exist, I simply refer to the numbers of the short sections.

15. Baron d'Holbach, *The System of Nature*, trans. H. D. Robinson (New York: Burt Franklin, 1979[1868]), 170.

16. Sigmund Freud, *The Future of an Illusion*, trans. James Strachey, in *The Complete Psychological Works* (London: Hogarth Press, 1961), 21:32.

17. David Hume, *Natural History of Religion*, N14.7, Bea 83, https://davidhume.org/texts/n/14#7.

18. Michael Buckley, *To the Origins of Modern Atheism* (New Haven, CT: Yale University Press, 1987).

ESSAY 5

1. Georg Wilhelm Friedrich Hegel, *The Phenomenology of Mind*, trans. J. B. Baillie (New York: Harper and Row, 1967) (emphasis added); Hegel, *The Phenomenology of Spirit*, trans. A. V. Miller (Oxford: Clarendon Press, 1977).

2. What distinguishes the (1984–85) edition and translation is that it reprints the notes of each lecture year separately on the basis of the still-available transcripts. The translators of the English edition, working under the direction of Professor Peter Hodgson, follow the policy of the new German edition, which appeared under the direction of Walter Jaeschke with the collaboration of the English and Spanish translators.

3. Georg Wilhelm Friedrich Hegel, *Lectures on the Philosophy of Religion*, Vol. 3, *The Consummate Religion*, ed. and trans. Peter Hodgson (Berkeley: University of California Press, 1985), 77–78.

4. Hegel, *Lectures*, 3:63n.

5. Hegel, *Lectures*, 3:195.

6. Cyril O'Regan, *The Anatomy of Misremembering*: Von Balthasar's Response to Philosophical Modernity, Vol. 1, *Hegel* (Chestnut Ridge, NY: Crossroad, 2014), 204.

7. Georg Wilhelm Friedrich Hegel, *Vorlesungen über die Beweise des Dasein Gottes*, ed. Georg Lasson (Hamburg: Felix Meiner, 1966[1930]), 117; Hegel,

Lectures on the Philosophy of Religion, trans. E. B. Speirs and J. Burdon Sanderson (1895), 3:303–4.

ESSAY 6

1. Cornelio Fabro, *Participation et Causalité* (Louvain: Publications universitaires de Louvain, 1961).

2. In a Note (*Zusatz*) attached to §573 of the *Encyclopedia of Philosophy*, Hegel explicitly states that the speculative nature of his treatment is due to its religious origin. Only through revelation has the metaphysics of Being attained its full meaning, namely, God in his self-relatedness. All finite entities participate in that divine Being: "The entire course of philosophy and more specifically of the *Logic* has not only disclosed this distinction [between religion and philosophy] but also judged, or rather the nature of this distinction established, in those categories through which it has developed and allowed itself to be judged."

3. Jean-Paul Sartre, "Introduction," in *L'être et le néant*, 2nd ed. (Paris, Librairie Gallimard, 1943), n.p.

4. Joseph Maréchal, *Le point de départ de la métaphysique* (Louvain: Museum Lessianum, 1944).

ESSAY 7

An earlier version of this chapter was originally published as "Evil—A Religious Mystery: A Plea for a More Inclusive Model of Theodicy," *Faith and Philosophy: Journal of the Society of Christian Philosophers* 7, no. 3 (1990): 261–80.

1. Arthur Schopenhauer, "'Supplemental' to Chapter 18," in *The World as Will and Idea*, trans. R. B. Haldane and J. Kemp (London: Kegan Paul, 1906).

2. Immanuel Kant, *Werke* (Berlin: Akademie, n.d.), 8:255.

3. I have developed this point in Louis Dupré, "Transcendance et objectivisme," *Archivio di Filosofia* 45 (1977): 265–72.

4. John Hick, *Evil and the God of Love* (San Francisco: Harper & Row, 1978), 70–78.

5. Cf. the critical analysis in William Rowe, "Rationalistic Theology and Some Principles of Explanation," *Faith and Philosophy* 1, no. 4 (1984): 361.

6. Leszek Kolakowski, *Religion* (Oxford: Oxford University Press, 1982), 25.

7. Henri Bergson, *The Two Sources of Morality and Religion*, trans. Ashley

Andra and Cloudesly Brereton (Garden City, NY: Doubleday, 1951), 261. See also the pertinent remarks in James Felt, "God's Choice: Reflections on Evil in a Created World," *Faith and Philosophy* 1, no. 4 (1984): 370–77.

8. Antony Flew, "Divine Omnipotence and Human Freedom," in *New Essays in Philosophical Theology*, ed. Antony Flew and Alasdair MacIntyre (London: SCM Press, 1965), 152.

9. J. L. Mackie, "Evil and Omnipotence," *Mind* 64, no. 254 (1955): 200–212; reprinted in *God and Evil*, ed. Nelson Pike (Englewood Cliffs, NJ: Prentice Hall, 1964), 46–60, see 57.

10. See Alfred North Whitehead, *Religion in the Making* (New York: Meridian Books, 1961), 92.

11. Nicholas Berdyaev, *The Divine and the Human*, trans. R. M. French (London: Geoffrey Bles, 1948), 92.

12. David Hume, *Dialogues concerning Natural Religion*, ed. Norman Kemp Smith (Indianapolis: Library of the Liberal Arts, 1947), 202.

13. I owe the comparison with Newman's "illative sense" (which was undoubtedly influenced by Hume) to my former student Stephen Fields.

14. John Stuart Mill, *An Examination of Sir William Hamilton's Philosophy* (London: Longmans, Green, 1872), 128.

15. Alfred North Whitehead, *Process and Reality* (New York: Macmillan, 1929), 523.

16. Whitehead, *Process and Reality*, 374.

17. Peter Bertocci, *The Goodness of God* (Washington, DC: University Press of America, 1981), 267. John Dewey made the same point in a more general way: "No mode of action can ... give anything approaching absolute certitude; it provides insurance but no assurance"; see Dewey, *The Quest for Certainty* (New York: G. P. Putnam's Sons-Capricorn Books, 1960[1929]), 33.

18. Jacques Maritain, *God and the Permission of Evil*, trans. Joseph Evans (Milwaukee: Bruce, 1966), 86.

19. A more extensive discussion appears in Louis Dupré, *The Other Dimension* (New York: Doubleday, 1972), chap. 3, "Religious Faith and Philosophical Reflection."

20. Alvin Plantinga, "The Probabilistic Argument from Evil," *Philosophical Studies* 35 (1979): 46–47, argued for this position.

21. Luigi Pareyson, "*La sofferenza inutile in Dostoevsky*," *Giornale di metafisica* 4 (1982): 123–70.

22. Cf. Hans Jonas, *The Gnostic Religion* (Boston: Beacon Press, 1963); Cyril O'Regan, *Gnostic Return in Modernity* (Albany: State University Press of New York, 2001), and O'Regan, *The Heterodox Hegel* (Albany: State University Press of New York, 1994), chaps. 4 and 5.

23. Karl Jaspers, *Philosophy*, trans. E. B. Ashton (Chicago: Chicago University Press, 1971), 3:90–116.

ESSAY 8

An earlier version of this chapter appeared as "Intimations of Immortality," *Filosofia e religione di fornte all morte Archivio di Filosofia* 49 (1981): 259–77.

1. William E. Hocking, *The Meaning of God in Human Experience* (New Haven, CT: Yale University Press, 1961), 49.
2. John Baillie, *And the Life Everlasting* (New York: Oxford University Press, 1934), 204.
3. Jacques Maritain, *The Range of Reason* (New York: Scribner, 1952), 62.
4. H. H. Price, "Survival and the Idea of Another World," *Proceedings of the Society for Psychical Research* 50, no. 182 (1953): 11–25; reprinted in John Hick, *Classical and Contemporary Readings in the Philosophy of Religion* (New York: Prentice Hall, 1964), 364–86. I shall refer to this reprint.
5. J. P. Strawson, *Individuals* (New York: Doubleday, 1963), 97–98.
6. Strawson, *Individuals*, 112. On Schlick's position, see Virgil C. Aldrich, "Messrs. Schlick and Ayer on Immortality," in *Readings in Philosophical Analysis*, ed. Herbert Feigl and Wilfrid Sellars (New York: Appleton-Century-Croft, 1949), 172.
7. Roland Puccetti, *Persons* (New York: Herder, 1969), 5.
8. Puccetti, *Persons*, 12–15.
9. Joseph Maréchal, *Studies in the Psychology of the Mystics*, trans. Algar Thorold (New York: Magi Books, 1964), 55–145.
10. Henri Bergson, *Matter and Memory*, trans. Margaret Paul and W. Scott Palmer (London: Macmillan, 1911), xiii.
11. William James, *Human Immortality* (Boston: Houghton-Mifflin, 1898), 22.
12. Maurice Merleau-Ponty, *Phenomenology of Perception*, trans. Colin Smith (New York: The Humanities Press, 1962), 431; "this" and "for-itself" are in italics in the original; italics added for "my."
13. Merleau-Ponty, *Phenomenology of Perception*, 93.
14. William E. Hocking, *The Meaning of Immortality in Human Experience* (New York: Harper, 1957), 233–34.
15. 1 Cor. 15:8. Cf. Baillie, *And the Life Everlasting*, 154.
16. Derek Parfit, "Personal Identity," *The Philosophical Review* 80, no. 1 (1971): 3–27.
17. Terence Penelhum, "The Importance of Self-Identity," *Journal of Philosophy* 68, no. 20 (1971): 689.

18. Hocking, *Meaning of Immortality in Human Experience*, 56.

19. Alan Donagan, "Spinoza's Proof of Immortality," in *Spinoza: A Collection of Critical Essays*, ed. Marjorie Grene (Notre Dame, IN: Notre Dame University Press, 1973), 241–59.

ESSAY 9

1. Edmund Husserl, *Ideen I*, in *Husserliana III*, trans. W. R. Boyce Gibson (The Hague: Martinus Nijhof, 1950), 128; in English as *Ideas* (London: Allen and Unwin, 1958), 162.

2. I found it, partly read, in Husserl's library, which, since the war, has been at the University of Leuven.

3. Gerardus van der Leeuw, *Religion in Essence and Manifestation*, trans. J. E. Turner (London: Allen and Unwin, 1938; repr. New York: Harper and Row, 1963), Vol. 2, chap. 109, p. 682.

4. Max Scheler, *On the Eternal in Man*, trans. Bernard Noble (New York: Harper and Brothers, 1960[1921;1954]), 134.

5. Louis Dupré, "Husserl's Intentions of Experience," in *A Dubious Heritage: Studies in the Philosophies of Religion after Kant* (New York: Newman Books, 1973), 75–93.

6. Henri Duméry, *La foi n'est pas un cri*, 2nd ed. (Paris: Presses universitaires de France, 1957). An English anthology of representative texts is *Faith and Philosophy*, ed. Louis Dupré, trans. Stephen McNierney and M. Benedict Murphy (New York: Herder, 1968).

ESSAY 10

An earlier version of this essay was originally published as "Truth in Religion and Truth of Religion," *Teodicea oggi? Atti del Colloquio 1988 dell'Instituto di Studi Filosofici di Roma*, Archivo di Filosofia 56 (1998): 493–518.

1. Mohandas K. Gandhi, *Yeraoda Mandir*, in *Gandhi: Selected Writings* (New York: Harper, 1972), 41.

2. He himself coined a new word based on truth-being to articulate his life project: *satyagraha*. Because *agraha* means "firmness, determination," we could understand it as "remaining faithful to the truth of being." For Gandhi, truth implies a single-minded devotion to authenticity in speaking, thinking, acting, and a willingness to suffer persecution for it. Only after having pursued it morally may we hope that it will reveal itself cognitively. Cf. D. M. Datta, *The Philosophy of Mahatma Gandhi* (Madison: University of Wisconsin Press, 1953), 128.

3. Augustine, *Confessions* 5.3. The reason is eloquently stated in *De vera religione:* "There is no lack of value or benefit in the contemplation of the beauty of the heavens, the arrangement of the stars, the radiant crown of light, the change of day and night, the monthly courses of the moon, the fourfold tempering of the year to match the four elements, the powerful force of seeds from which derive the forms of measure and nature in its kind. Yet such a consideration must not pander to a vain and passing curiosity, but must be turned into a stairway to the immortal and enduring" (#52).

4. Not until the high Middle Ages did Western theologians clearly accept *all* knowledge as intrinsically good and destined to find its fulfillment in God.

5. Anselm, *Cur Deus Homo?*, trans. Jasper Hopkins and Herbert Richardson (Toronto: University Press, 1976), bk. 1, chap. 2.

6. On the ambivalence of Anselm's attitude, cf. William Collinge, "Monastic Life as a Context for Religious Understanding in St. Anselm," *American Benedictine Review* 35, no. 4 (1984): 378–88.

7. "For Thomas, neither Christian doctrine nor the miracles that attest to it would teach man anything without the interior *instinctus et attractus doctrinae* (*In John*, c. 6, I. 4, n. 7; c. 15, I. 5, n. 5; *In Rom.* c. 8, I. 6), which he also calls *inspiratio interna* and *experimentum*"; Hans Urs von Balthasar, *The Glory of the Lord* (San Francisco: Ignatius, 1983), 1:162.

8. Edmund Husserl, *Logische Untersuchungen* (Halle: Niemeyer, 1913), 1:228 (emphasis added).

9. Harold Joachim, *The Nature of Truth* (Oxford: Clarendon, 1969 [1906]), 68. The importance of Joachim's expression lies in its distinguishing "the determining characteristic of the 'significant whole'" from a logical nexus that secures a certain cohesion of various elements without intrinsically relating them.

10. C. D. Broad, *Religion, Philosophy, and Psychical Research: Selected Essays* (London: Routledge and Kegan Paul, 1953), 235.

11. Martin Heidegger, *On the Essence of Truth*, in *Basic Writings*, ed. David F. Krell and trans. John Sallis (New York: Harper, 1976), 129–33.

12. Hans-Georg Gadamer, *Wahrheit und Methode*, 2nd ed. (Tübingen: Mohr, 1965), xxv.

13. Georg Wilhelm Friedrich Hegel, *Vorlesungen* über *die Philosophie der Religion*, ed. Walter Jaeschke (Hamburg: Felix Meiner, 1981), and Hegel, *Lectures on the Philosophy of Religion*, Part 1, *The Concept of Religion*, ed. and trans. Peter C. Hodgson (Berkeley: University of California Press, 1984), 1.

14. Max Scheler, *On the Eternal in Man*, trans. Bernard Noble (New York: Harper & Brothers, 1960), 261; Gerardus van der Leeuw, *Religion in Essence and Manifestation*, trans. J. E. Turner (New York: Harper, 1960), 61.

ESSAY 11

An earlier version of this chapter was published as "The Enigma of Religious Art," *Review of Metaphysics* 29, no. 1 (1975): 27–44.

1. F. David Martin, *Art and the Religious Experience* (Lewisburg, PA: Bucknell University Press, 1972), 69.

2. Georg Wilhelm Friedrich Hegel, *Vorlesungen über die Ästhetik: Jubiläumausgabe* (Frommann-Holzboog, 1964–71), 7:32. Comments in Karsten Harries, "Hegel on the Future of Art," *Review of Metaphysics* 27 (1974): 677–99.

3. Ernst Bloch, *Das Prinzip Hoffnung* (Frankfurt: Suhrkamp, 1959), 248 (my translation).

4. Exceptions are more apparent than real. Thus when a French art critic hesitated to call El Greco a religious painter, he referred to the Spanish artist's ability to evoke religious depth, not to his personal feelings while painting a religious subject: "He knew the sense of mystery, but he never entered it himself: he underwent its fascination and possessed the marvelous power to render this fascination sensible. But it all leaves one outside, while this is a realm which one must enter oneself"; Marie-Alain Couturier, *Art Sacré* (Paris, 1937), 89.

5. Benjamin Rowland, selected by, *Evolution of the Buddha Image* (New York: The Asia Society, 1963).

6. Gerardus van der Leeuw, *Sacred and Profane Beauty: The Holy in Art*, trans. David E. Green (New York: Holt, Rinehart and Winston, 1963), 206–7.

7. Walter Oakeshott, *The Mosaics of Rome* (Greenwich: New York Graphic Society, 1967), 61.

8. André Grabar, *The Art of the Byzantine Empire* (New York: Greystone Press, 1967), 28.

9. Dietrich Seckel, *The Art of Buddhism* (New York: Greystone Press, 1968), 186–87; 204–5.

10. *Enchiridion Symbolorum*, eds. Heinrich Denziger et al. (Barcelona: Herder, 1957), no. 337.

11. In depicting religious subjects, Rembrandt selected the moment of inner drama—such as Abraham answering Isaac's question about the sacrificial victim—rather than the outer event.

12. Karsten Harries, *The Meaning of Modern Art* (Evanston, IL: Northwestern University Press, 1968), 107.

13. Cf. Jacques Claes, *De dingen en hun ruimte* (Antwerp: De Nederlandsche Boekhandel, 1970), 91–208.

14. Michael Fried, "Art and Objecthood," in *Minimal Art*, ed. Gregory Battock (Berkeley: University of California Press, 1968), 147.

15. The disappearance of the subject has, quite naturally, led to a decline of the subjective perspective. A multiplicity of centers and perspectives has

come to replace the one center of the Renaissance. Often, particularly in architecture, the viewer feels disoriented, unable to synthesize the complexity of his experience.

ESSAY 12

An earlier version of this chapter was published as "Ritual: The Sacralization of Time," *Revue de l'Université d'Ottawa* 55 (October–December 1985): 261–69. Reproduced with permission from the University of Ottawa Press.

    1. Friedrich Nietzsche, *Thus Spoke Zarathustra*, in *The Portable Nietzsche*, ed. Walter Kaufman (New York: Viking Press, 1956), 281.

    2. Virgil, *Eclogues* 4.34–56.

    3. By this thesis, implied in Karl Kerenyi's studies on Roman religion, Mario Perniola forcefully opposed Eliade's intrinsically mythical interpretation of ritual, in a paper on Roman rites, in Perniola, "Mort et naissance dans la pensée rituelle," in *Filosofia di fronte alla morte* (Padua: Cedam, 1981), 461–68.

    4. Ernst Cassirer, *The Philosophy of Symbolic Forms* (New Haven, CT: Yale University Press, 1955), 2:39.

    5. Mircea Eliade, *The Myth of Eternal Return* (New York: Pantheon, 1954), 140.

    6. Henri Hubert and Marcel Mauss, *Mélanges d'histoire des religions* (Paris: Felix Alcan, 1909), 213ff.

    7. Victor Turner, *Dramas, Fields and Metaphors* (Ithaca, NY: Cornell University Press, 1974), 52–53.

    8. Louis Dupré, *The Other Dimension* (New York: Seabury Press, 1979), 128.

    9. Cornelis Verhoeven, "Wat is een ritus?," in *Rondom de leegte* (Utrecht: Ambo, 1965), 9–49.

    10. Paul Claudel, *La Ville* (Mercure de France, 1967), 348.

    11. Richard Rubenstein, *After Auschwitz* (Indianapolis: Bobbs-Merrill, 1966), 97.

    12. Peter Berger, *Facing up to Modernity* (New York: Basic Books, 1977), 74. Emile Durkheim made the same observation around the turn of the century when he described the modern individual's life as guided by "a restless movement, a planless . . . self-development, an aim of living which has no criterion of value and in which happiness lies always in the future, and never in any present achievement"; Durkheim, *Le suicide* (Paris: Felix Alcan, 1897),

quoted in Erich Fromm, *The Sane Society* (New York: Holt, Rinehart, Winston, 1955), 191.

13. It was nevertheless Euripides who wrote the drama that most directly revived the ancient rite. Still, as Jan Kott has observed, even in *The Bacchae*, two separate and contradictory structures exist—one sacred, the other profane: "The eating of the god, the rite of death and renewal, becomes in the end a cruel killing of son by mother. . . . Dionysus has been torn to pieces *in illo tempore*, in cosmic time; the dismemberment of Pentheus is carried into historic time, made visible in violent close-up"; Jan Kott, *The Eating of the Gods* (New York: Random House, 1970), 207–20.

ESSAY 13

An earlier version of this chapter was originally published as "On the Natural Desire to See God," *Radical Orthodoxy: Theology, Philosophy, Politics* 1, nos. 1 and 2 (2012): 81–94.

1. W. D. Ross, *Aristotle: A Complete Exposition of His Works and Thought* (New York: Meridian Books, 1959), 147.

2. Georges Cottier, O.P., "Désir naturel de voir Dieu," *Gregorianum* 78, no. 4 (1997): 695–96.

3. Nicolas of Cusa, *De filiatione dei* (*On Being a Son of God*), III.64.

4. Cusanus, *Idiotae de mente*, VII, 106, in *On Wisdom and Knowledge*, trans. Jasper Hopkins, (Minneapolis: Arthur J. Banning Press, 1996), 237.

5. Cusanus, *Idiotae de sapientia*, I, 10, in *Nikolaus von Kues, Werke*, ed. Paul Wilpert (Berlin: Walter De Gruyter, 1967), 1:220.

6. Cusanus, *Idiotae de mente*, IX, 123, in *Nikolaus von Kues, Werke*, 1:262.

7. Louis Dupré, "The Mystical Theology of Cusanus's *De Visione Dei*," in *Eros and Eris: Liber Amicorum for Adriaan Peperzak*, ed. Paul van Tongeren et al. (Dordrecht: Kluwer, 1992), 105–17.

8. A summary and defense of the Scholastic efforts appears in the massive study by Lawrence Feingold, *The Natural Desire of God according to St. Thomas Aquinas and His Interpreters* (Rome: Appolinare Studies, 2001). According to Feingold, the recent attempts by Henri de Lubac and his followers to restore Aquinas's alleged position, while ignoring the work of the commentators during half a millennium, rests on a mistaken principle. Feingold's study starts with a careful analysis of Aquinas's texts. A lengthy analysis of the commentaries written by Scotus, Denys the Carthusian, Caietanus, and Suarez follows it. I have profited greatly from Aaron Richess's intelligent analysis of Feingold's work.

9. Cf. Heidegger, *Gelassenheit* (Pfullingen: Günther Neske, 1959).
10. Max Scheler, *Vom Ewigen im Menschen* (Bern: A. Francke, 1954); in English, *On the Eternal in Man*, trans. Bernard Noble (New York: Harper and Brothers, 1960), 261.
11. Karl Rahner, *Hörer des Wortes* (München: Kösel Verlag, 1963), 176.

ESSAY 14

1. Exod. 3:14.
2. Robert Spaemann, "Mysticism and Enlightenment," in *The Crisis of Religious Language* (New York: Herder and Herder, 1973), 70–83 (emphasis added).
3. *Tractatus Logico Philosophicus*: Ludwig Wittgenstein, *Logisch-Philosophische Abhandlung*, trans. D. F. Pears and B. F. McGuinnes (New York Routledge and Kegan Pau, 1961), 147.
4. Jacques Maritain, *Les degrés du savoir* (Paris: Desclée de Brouwer, 1946), 515–18.
5. Jacques Maritain, "L'Expérience mystique naturelle et le vide," *Études Carmélitaines* (October 1938).
6. Joseph Maréchal, S.J., *Études sur la psychologie des mystiques*, 2 vols. (Paris: Desclée de Brouwer, 1924); Maréchal, "On the Feeling of Presence," in *Studies in the Psychology of the Mystics* (London: Burns, Oates and Washbourne, 1927), 57–145.
7. William Ernest Hocking, *The Meaning of Immortality in Human Experience* (New York: Harper, 1957), 44–59.
8. Of course, much of what Hocking writes about the two souls might have been more clearly expressed in the language of Freud. But he preferred to stay with the mystical expression and deliberately chose to avoid Freud's underlying materialism.
9. Wilhelm Bousset, "Die Himmelsreise der Seele," *Archiv fur Religionswissenschaft* 4 (1901): 253ff.
10. Erwin Rohde, *Psyche*, trans. W. B. Hillis (New York: Harper Torchbooks, 1966), 264, 291.
11. *The Bhagavad Gita*, trans. Eliot Deutsch (New York: Holt, Rinehart and Winston, 1968), 2, 29 (p. 49). R. C. Zaehner translates the term *ascaryam* (marvelous) as "*By a rare privilege* may someone behold it . . . ."; *The Bhagavad Gita* (New York: Oxford University Press, 1969), 50; Rudolf Otto reads "*As wholly other* does one gaze upon it . . . ," in *The Idea of the Holy* (London: Oxford University Press, 1925), 195.

12. Jan van Ruusbroec, *The Mirror of Eternal Blessedness*, in *The Spiritual Espousals and Other Works*, trans. James A. Wiseman, O.S.B. (New York: Paulist Press, 1985), 238.

13. Plotinus, *Enneads* 6.9.11.

14. John of the Cross, *The Dark Night of the Soul*, 2.23.11. Also see *The Living Flame of Love* (trans. A. Peers), stanza 2.16.

15. *The Living Flame of Love*, stanza 2.7.

16. Johann Tauler, O.P., *Sign Posts to Perfection*, ed. and trans. Elizabeth Strakosch (St. Louis: Herder, 1958), 95–96.

17. Pseudo-Dionysius, *Mystical Theology*, in Migne, *PG* 3:1009.

18. *Obras Completas de san Ignacio de Loyola* (Madrid: La Editorial Católica, 1952), 49–50, translated into English by Elmer O'Brien, in *Varieties of Mystic Experience* (New York: Holt, Rinehart, Winston, 1964), 247.

19. John of the Cross, *The Ascent of Mount Carmel*, 2.23.3.

20. Teresa of Avila, *Relations*, in *Works*, 1:364 (emphasis added).

21. John of the Cross, *Dark Night of the Soul*, 2.23.11.

22. Jacques Maritain, *Redeeming the Time* (London: Geoffrey Bles, 1946), 242.

ESSAY 15

1. Vincent of Aggsbach, his main opponent, had also criticized his earlier *De docta ignorantia*. For the historical context of the beginning of *De visione Dei*, I have followed Jasper Hopkins's "Interpretive Study," which prefaces (91–97) his translation in Hopkins, *Nicholas of Cusa's Dialectical Mysticism: Text, Translation, and Interpretive Study of "De visione dei"* (Minneapolis: The Arthur J. Banning Press, 1988[1985]). I follow Hopkins's translation.

2. Prologue to *De visione Dei*, text and trans. Hopkins, 112–15.

3. Birgit Helander, *Die visio intellectualis als Erkenntnisweg und -ziel des Nicolaus Cusanus* (Stockholm: Almqvist & Wiksel, 1988), chaps. 1 and 7, has shown this intellectual teleology.

4. The following passage taken from a dialogue with a "Pagan" shows this. *Pagan*: Nothing then is God? *Christian*: He is not nothing, for nothing still bears the name "nothing." *Pagan*: If God is not nothing, then He is something? *Christian*: No, because something is not identical to everything. God is no more something than everything"; *De deo abscondito* (*The Hidden God*), ed. Elisabeth Bohnenstaedt (Hamburg: Felix Meiner, 1967), #9.

5. Cf. Rudolf Haubst, "Albert, wie Cusanus ihn sah," in *Albertus Magnus Doctor Universalis 1280–1980*, ed. Gerbert Meyer, O.P., and Albert Zimmerman

(Mainz: Grünewald, 1980). On the variations in the acceptance of Platonic philosophy by Western mystics, see Bernard McGinn, *The Presence of God: A History of Western Christian Mysticism*, 3 vols. (New York: Crossroad, 1991–2005).

6. Herbert Wackerzapp, *Der Einfluss Meister Eckharts auf die ersten philosophischen Schriften des Nikolaus von Kues (1440–1450)* (Münster: Aschendorff, 1962).

7. I owe this information to Peter Casarella, and saw it confirmed in the Carthusian's *Tractatus de Donis Sancti Spiritus*, 2.13, in *Opera*, Vol. 41.

8. Rudolf Haubst, "Der junge Cusanus war im Jahre 1428 zu Handschriften-Studien in Paris," *Mitteilungen und Forschungen der Cusanus-Gesellschaft* 14 (1980): 198–205. See also Theodor Pindl-Buechel, "The Relationship between the Epistemologies of Ramon Lull and Nicholas of Cusa," *American Catholic Philosophical Quarterly* 64 (Winter 1990): 73–87.

9. Nicholas of Cusa, *De dato patris luminum* (Hamburg: Felix Meiner, 1932–). Cf. also Siegfried Dangelmayr, *Gotteserkenntnis und Gottesbegriff in den philosophischen Schriften des Nikolaus von Kues* (Meisenheim-am-Glan: Anton Hain, 1969), 197–204.

10. E. Bohnenstaedt, "Einführung," in *Nikolaus von Kues: Drei Schriften vom verborgenem Gott* (Hamburg: Felix Meiner, 1958), xix.

11. For a comparison of Cusanus's notion of form with that of St. Thomas, see Dangelmayr, *Gotteserkentnis*, 208–14.

12. Although unambiguously in the Neoplatonic camp with his theory of *form*, Cusanus nevertheless insists that each mind is created singularly and individually: "Factum autem semper est singulare et implurificabile, sicut omne individuum" (*De venatione sapientiae*, chap. 37). Hildegard Menzel-Ragner therefore calls the cardinal's concept of individuality *durchaus christlich*. See the introduction to the German edition of *Idiota de mente: Der Laie über den Geist* (*The Layman on Spirit*) (Hamburg: Meiner, 1949), 50.

INDEX

A
Absolute: consciousness of, 54; expressive nature of, 99; good and evil in, 74–75; Hegelian philosophy of, x, xi, 57, 58; Neoplatonic theology of, 93; personalist interpretation of, 71; self-identity of, 56
Absolute Spirit, xii, 49, 50, 53
abstractionist paintings, 123, 124
Aeschylus, 132
Akhenaton, king of Egypt, 119
Alberti, Leon Battista, 29
angels, 14
Anselm of Canterbury, on quest for truth, 101–2
Arendt, Hannah, 17, 19
Aristotle: on *catharsis*, 132; *De anima*, 136; definition of God, 72; on forms, 13; idea of soul, 142; on knowledge, 18; legacy of, xi, xvi; *Nicomachean Ethics*, 136; *Peri Philosophias*, 14; *Physics*, 136; view of philosophy and religion, 1
art: criterion of, 28, 29; dehumanization of, 122–23; feelings expressed in, 116; fundamental principle of medieval, 24; mission of, 30; ontological vision of, xiv–xv, 114–15; self-sufficiency of the work of, 122; viewer and, 28, 121–22, 123. *See also* religious art
atheism: genesis of, 35, 40; meaning of, 35; religion and, 45; studies of, x, 43; transition to, 41

Augustine, Bishop of Hippo, Saint: *City of God*, 15; on God's creation, 64–65; on God's indifference to the suffering of creatures, 70; rejection of philosophical learning, 100, 172n3; on truth, 100–101, 103
Avicenna, 36, 56, 104

B
Bacon, Francis, 17–18, 20, 123
Balthasar, Hans Urs von, 139, 140
Baroque culture, 119, 121
Barth, Karl, 95
Baudelaire, Charles, 32
Bauer, Bruno, 52
Baur, Ferdinand Christian, 49
Beauvoir, Simone de, 77
Being: all-comprehensive idea of, 58; finite and infinite, 72; metaphysics of, 56, 59; philosophical study of, 56, 59, 104; pre-apprehension of, 4; transcendent, 104
Berdyaev, Nikolai, 69
Bergson, Henri, 67, 79
Bernard of Clairvaux, 15
Bertocci, Peter: *The Goodness of God*, 70; interpretation of the Absolute, 71
Bérulle, Pierre de, 27
Bhagavad Gita, 148
Biel, Gabriel, 146
Bloch, Ernst, 115, 118
Blondel, Maurice, 4, 5, 59, 71, 140
Boccaccio, Giovanni, 25

body: consciousness and, 79; of
    Jesus, 82; meaning of the term,
    82; memory and, 79; mind and,
    79–80, 85–86, 87; in theories of
    immortality, 80
Boethius, Anicius, 14
Borobudur temple in Java, 118
Britten, Benjamin, 130
Broad, C. D., 108
Bruno, Giordano: idea of the universe,
    27; view of creation, 16–17
Buckley, Michael, x; *To the Origins of
    Modern Atheism*, 43
Buddha statues, 118, 119, 120
Byron, George Gordon: *Don Juan*, 31
Byzantine mosaics, 119, 120

C
Calvin, John, 65, 146
Caravaggio, 120
Casel, Odo, 129
catharsis, 132
Catherine of Siena, 149
causal dependence, 44
causal determinism, 65
causality, 40, 57, 65, 135. *See also* divine
    causality
Cézanne, Paul, 121
Chagall, Mark, 124
Chapelle, Albert, 8
Chinese landscape paintings, 118
Christian faith: as "necessary hy-
    pothesis," 5; rites of, 129
Cicero: *Hortensius*, 100
Claudel, Paul, 130
Clement of Alexandria, 100
cognition, 17, 136
coherence, 107–9
Collingwood, R. G., 114
comedy, 51
computer, 19
connatural knowledge, 147
consciousness, 79, 89
contemplation, 142
Copernicus, Nicolaus: *Revolutiones*, 27
cosmos, theories of, 13–14, 17, 27
Cottier, Georges, 136
creation: ancient religions view of, 158;
    causal model of, 21; meaning
    of, 57; medieval view of, 17, 20;
    monotheist concept of, 159. *See
    also* divine creation
creative insecurity, 71
Critique of Pure Reason (Kant), 21
Crusaders, 50
Cullmann, Oscar, 80
Cusanus. *See* Nicholas of Cusa

D
Dante Alighieri: *De monarchia*, 14;
    humanism of, 15; on language,
    25–26
deism, 36, 37, 38–40, 41
de Kooning, Willem, 123
de Lubac, Henri, xvii, 139, 175n8
Denis the Carthusian, 153, 155
Descartes, René: on infinite horizon,
    141; proof for God's existence,
    xvii; theory of universe, 16; *Third
    Meditation*, xvii; view of causality,
    40
desire: fulfillment of, 137; for life after
    death, 76; of seeing God, 139, 140;
    for spiritual knowledge, 137
Dialogues concerning Natural Religion
    (Hume), 69
Diderot, Denis: on origin of life, 40–41;
    on self-moving cosmos, 17; spiri-
    tual development of, 43–44; the-
    ism of, x
Dionysius, 146; *Mystical Theology*, 153
disclosure, concept of, 109–10, 111
divine causality, 65
divine creation, 44, 66, 135
divine light, 119–20
divine predestination, 65
Donagan, Alan, 86
Don Quixote (Cervantes), 30
Dostoevsky, Fyodor: *The Brothers Kara-
    mazov*, 74
doxic modality, 111
Duccio, 123
Duméry, Henri, viii, xiii, 2, 92, 93, 94
Duns Scotus, John, 3
Dupré, Louis: on aesthetic and religious
    experience, xiv; career of, xix;

hypothesis of "inverted analogy," xix; on idea of God, x, xi–xii; interpretation of Cusanus, xviii–xix; legacy of, viii, xx; *Metaphysics and Culture*, ix; on modern atheism, x; on mysticism, xvi; on nature of truth, xiv; on phenomenological method, xiii–xiv; philosophical journey of, vii–viii; on possibility of God, xvii; relationship to Hegel, x–xi; on religious art, xv; on ritual, xv; on ritualization of time, xiv, xv–xvi; on Spirit, xi; study of the mystics, xvii–xviii; theory of the symbol, ix, xiv
Durkheim, Émile, 128, 174n12

E
Easter rite, 129–30
Eckhart, Meister, 56, 145, 153, 154, 157, 158
Edwards, John, 38
efficient causality, 135
egological reduction, 93
Egyptian pyramids, 118
eidetic reduction, 93, 96
El Greco, 119, 173n4
Eliade, Mircea, 92, 174n3
Emerson, Ralph Waldo, xix
Enlightenment, 51
Epicurus, 35
Eucharist, 129
Euripides, 132, 175n13
evil: denial of, 63; freedom and, 69; God and, 62, 70; magnitude of, 61–62; in monotheism, possibility of, 63–64, 74–75; Neoplatonic interpretation of, 64; origin and significance of, 63, 74; overcoming of, 63–64; reversal to goodness, 73

F
Fabro, Cornelio, 58
faith: disclosure of, 111; gnostic drive of, 8; intellect and, 159–60; metaphysical implications of, viii, 6; philosophy and, 1–9; as source of meaning, 55

Farabi, Abu Nasr Muhammad al-, 36
fear, 42
Feingold, Lawrence, 175n8
Fichte, Johann Gottlieb, 35, 58
Ficino, Marsilio, 36, 139, 143
fideism, 69
finite beings, 56–57, 67
finite freedom, 68
Fink, Eugen, 94
Flew, Antony, 67, 68
Florensky, Pavel, 146
form, 13, 158
formal causality, 135
Foucault, Michel, 30
Fourth Council of Constantinople, 120
Francis of Assisi, 15
freedom, 21, 67, 68, 69
Frei, Hans, xvii
Freud, Sigmund, 43, 176n8
future, North American turn to, 131–32

G
Gadamer, Hans-Georg, xiv, xv, 110
Galilei, Galileo, 16, 29
Gandhi, Mahatma, 99, 171n2 (essay 10)
Gelassenheit (resignation), 144
Gerson, Jean, 152
Gilson, Etienne, 7, 37
gnosis, 5, 8, 53, 100
God: as absolute form, 157; *a priori* opposition to the idea of, 21, 141; Being of, 56–57, 71, 72, 155–56, 157; Christian doctrine of, 157; creative act of, 56, 57, 65, 72; efficacious grace of, 65; eternal wisdom of, 138; as invisible source of all the visible, 157; limits of metaphysical knowledge of, 3–4; love of, 159, 160; in modern philosophy, x, xiii, 91–92, 162n13; monotheist idea of, 93–94; natural desire for, xix, 135, 136, 141; omnipotence of, 16, 65–66; passivity of, xi–xii, 71, 72, 75; proofs of the existence of, 3, 5, 39, 58, 63; as pure actuality, xii; relation to the world, 70, 144; response to the creature's initiative,

God *(cont.)*
    72–73; seeing-as-creating, 156–57; as Spirit, 51, 52, 54; suffering, 71; transcendent, 2; unity between creatures and, 63, 156; will and essence of, 66–67
Goethe, Johann Wolfgang von: on art and religion, 114; *Faust*, 118; on God, 74; *Wilhelm Meister*, 30–31
good, 65
Gorky, Arshile, 123
Gothic cathedral, symbolic interpretation of, 23
Grassi, Ernesto, ix
Greek mythology, 51, 126
Greek philosophy, 13, 143
Greek sculptures, 118
Gregory Nazianzen, 20
Gregory of Nyssa, 20; "On the Creation of Man," 125
Grünewald, Matthias: *Crucifixion*, 119
Guyon, Jeanne, 144

H
hallucinations, 79
Harries, Karsten, 121
Hegel, Georg Wilhelm Friedrich: on Christian religion, 52; concept of the Trinity, 53, 59; critique of, xi; on Crusaders, 50; on disclosure of religious truth, 110–11; on faith, 8; on God as Spirit, 52, 54; on Holy Spirit, 49, 50, 53; idea of Being, 58–59, 168n2 (essay 6); idea of the Absolute, x, xi, xii, 58; *Lectures on the Philosophy of Religion*, 52; on overcoming evil, 61; *The Phenomenology of Spirit*, xi, 50, 51–52; on philosophy, 7; on proofs of the existence of God, 3; on religion and philosophy, viii, 49–50, 53, 110; on revelation, 7; on theology and philosophy, 47
Heidegger, Martin: *Being and Time*, 59; denial of transcendence, xiv; on God, 6; idea of Being, 59; on language, ix; on link of philosophy to mysticism, 144–45; on primary task of philosophy, 140; on truth, 19, 109
heliocentric theory, 27
henological reduction, 93, 94
Herbert of Cherbury, 38
Héring, Jean, 92
Hessen, Johannes, 2
Hick, John, 64
Hinduism, 158
historical novel, 31
Hocking, William Ernest, xii–xiii, 76, 81, 84, 86, 176n8
Hodgson, Peter, 167n2
Holbach, Paul-Henri Thiry, Baron d', x, 42
Holy Spirit, 53, 54
Hopkins, Jasper, 151
Horkheimer, Max, 20
Hugo, Victor: on art, 29–30; *Cromwell*, 29
humanism, 25, 26–27
humans: autonomy of, 69; as creators, 68; primacy of, 27, 28
Hume, David: *Dialogues concerning Natural Religion*, 42, 69; on idea of God, 42; *Natural History of Religion*, 41–42; on religion, 43; on selfhood, 85
Husserl, Edmund: concept of *epoché*, 111; *Logical Investigations*, 106; phenomenological method of, 59, 93, 94; on problem of God, xiii, 91–92, 162n13; on transcendental reduction, 96; view of religion, 91–92

I
Ibn-Sina. *See* Avicenna
iconoclastic movements, 120–21
ideal deed, 128
Ignatius of Loyola, 148, 149–50
ignorance, 42
"imitate" nature, 29, 30
immediacy, 33
immortality: anti-Platonic idea of, 80; *a priori* argument for, 83; religious

belief in, 76; self-identity and, 83, 84; of the soul, xii; study of, xii–xiii
infinite Being, 72, 75, 140, 141
infinite horizon, 141
infinite universe, 27
infused rationality, 17
Ingarden, Roman, 91
intellect, 159–60
intellectual apprehension, 150, 152
intentionality, 106
intuition, 146, 147
irony, 31–32

J
Jacobi, Carl Gustav Jacob, 35
Jaeschke, Walter, 167n2
James, William, 79, 133, 148, 151; *Varieties of Religious Experience*, xviii, 144
Japanese Oxcart pictures, 118
Jaspers, Karl, 74, 140
Jesus Christ: body of, 82; life after death, 87
Joachim, Harold: *The Nature of Truth*, 108; on "significant whole," 108, 172n9
John of the Cross, xvii, 148, 149, 150
Jonas, Hans, 17, 19
journey, as symbol of spiritual development, 31
Judaism: animal sacrifice in, 131; concept of evil in, 63

K
Kandinsky, Wassily, 123
Kant, Immanuel: *Critique of Pure Reason*, 21, 58; on existence of God, 58; philosophy of, 49, 55; reversal of the correspondence theory, 106; on theodicy, 63; on transcendental ego, 93
Karrer, Otto, 6, 7
Kerenyi, Karl, 174n3
Kindi, al-, 36
knowledge, 102
Kolakowski, Leszek, 66

Kortrijk, Belgium, vii
Kott, Jan, 175n13

L
La Mettrie, Julien Offray de, 41
language: as foundation of a new culture, 25; as house of Being, ix; as integral part of creation, 24; nature and, 24, 25, 32–33; new theology of, ix; primary function of, 24–25; symbolic power of, 26
Lazarus (biblical figure), 88
Lectures on the Philosophy of Religion (Hegel), 52
Lefebvre, Henri, 32
Leibniz, Gottfried Wilhelm, 65–66
Leonardo da Vinci, paintings of, 118
Lessing, Gotthold Ephraim, 35
Levesque, Paul, ix
life, origin of, 40–41
life after death: desire for, 76; personal identity and, 77; philosophical reflections on, 77–79; possibility of, 77, 87–88; religious doctrine of, 80, 88; sensations and emotions in, 78, 79
Lille, Alain de, 24
Limbourg brothers, 28
Lindbeck, George, xvii
literary criticism, 32, 33
lived religion, xiii
Locke, John: on faith, 38; religious deism of, x, 37–38; on revelation, 37; works of, x, 36, 37, 38
logos, 14
Lorenzetti, Ambrogio, 28
Lossky, Vladimir, 146
love, 159, 160
Lukács, György, 30
Lullus, Raymundus, 155
Luther, Martin: *Theologia germanica*, 146

M
Mackie, J. L., 68
Maimonides, 104
Mâle, Émile, 23

Marcel, Gabriel, 110
Maréchal, Joseph, 4, 60, 78, 79, 147
Marheineke, Philip, 52
Marion, Jean-Luc, xiii
Maritain, Jacques, xviii, 73, 77, 146–47
Martin, F. David, 114
Mary Magdalene, 88, 117
Matisse, Henri, 123, 124
Maximus the Confessor, 20, 146
medieval culture, rationality of, 14
medieval symbolism, 23–24
medieval theology, 16
Memphite theology, 158
Menzel-Ragner, Hildegard, 178n12
"mere nature" (*natura pura*), 133
Messiaen, Olivier, 124
metaphysics, viii, 60
Mexican temples, 118
Michelangelo Buonarroti, 118
Milbank, John, 139
Mill, John Stuart, 70
mind: after death, 86–87; desire of God, 138–39; immortality and, 81–82; object and, 106–7
mind-body relation, 79–80, 87
minimal art, 122
mirror image, 28–29
modern age: historical awareness of, 131; secularization of, 130
modern culture: crisis of meaning in, 20, 30; role of self in, 20; secularization of, 35–36, 51, 116, 141
monotheism: divine revelation and, 96; emergence of, 43; possibility of evil in, 74–75; theoretical and practical norms of, 96; truth in, 100
Moses (biblical figure), 56
mystical consciousness, 144, 154
mystical desire, 142
mystical enlightenment, 144
mystical experience, 151, 152, 158
mystical knowledge, 147
mysticism: Christian, 148; elements of, 151; evolution of, 145–47; negative connotation of, 145; return of philosophy toward, 143; study of, xvi, xvii–xviii; Trinitarian, 145; without philosophy, 145–50

N
Nabokov, Vladimir, 165n16
Natorp, Paul, ix
natural desire of God, xix, 135, 136, 137, 139, 141, 146, 153
Natural History of Religion (Hume), 41–42
naturalism, 15, 121
natural law, 14
natural theology, 1, 37, 69
nature: Aristotelian concept of, 138; language and, 24; modern technology and, 18
Neoplatonic philosophy, 142, 143, 155–60
Newman, Barnett, xv, 124
Newton, Isaac, principle of inertia, 17, 40, 57
Nicholas of Cusa: on aesthetic experience of the icon, 152–53; alma mater of, 154; on Being of God, 155–56, 157; career of, 134; concept of form, 158; concept of individuality, 178n12; deism of, 36; on desire to comprehend God, xix, 138, 153; on God's relation to creatures, 157; on intellect, 159; justification of mystical experience, 158; on language, 26; *The Layman on Wisdom*, 138; on love of God, 159; mystical theology of, 151, 153–55, 159, 160; *On Seeking God*, 153; *On the Gift of the Father of Lights*, 155, 158; *On the Sonship of God*, 138, 153; philosophy of Being, 56–57; on poet's creativity, 44; synthesis of philosophy and theology, 138; theology of creation, 57; Trinitarian theology of, 155, 159; *The Vision of God*, xviii, 151, 152, 155, 156, 159; visual metaphors of, 157–58
Nietzsche, Friedrich, 125
night, as negative desire, metaphor of, 74

Nominalist theology, 15, 20, 24, 25, 35–36, 103
Novalis, 31
novel, 30–31

O
object and mind, 106–7
O'Regan, Cyril, xi, 53
Origen, 100
Orsi, Robert, xiii
Ortega y Gasset, José, 122

P
paradox of omnipotence, 68
Parfit, Derek, 83
Parmenides, 56, 58, 109
past, 131
Paul, Jean: *Titan*, 31
Paul III, pope, 27
Penderecki, Krzysztof, 124
Penelhum, Terence, 83
Perniola, Mario, 174n3
personal identity, 77, 80, 83
Petrarch, 25
phenomenology, xiii, xiv, 89, 92, 93, 94, 95–96
phenomenon of existence, 59
philosophy: contemplation and, 142; elements of, 141; idea of God and, 1–2; mystical elements in, 142–45; mysticism without, 145–50; origin of, 133, 142; religion and, viii, 1–9, 49–50, 55, 134; theology and, 47, 138, 143
philosophy of religion, viii, xvi, 5, 7, 8–9
physis, 13
Pico della Mirandola, Giovanni, 27
Plato: on divine causality, xi; followers of, 139, 142; on forms, 13; on Good, 56; idea of *anima mundi*, 14; on knowledge, 18; nostalgia for an ideal world, 142; *Republic*, 56; *Timaeus*, 14, 20; translation of works of, 158; view of cosmos, 135
Plotinus, 56, 93, 119, 142, 158
poetic language, 32

postmodern art, 122, 123
Praz, Mario, 25
pre-apprehension of Being, 4
Price, H. H., 77
principle of value, 2
process philosophy, 70
Pseudo-Dionysius, 56, 119, 149, 153
Puccetti, Roland, 78

R
Rahner, Karl, xvii, 4, 140
rationalism, 1, 45
rationalist deism, 36, 38–40
rational knowledge, 104
reality: idea and, 106; -in-itself, 33; reduced, 16; of value, 2
redemption, 72, 73, 74
Reform Judaism, 131
religion: as-experience, xiii, xiv, 22, 94, 95, 105; as-transcendent, xiii, 94, 95; definitions of, 76; development of, 6–7, 15; as feeling, 105; genetic explanation of, 43; historical origin of, 42; "locative" theory of, xiii; metaphysics and, 7, 8; morality and, 38, 39; phenomenology of, xiii, 92, 93, 95–96; philosophy and, viii, 1–9, 49–50, 55, 134; process of interpretation and, 107; vs. science, 6
religious act, 97, 111–12
religious art: abstractionist, 124; aesthetic experience of, 118, 119, 120, 152–53; definition of, 113–14, 115, 116; incompleteness of, 118; interpretation of, 124; of the past, 124; profane darkness in, 119, 120; religious symbols in, 117–18, 119–20
religious buildings, 122
religious consciousness, 90
religious creativity, 44
religious mysticism, 133, 138, 141, 147
religious truth: divine origin of, 99–100; justification of, 106, 111, 112; rationalist interpretation of, 104; reinstatement of the notion of, 105; scientific definition of, 102–3

Rembrandt (Harmenszoon van Rijn), 121
Renaissance art, 28
representational narrative, 32
res cogitans, 16
res extensa, 16
Resurrection, 82
Revelation, 36, 37, 52–53
revolution in sensibility, 25
Richier, Germaine, 124
ritual: *catharsis* of, 132; Christian, 129–30; churches and, 132; effectiveness of, 126; meaning of, 128, 129; vs. myth, 126; orientation toward a past, 129–30, 131; relation to the future, xv; secularization of the modern age and, 130; social function of, 127–28; symbolism of, 130; time of, 127, 128–29
ritualization of time, xiv, xv–xvi
Rohde, Erwin, 148
Roman religion, 126
Romantic art, 29
Ross, W. D., 136
Rothko, Mark, xv, 123, 124
Rouault, Georges, 124
Rubenstein, Richard, 131
Russell, Bertrand, xvii; *Mysticism and Logic*, 143
Ruusbroec, Jan van, xviii, 145, 148, 154–55

S

sacred: category of, 7; as distinct sphere of being, 117; vs. profane, 113, 116, 175n13
Salutati, Coluccio: "On the Works of Hercules," 26
Santa Constanza mosaics, 119
Santayana, George, 113
Sartre, Jean-Paul, 21
satyagraha, 171n2
Scheler, Max, 94, 112, 140, 162n13; *On the Eternal in Man*, 92
Schelling, Friedrich Wilhelm, 5, 58
Schleiermacher, Friedrich, 49, 105

Schlick, Morris, 77
Scholasticism, xvi, 3, 4, 20, 70
Schopenhauer, Arthur, 62
science, 6, 18, 44
seeing-as-creating metaphor, 156–57
Seinszuwachs (increase in density of Being), 110
self: *a priori* concept of, 84; awareness of, 150; body and, 85–86; conscious and unconscious, 84, 85, 86; definition of, xviii, 147; empirical notion of, 84, 85; excursive, 147; nature of, 150; philosophical views of, 20; reflective, 147
self-consciousness, 147
self-motion, 16
self-realization, 77
significant whole, 108, 172n9
Skinner, B. F., 69
Smart, Ninian, 83
Soloviev, Vladimir, 146
soul, xii, 51, 148, 149, 153
Sozzini, Fausto, 36
Spaemann, Robert, 144
Spinoza, Baruch, xii, 35, 79, 86
Spirit, xi, 49, 50, 53
spiritual body, 82
spiritual consciousness, 53–54
spiritual experience. *See* mysticism
Stella, Frank, 123
Strawson, P. F., 77, 78
subconsciousness, 84
subject, disappearance of, 123, 173n15
subjectification of the real, 20
suffering, 71, 73, 74
Sylvester of Ferrara, 139
symbolic structures, 30–34
symbolic world, 23–26
symbols, ix, xiv, 33–34

T

Tauler, John, 149
technology, 18–19
Teresa of Avila, xvii, 146, 150
Tertullian, 100
theism, x, 44
theodicy, 1, 61, 62, 63, 66, 69

theology, xiv, 138, 143, 145
Thomas Aquinas: on Aristotle's natural virtues, 137; on beings, 71; criticism of, 138; *De regimine principum*, 14; on distinction between essence and existence, 158; on existence of God, 39; formation of philosophical views of, 36; on highest knowledge, 136; idea of Being, 58; impact on modern thought, 60; on knowledge, 18; on mind, 80; on natural desire of God, xvi–xvii, 137, 175n8; on origin of the universe, 57, 159; scientific presentation of religious truth, 102–3; *Summa Theologiae*, 7, 39, 102
time, 125, 126–27, 128
Tindal, Matthew: *Christianity as Old as Creation*, 36
Toland, John: *Christianity Not Mysterious*, 38
transcendent, meaning of, 2
transcendental ego, 93, 97
transcendental reduction, 93, 96
transcendental Thomism, ix, xvii, 60
Trinity, 52, 53, 59, 153, 154
truth: coherence as criterion of, 107–9; correspondence theory of, 106–7; definitions of, 171n2 (essay 10); disclosure theory of, 109–12; experience of, xv; about God, 103; quest for, 101–2; rationality and, 99, 103; about religion, 104–6; of religion, 97–98, 103, 107; within religion, 100–104; traditional and modern conceptions of, xiv, 99, 100; worldly wisdom and, 100. *See also* religious truth
Tweed, Thomas A., xiii
Tylor, Edward B., 7, 148

U
unhappy consciousness, 50, 51
universe, 15, 57–58

V
value systems, 73
van der Leeuw, Gerardus, xiii, 94–95, 112; *Religion in Essence and Manifestation*, 92
van der Weyden, Rogier, 119, 123, 152; *Deposition*, 124
Vedantic writings, 148
Verwilderung (feralization), 6
Vincent of Aggsbach, xix
Virgil, 125
Voltaire, 38, 39; *Questions on the Encyclopédie*, 39
von Hügel, Friedrich, 134

W
Whitehead, Alfred North, 14; *Science and the Modern World*, 1
Wilder, Thornton, 78; *Our Town*, xvi
Windelband, Wilhelm, 6
Wittgenstein, Ludwig, xvii, 107, 143, 144
Woolston, Thomas, 38
Wordsworth, William: *The Prelude*, 31
world order, 17, 20

Y
Yom Kippur liturgy, 131

LOUIS DUPRÉ was the T. Lawrason Riggs Professor Emeritus of Religious Studies at Yale. He was the author of *Religion and the Rise of Modern Culture* and *The Quest of the Absolute: Birth and Decline of European Romanticism*.

PETER J. CASARELLA is a professor of theology at Duke Divinity School. He is the author of multiple books, including *Reverberations of the Word: Wounded Beauty in Global Catholicism*

www.ingramcontent.com/pod-product-compliance
Lightning Source LLC
Chambersburg PA
CBHW051711060225
21549CB00004B/123